Risky Relations

Risky Relations

Family, Kinship and the New Genetics

Katie Featherstone, Paul Atkinson,
Aditya Bharadwaj and Angus Clarke

Oxford • New York

English edition
First published in 2006 by
Berg
Editorial offices:
First Floor, Angel Court, 81 St Clements Street, Oxford OX4 1AW, UK
175 Fifth Avenue, New York, NY 10010, USA

Berg is the imprint of Oxford International Publishers Ltd.

Library of Congress Cataloging-in-Publication Data
Risky relations : family, kinship and the new genetics / Katie
Featherstone ... [et al.].— English ed.
    p. cm.
Includes bibliographical references and index.
ISBN-13: 978-1-84520-178-4 (cloth)
ISBN-10: 1-84520-178-7 (cloth)
ISBN-13: 978-1-84520-179-1 (pbk.)
ISBN-10: 1-84520-179-5 (pbk.)
  1. Communication in the family. 2. Family—Health and hygiene. 3.
Genetic disorders—Psychological aspects. I. Featherstone, Katie.

HQ519.R57 2006
306.8709′0511—dc22   2005026979

British Library Cataloguing-in-Publication Data
A catalogue record for this book is available from the British Library.

ISBN-13 978 1 84520 178 4 (Cloth)
            978 1 84520 179 1 (Paper)

ISBN-10 1 84520 178 7 (Cloth)
            1 84520 179 5 (Paper)

Typeset by Avocet Typeset, Chilton, Aylesbury, Bucks
Printed in the United Kingdom by Biddles Ltd, King's Lynn.

www.bergpublishers.com

Contents

Preface

Genetics play an increasingly important part in contemporary medicine. The genetic basis of some medical conditions is now firmly established, and specialist services provide advice to individuals whose genetic make-up means that they or their relatives have a likelihood of developing a disease and can help people make decisions about their reproductive behaviour. Genetic tests can be used to diagnose a wide range of conditions, or to predict the genetically based risks that people face. Familial cancers (such as breast and ovarian cancer or colorectal cancer), Huntington's disease, cystic fibrosis, myotonic and Duchenne muscular dystrophy are among the conditions that have been thoroughly documented from both a medical and a sociological perspective. New research is constantly introducing new medical conditions into the ambit of genetic science and medicine. There is now a huge range of diseases and syndromes that have been identified as having a genetic basis. Common conditions such as diabetes and heart problems have an inherited component. Thalassaemia and sickle-cell disease are related to the genetics of particular ethnic groups. The genetic basis of psychological illness is being increasingly identified, with suggested genetic bases for schizophrenia, Alzheimer's, and severe depression. Large-scale programmes of biomedical and social research, on a global scale, contribute to and reflect medical and societal interests in new genetic technologies.

New genetic technologies mean that the biological basis of family and kinship is – potentially – of increasing significance. The identification of a genetic mutation or deletion within a kindred can have far-reaching implications for its members. If my own genes suggest that I have a genetic condition, am a 'carrier' for one, or have a heightened risk of developing one, then that has potential consequences for other members of my family. Precisely which members of my family are or might be affected by the genetic disease varies, depending on the biology of the condition itself and its mode of inheritance, and we discuss these issues throughout the book. For now, we need to note that the increasing identification of genetic disease and genetic risk implies a heightened salience of biological relatedness among family members. Kinship could become increasingly identified with common ancestry, shared genetic material, and shared risks.

This is not, of course, entirely novel. We have not had to wait for modern genetic science, still less the results of the Human Genome Project, to recognize that family members can share common characteristics, and that they are inherited. Family resemblances – physical and moral – have been recognized for centuries: one need only see how successive portrait painters have captured the family 'look' of generations of noble and royal families, for instance. Selective breeding of domestic animals and foodstuffs has been going on for generations. Pedigree pigs and thoroughbred horses, noble lineages and royal successions have all depended on a practical understanding of inheritance, bloodlines and lineages, quite independently of contemporary scientific understandings of genetics. The scientific contributions of Gregor Mendel (and his rediscovery in the early twentieth century), the discovery of the structure of DNA by Francis Crick, James Watson, Rosalind Franklin and Maurice Wilkins, in the middle of the twentieth century, and the various genome projects at the century's end and the beginning of the twenty-first century have signalled the rise of genetic science. However, a general sense of biological relatedness and inheritance has not rested on that science alone. Indeed, Mendel himself had no biological basis for the patterns of inheritance he identified, and Darwin's theory of evolution was developed in the absence of a clear biological mechanism of inter-generational inheritance and mutation. Likewise, there is nothing novel about the idea of inherited susceptibility to ill health. Family resemblances have long included the perception of general physical constitution, robustness or weakness. The inheritance of specific conditions is not a new idea. The distribution of haemophilia among the royal families of Europe is a well-known case in point. While the identification of a genetic basis for psychological problems may be challenging for contemporary psychiatry, it is by no means alien to a more general array of beliefs about families and their characteristics that are independent of genetic science.

While the new genetic science has important implications for medicine, and for how we think about families, it would be quite wrong to think that everything about genetic medicine and the biological basis of inheritance is totally new. It would be equally wrong to think that current beliefs, attitudes and practices about these things are governed entirely by the tenets of contemporary genetic science itself. There are complex interplays between scientific research, medical practice, mass media reportage and everyday understandings. Everyday knowledge is by no means determined by scientific knowledge. It is not even determined by the style and content of mass media representations. We have to recognize that scientific knowledge is always received and interpreted against the backcloth of rich, varied and adaptable repertoires of everyday culture.

Our book reports research that is part of a long-standing and continuing collaboration between social scientists and specialists in genetic medicine. It reflects a number of strands in sociology, anthropology and cultural studies that in turn have been affected by rapid changes in biomedical science. Our research maintains a clear commitment to fundamental social-science concerns. Indeed, it is our shared contention that the current state of genetic knowledge and practice urgently demands the insights that can only be provided by a thorough commitment to the ideas of sociology, anthropology, and cognate disciplines.

Our book derives from intensive work with members of several families who had been identified as having (or at risk of sharing) a genetic condition. We introduce these medical conditions as we introduce our data, and the families and the genetic conditions or syndromes involved are described within Chapter 2 and in more detail in an Appendix. We do not include some of the most common diseases, which have been extensively documented by other social scientists, as we acknowledge later in the book. However, the analytic issues thrown up by our research are generic. They are not confined to the medical circumstances experienced by our research informants alone. Equally, the issues we explore are not limited geographically. Our fieldwork was conducted primarily in South Wales, but the issues transcend regional and national boundaries. We do not for one moment imply that the cultural contexts of professional and lay knowledge are undifferentiated, and we insist that the cultural bases of ideas about inheritance, health and disease need empirical research across multiple sites and cultural milieux. The contents of belief systems and practices may vary; the broader analytic themes that we identify are salient globally. There remains much work to be done to document the ethno-genetic knowledges of many populations around the world. Our own research and research like it need to be developed across a broad spectrum of social groups. Our research has been with white families living in South Wales. The absence of other ethnic groups does not reflect a deliberate decision to exclude them from our research in general, but rather the fact that the particular projects on which this book is based did not specifically include minority communities or medical conditions specific to them.

The location of our research in South Wales partly reflects the fact that there is an unparalleled degree of collaboration between social scientists and geneticists there, and a substantial concentration of research investments at Cardiff University, where this work was undertaken. Families in Wales are especially important in the context of sociological and anthropological research more generally. There is now a long and extensive tradition of work, spanning many decades, documenting family and community life in Wales. Family research, together with research on health and illness, has long been a core theme of the social sciences in Welsh universities. It is, therefore, especially appropriate that newer concerns with biomedical and social relations should be added to that research heritage.

In Chapter 1, we locate our research within the broader intellectual context. We elaborate on the renewed interest in 'kinship' among anthropologists and sociologists, and how this has been given particular urgency by recent developments in biomedical science. We suggest that those developments and their social, interpersonal consequences have not all had the same implications for family life and kinship practices. Innovations such as new reproductive technologies have the capacity to destabilize the taken-for-granted relations between kinship, family, reproduction and biology. New genetic technologies, by contrast, tend to reinforce the implied relationships between kinship and biological relatedness. It is, however, important to recognize that family and kinship are social, culturally defined categories. They are not determined by biological 'facts' of procreation and generation. Even though there is a homology between the social and biological categories of Anglo-American kinship, that must not blind us to the fact that these categories are culturally defined. Congruence or overlap between the two category systems – the cultural and the biological – is something that is made to happen, in various different social contexts, rather than a reflection of naturally given phenomena.

In Chapter 2, we develop these themes by introducing various sites in which the facts of kinship and the facts of genetics are brought together. We introduce, therefore, the clinical setting in which genetic counselling is conducted. It is here that practitioners and their clients collaborate to construct one version of kinship – the pedigree or family tree – that is the basis of much genetic interpretation. This is an artefact that straddles the two domains of medical practice and everyday family life. It is grounded simultaneously in the socially constructed facts of biological relations and the equally constructed facts of family relations. It is within the genetics clinic also that the phenomena of the clinic and the findings of the genetics laboratory are brought together to create predictions of genetic risk or diagnoses of genetic conditions. It is here, too, that – through genetic counselling – these assessments and their implications are discussed with 'patients'. Here, then, is a major site of knowledge production and reproduction. It is also one starting point in the varied processes whereby understandings of genetic conditions are distributed within family networks.

We recognize that there is another major site in which 'families' and genetic knowledge are assembled – and that is the research process that we ourselves initiate as social scientists. When we interview family members we and they are engaged in the co-production of family, kinship and genetics. We do not believe, therefore, that there exist 'families' as naturally given entities that are independent of these occasions of talk. (There are, of course, many other occasions in which families are rendered visible: the ceremonies of status passage and calendar rituals are cases in point.) Equally, we do not subscribe to the view that there is no relationship between the everyday experience of family life and the accounts of family relations generated in the clinic or in the research interview. We do not, therefore, subscribe to the view that the research interview can refer to nothing but itself. However, we do recognize that on all occasions of its construction, the 'family' does not correspond to an ideal type, but is grounded in the social realities of 'practical kinship'. By that, we refer to the practices that transform a variety of possible relations – given by kinship or marriage – into the social realities of mutual recognition and obligation, including the potential sharing of genetic information derived from the clinic.

In Chapter 3, we go on to examine our family members' beliefs about inheritance. We examine how they make sense of the processes of inter-generational transmission of traits and characteristics. We discuss how their ideas about their specific medical conditions and risks are embedded within a broader cultural context of beliefs and understandings. Members may trace how a condition 'came into' the family and identify it with 'sides' of the family, associating it with the distinctive characteristics of their relatives. Their explorations are associated with ideas about fate and chance. It is characteristic of new genetic medicine that it provides particular kinds of answer to the perennial questions of chance and determinism, and a distinctive aetiology of personal misfortune that is grounded in shared social relations. We examine how the particular ideas about inherited disease are related to broader ideas about personal traits and characteristics.

Chapter 4 explores the processes of 'mutual surveillance' among family members. Genetic conditions occasion alertness and monitoring in various ways. Older members of a family may observe members of the next generation, in order to try to detect if a medical condition is 'coming out'. Likewise, if they are aware of the familial nature of the condition, members of the younger generation may implicitly survey their older relatives, in order to try to assess their own possible fate. Over and above the processes of medicalized surveillance that is often a consequence of genetic counselling, therefore, there is an everyday, mundane form of mutual surveillance. Beliefs about who is 'at risk' within the family may follow *social* rather than biological categories. The assessments of genetics professionals are thus assimilated into the broader systems of belief and practice that form the context of ideas about kinship and inheritance.

As we have already pointed out, genetic information is always – in principle – information about relations and 'others' within the kindred. In Chapter 5, we therefore turn to examine how knowledge and information about genetic diagnoses and risk assessments are shared and distributed within families. It would be naïve to assume that family networks are entirely 'open' when it comes to sharing genetic knowledge. Indeed, everything we know about family life in general should lead us to predict the reverse: families are proverbially sites of secrets, evasions and half-truths. Families have skeletons in the cupboard, and black sheep among the various generations. The distribution of knowledge and awareness of genetic matters is certainly uneven within the families we worked with. Genetic 'information' does not flow evenly and uninterrupted across the generations or across degrees of kinship. Individuals who do have an awareness of their genetic constitution – because they have had direct experience of genetic testing and counselling – often have to make decisions about whom they tell and how they tell them. This means that they are often engaged in what we call 'practical ethics'. The ethics of genetic disclosure are by no means restricted to medical practitioners and counsellors. They are matters of everyday decision-making for family members themselves. Family members may need to assess how individuals will cope with the information, for instance. Alongside the calculus of genetic risk, therefore, there is a moral calculus of disclosure.

Up to this point in the book, we describe our research thematically. These themes are, of course, intertwined in the real lives of family members. We separate them out for analytic purposes. In order to demonstrate more graphically how they can all fit together to inform the realities of practical kinship, in Chapter 6 we present an extended case study of one kindred. In doing so, we are able to put together several of the themes already discussed in the book and to see them in their concrete detail. We provide a thick description of how the cultural categories and practices of inheritance, practical kinship and everyday ethics are linked in the accounts from this one family.

We conclude by recapitulating the broader analytic issues thrown up by this empirical research. Although our book is not intended primarily as a guide for professional practice, our conclusion includes observations about the professional utility of research like ours. It is, we insist, vitally important that as genetic knowledge assumes increasing significance, the cultural context in which it is imparted is understood. Genetic counsellors, however sensitive and painstaking their work with their clients, can only spend very limited amounts of time with them. They cannot determine how the genetic information they provide will be understood, shared and acted upon (or not acted upon). They certainly should not base their professional work on unrealistically simple or idealized models of family life. A sound appreciation of everyday social reality is of profound importance for professional practice. Empirical social research like ours must continue to inform professional work.

Reductionism of various sorts haunts contemporary discourse about genetics and post-genomic science. It is clear that we cannot endorse reductionist arguments that collapse all of social and cultural life into the oversimplified categories of evolutionary psychology or other forms of sociobiology. The realities of genetic science are much more complex than vulgar versions of genetic determinism would allow. Equally, we cannot explain away such biomedical phenomena by suggesting that genetic scientists and medical practitioners are mere cultural artefacts. It is vital that social scientists and medical scientists recognize and remain faithful to the indigenous complexities of natural and cultural domains. The world of genetic medicine and the everyday lifeworlds of the families involved are correspondingly complex. They are traversed by the new knowledge of genetic medicine and the cultural knowledge of family, kinship and inheritance. In presenting our field research in this book, we have tried to remain faithful to that complexity.

Acknowledgements

This book and the research on which it is based would not have been possible without the financial and intellectual support of a large number of people. Our research on families in Wales was made possible by a research grant from the Wellcome Trust, whose financial support is gratefully acknowledged. The research was undertaken and the book prepared under the auspices of the Economic and Social Research Council's Centre for Economic and Social Aspects of Genomics (CESAGen), a collaboration between Cardiff and Lancaster Universities. The support of the ESRC is gratefully acknowledged.

The research is itself part of a much wider series of collaborations between social scientists, geneticists and other health professionals at Cardiff University. We are grateful to them, in particular Sir Peter Harper, whose vision of genetic medicine extends to incorporate research on its social and ethical implications. While lip service is paid to interdisciplinary research in many quarters, it remains rare to find genuinely interdisciplinary research collaborations. We are fortunate to have benefited from the long-term commitment of colleagues in the social and bio-medical sciences. We have also gained greatly from our regular contact with Professor Martin Richards and his colleagues at Cambridge University, whose work on genetics, health and families has informed our own in many ways.

Our colleagues in CESAGen at Cardiff have provided a regular source of social and intellectual stimulation. We are grateful for their colleagueship and friendship. In particular, we would like to thank Mel Evans and Maggie Gregory, who supported us through the various draft stages of this book.

Our greatest debt is to the family members themselves who allowed us to interview them in their homes, and to observe their encounters with genetic counsellors. Social research in this area is not only a matter of cross-disciplinary dialogue between academics in medicine and the social sciences. It is also about the collaboration and support of individuals and their families under the clinical gaze. If we are to understand the nature of inherited medical conditions, then the full participation of families is a vital resource. We cannot acknowledge participants individually, as they have been granted anonymity. However, our research would simply not be possible if people were not willing to give up their time to talk to us and help us talk to other members of their families. Last but not least we would like to thank our own families for their patience and unstinting support.

–1–

Risky Relations and Other Complexities

Introduction

The ties of kinship and family have been thrown into sharp relief by the most recent developments in the new genetics and other medical technologies. Every relationship is risky, in multiple senses, whether it be a marriage, an illicit affair, a friendship or a working collaboration. The 'risky relations' we shall be documenting in this book are the relationships of family and kinship among the networks of related people who share, or potentially share, the risk for a genetically transmitted disorder. As genetic medicine increases in prominence and significance, and as more and more disorders are identified as having at least a genetic component, it becomes increasingly pressing that we should understand the social relationships of family and kinship into which genetic risks are, as it were, introduced by the work of geneticists and other professionals.

Seen from the point of view of the social scientist, the new genetics introduces and reinforces well-established analytic topics: how do people trace their relationships and how do they express them? What does 'family' mean in everyday terms and how do people maintain familial ties in practical terms? How do people conceptualize the familial resemblances and individual differences that are observable among family members? These and related themes are among the stock-in-trade of anthropologists and sociologists, and have been for many decades. Biomedical innovations have given many of these long-standing topics new significance. Seen from the point of view of the geneticist, the social sciences can help to address some urgent practical and ethical issues: if we tell an individual that she or he is a carrier of a genetic disease, or has a risk of inheriting or transmitting such a disease, what does that imply for other members of the family? How do professionals and family members communicate such genetic news to other members of the same kinship network? How do people interpret the sort of genetic information they are given by genetic counsellors and how do they act in the light of such knowledge? How is professional knowledge refracted through everyday understandings of inheritance and kinship?

As a consequence of recent innovations in biomedical knowledge and medical practice, geneticists and social scientists find common ground in a number of research topics. Developments in biomedical science constitute one of many areas where the issues that derive from professional practice are congruent with the analytic interests of social science. Such congruence does not imply identity. The practical and theoretical concerns come together, but they derive from different disciplinary interests. It is important that in working on shared topics, the social scientists and the biomedical scientists do not lose sight of the disciplinary frameworks within which they work. There is a danger of focusing prematurely on joint 'problem-solving' rather than bringing to bear the distinctive and well-founded expertise within each academic tradition.

Family and Kinship

Kinship and the family have long been of interest to social scientists. For many decades, the study of kinship was a core aspect of the discipline of social anthropology. Indeed, it was held to be one of the defining characteristics of many 'non-Western' societies that social relations of many sorts were grounded in the rights and obligations conferred by kinship and marriage. The documentation and analysis of kinship systems was, therefore, a central feature of the discipline of anthropology. Understanding the complexities of kinship nomenclature was in turn a distinctive feature of the apprenticeship of the young anthropologist, while mapping the systems of kinship and marriage was among the standardized practices that helped to define the normal ethnography of any given society. Likewise, it was a tenet of community studies (a domain of work that straddled anthropology and sociology) that family and kinship were key aspects of the smaller-scale arrangements characteristic of rural villages, urban neighbourhoods, and settlements based on traditional industry (such as mining or fishing). Multiple strands of relatedness within such face-to-face societies, with strong ties based on family and kin, were normally seen as especially characteristic of the *Gemeinschaft* quality of such social arrangements.

In contrast, there has been an equally long preoccupation with the apparently diminishing significance of such primary ties within the more complex and fluid environments of advanced urban and metropolitan societies. The origins of urban sociology in the United States, for instance, repeatedly contrasted the strength of primary groups (such as the family) in the 'old' settlements of the rural South and among the European peasantry who constituted the immigrant populations of the industrializing United States with the anonymous and disorganized way of life in the expanding metropolis (Atkinson and Housley, 2003). The family was widely portrayed as a basis for social order, and was under threat from conditions of rapid social change. The alleged instability of the family among ethnic groups –

especially among African Americans – was a recurrent preoccupation. Within such an intellectual framework, the family was often assimilated in the study of social problems (such as domestic violence).

The importance of family and kinship studies to mainstream branches of anthropology and sociology became diminished for a significant period of time. The formal study of kinship systems was perceived to be among the more sterile aspects of anthropological discourse. There were several reasons for that. The classic period of kinship studies – especially in British social anthropology – was identified with a tendency to essentialize the differences between Western societies and 'other cultures' and to exoticize the 'others' (Rosaldo, 1989). Moreover, that period was associated with the high point of structural-functional modes of analysis, which tended to promote an ahistorical and static portrayal of non-Western cultures. The careful description of 'systems' of kinship and marriage within such an analytic framework also underplayed the analysis of social action and practice, which, in turn reinforced the apparent timelessness of the exotic other. There was, in addition, a more general sense that the typologies of kinship systems that had been so characteristic of social anthropology in its early decades were redolent of the more general museum-culture of expeditions and fieldwork of the late nineteenth and early twentieth centuries.

The significance of kinship, in other words, was severely reduced in general anthropological discourse. The traditional categories of ethnography and the equally traditional anthropological monograph were called into question. Anthropology went through a period of radical self-questioning, not least as a consequence of the so-called crisis of representation (Clifford and Marcus, 1986). In that process, the previously core preoccupations of the discipline underwent a period of radical re-examination. The apparently arid examination of systems of kinship in traditional societies was diminished in its relevance and significance for the discipline as a whole. In many ways, the study of family and kinship seemed like a relic of a bygone period in anthropology.

Equally, the sociology of the family has not seemed to be especially central to contemporary sociology. Indeed, it has joined several empirical or substantive domains within sociology in being somewhat eclipsed. The American tradition of family studies has had very little impact outside the United States. Many sociologists have in recent years followed the cultural turn, finding material culture, cultures of consumption, the semiotics of space and place, and other exotica more congenial than the more traditionally central areas of family, community, education and the like.

In recent years, however, several trends have reinvigorated the study of families and kinship (Carsten, 2000, 2004). They have included the development of feminist scholarship on reproduction and generation, and new forms of biomedical technology and intervention. These trends have led us to re-evaluate the potential significance of family and kinship, and have in turn provided new ways of thinking about reproduction and kinship (Cussins, 1998; Edwards et al., 1999; Franklin, 1997; Ragoné, 1994; Strathern, 1992b). Kinship and the family have not merely returned to share centre stage with other issues among the social sciences: they have also been reconfigured. What counts as kinship and what counts as family have themselves become increasingly –and interestingly – problematic (Strathern, 1992b). Family and kinship have become unquestionably more complex matters in recent decades. The increasing pace of change in biomedical technologies is having a reciprocal effect on the relationships of blood and marriage that constitute the building blocks of family and kinship. Reproductive technologies and the social and medical implications of new genetic science have simultaneously revitalized the study of kinship, while having the potential to transform the very nature of kinship and inheritance themselves. The biological and social bases of relatedness and inheritance have become more prominent cultural objects of scrutiny, while the relationships between the biological and the social have become progressively less obvious. Indeed, the anthropological excitement lies precisely in the changing and fluid boundaries between nature and culture.

In addition, the anthropological re-evaluation of kinship studies owes a great deal to the revisionist work of the American cultural anthropologist David Schneider (1980, 1984). Schneider transformed his own contribution from a formalist analysis of kinship systems to an account of kinship as an array of culturally specific practices rather than a universal mode of organization or as a self-evidently given tool of comparative anthropology. Although subject to criticism himself (cf. Carsten, 2000), Schneider helped to revitalize the anthropological study of kinship, while undermining the foundations of traditional studies of kinship systems as ideal types.

New biomedical forms of intervention have disrupted some of the taken-for-granted foundations of biology and kinship. For example, technologically assisted conception creates different possibilities of configuring biological kinship (Cussins, 1998; Franklin and Ragoné, 1998). The late-20th- and early-21st-century 'natural parent' – who embodies the genetic and social kin credentials – may be dispersed either by fertilization outside the body (in vitro fertilization) or by the use of donated third-party gametes (eggs or sperm). For some people – including the creators of ethical and legal codes – contemporary biomedical science creates a new dilemma for modern kinship: 'How to make sense of new forms of assisted conception which create more flexible and uncertain relations' (Franklin, 1997). In contemporary technologically 'advanced' societies, therefore, the relationships between the 'natural' facts of procreation and the social arrangements of relatedness have become increasingly problematic (and analytically interesting).

A similar set of observations can be made in respect of sociology as a discipline. At one time, 'the family' was seen as one of the central topics in sociological research and theory (Walby, 1990). In particular, the family was a key element in the development of functionalist Anglo-American sociology and was seen as a social institution of fundamental significance. The eclipse of functionalism in turn implied a marginalization of family studies. However, a series of analytic interests have successively raised the profile of sociological research on domestic, generational and kinship issues. These have been led by feminist examinations of marriage, domestic relations and households (Oakley, 1974; VanEvery, 1995), by renewed sociological attention to relations between generations (Pilcher, 1995), and by transformations in the socio-biological bases of relatedness. Imperatives driving the latter have included the consequences of new reproductive technologies such as in vitro fertilization, gamete donation and surrogate parenting. Recent biomedical innovations such as pre-implantation diagnosis and the use of 'spare' embryos for the derivation of human stem cells have given yet greater urgency to the analysis of forms of kinship and their potential transformation. The emergence of sociological research on new genetic technologies and their potential consequences draws the sociology of 'kinship' and family relations back into the mainstream of contemporary sociology. Moreover, there has been a significant convergence between the sociology of medicine – always a major field in empirical sociology – and the sociology of science and technology. The latter domain, which was once characterized by a focus on the 'hard' laboratory sciences, has become increasingly devoted to sociological accounts of biomedicine and the life sciences. Studies in science and technology studies have explored processes of discovery and innovation in the biomedical sphere, including suggestions that the notion of *biomedicine* constitutes a new mode of knowledge-production in its own right (Keating and Cambrosio, 2001, 2003).

The (often-exaggerated) media reports of new post-genomic technologies (Hope, 2003) make ever more problematic our traditional and taken-for-granted categories of kinship. The new biological rhetoric of reproductive cloning and similar futuristic possibilities questioning the use value of the Y chromosome and whether men will have a role in reproduction in the future, emerge with the potential promise to transform further the cultural links between natural and social arrangements (Sykes, 2003). Reports of the possibility of taking eggs from embryos have created headlines warning that a baby's 'mother' may be an unborn embryo and similar rhetoric around the use of embryos in stem cell research has become a major media preoccupation (cf. Williams et al., 2003). The alleged possibilities of human cloning can clearly disrupt the accepted categories of procreation and generation. The boundaries between nature and culture, and their implications for relatedness and inheritance have become potentially more fluid and complex. It is far too soon to imply that all members of contemporary society are equally aware of these implications or are potentially affected by them. However, the realizations and possibilities of new biomedical technologies have placed certain issues concerning kinship and inheritance at the forefront of social-science research.

Recent anthropological literature on biomedical research has tended to assume that there is a general movement towards the problematization of kinship, families and blood relations. A recent case in point is the work of Finkler, who tends to assimilate all recent developments into one set of issues that trouble the conventional assumptions about kinship and family relations: 'A good argument could be made that the new reproductive technologies have done more than any other factor to call into question our traditional understanding of family and kinship, scientific innovations that can potentially manipulate and influence genetic transmission and inheritance require us to rethink our definitions of family and kinship' (2000: 38).

In several significant ways, however, this conflation of new reproductive technologies and the new medical genetics is unhelpful. From the point of view of the disciplines of sociology and anthropology there is no doubt that both the new reproductive technologies and the new genetics have helped to revive our collective interest in families and kinship. Nevertheless, the general effects of the two on general cultural categories are – in at least one crucial respect – diametrically opposed. New reproductive technologies have tended to *weaken* the relationships between the biological 'facts' of conception and the social categories of kinship. The complex possibilities created by the technologies of IVF, surrogate motherhood, reproductive cloning and the like all displace kinship. Family relations are supplemented by a variety of novel and alternative modes of creating persons and creating relations between persons. In sharp contrast, the new genetics tend, if anything, to *strengthen* the conventional categories of reproduction and biological relatedness. The biology of genetics reinforces the significance of traditional kinship categories, in reaffirming the biological relatedness of kindred.

This does not mean that the categories of kinship or of biological relationships are given, nor that they are immutable. On the contrary, the legacy of classical social and cultural anthropology reminds us that there are numerous ways in which kinship relations are recognized, and equally, numerous ways in which inheritance is recognized, conceptualized and managed. Clearly, there are numerous cultural, religious and judicial ways in which goods and offices are transmitted and inherited, and we are not primarily concerned with them in this book. (We should note, however, that the analytic topic of 'inheritance' is a broad one and incorporates many social and cultural arrangements: inheritance relates to a much wider range of phenomena than are covered by issues of biological relatedness.)

In the contemporary Western (that is Anglo-Euro-American) world, it is easy to assume that arrangements of biology and culture are self-evident and unremarkable. It is not exactly a historical accident, but it is remarkable that 'our' assumptions about kinship and relatedness imply a high degree of congruence between biological 'facts' and social categories (Strathern, 1992a). Our indigenous systems of kinship and our biomedical systems of representation are derived from a common stock of interpretations of the social and natural worlds. Our understandings of kinship and inheritance long pre-date the explorations of Gregor Mendel, of course, let alone the the rapid development of genetic understanding in the fifty years and more since Crick and Watson published their speculation concerning the structure of DNA. It is, however, little exaggeration to suggest that Mendel's work – and the early science of genetics that followed the rediscovery of Mendel – was possible in the form it took precisely because of the pre-existence of a distinctively European type of kinship. In most Anglo-European kinship systems, relations are 'bilateral' (Goody, 1983). No distinction is made categorically between blood relations on the mother's side and those on the father's side. Kinship nomenclature and categories recognize differences between generations and between degrees of relatedness (grandmother, mother, daughter, granddaughter, aunt, niece, cousin etc.). These degrees of relatedness correspond to Western scientific ideas about biological relatedness. Our biological models make similar kinds of distinction of generation and degree, but also do not distinguish between different lines of descent. Hence all 'uncles' are uncles, irrespective of whether they are our mother's brother or our father's brother. All offspring of aunts and uncles are cousins likewise. Our mother's mother and our father's mother are both our grandmothers, without formal distinction. (In everyday usage, we know that families often find pet names and the like to make such local distinctions.) The Western biological and cultural systems assume that one is equally related to both one's parents or all one's children, for instance.

To those who have no experience of the relevant anthropological literature, it might seem that the high degree of congruence of our own cultural and biological belief systems is entirely natural – and indeed that the cultural categories are unproblematically generated by the underlying biological realities. Tracing social relations equally through maternal and paternal relations of consanguinity *seems* to mirror what we know about the natural facts of biology, in that genetic inheritance is also bilateral. It needs to be borne in mind, however, that our shared kinship system pre-dates modern biology and that modern molecular biology mirrors cultural practice quite as much as social categories reflect biology (cf. Richards, 1996a, 2000). In other words, genealogical relations are not simply biological or genetic connections, but are derived from social systems that in turn include beliefs and practices concerning how biological relations come about.

Western systems of kinship and relatedness clearly pre-date even nineteenth-century biological theories. Our cultural history includes many contexts in which families, kinship and descent have been constructed. We are entirely familiar with the family tree, for instance. The iconography of Christianity includes representations of the descent of Jesus, tracing his ancestry through the House of David. The family tree of Jesus is among the many canonical tropes of

Christian representation. In a similar way, we are all familiar with the extended family trees of European royal houses and noble families. Among royal and aristocratic families, it is a matter of some moment that one can trace one's lineage and one's origins back over many generations, and thus establish one's ancestry among suitably noble forebears. Title, position and property depend upon such genealogical documentation, and have done so for centuries. In a parallel manner, prize farm animals and domestic pets have their own pedigree (Ritvo, 1987). Racehorses also have their own pedigrees, which have major consequences for their monetary value and the more symbolic values placed on them (Cassidy, 2002). Again, the social importance of animals and their pedigrees long pre-date modernity and modern genetics (Haraway, 1990, 2003; Macfarlane, 1986). (As we shall indicate below, they do not necessarily reflect modern biological thinking either.)

Our local understandings of kinship and descent carry mixed messages. On the one level, as we have already said, Anglo-American kinship does not distinguish between different lines of descent. We can trace kinship equally through female and male parents and ancestors, without formal differentiation between our mother's father and our father's father. In practice, however, we have various ways of superimposing more selective lines of descent. Traditionally in Anglo-American culture, our naming practices derive family names only through the male line, which – coupled with the convention of women taking their husband's family name – has created the appearance of clear family lines through the thickets of consanguinity. The recent practice of hyphenating family names, primarily as a feminist response to the patriarchal asymmetry, reflects simultaneously the widely shared convention, and the virtual impossibility of resisting some degree of asymmetry. In practice, one cannot go on combining hyphenated names beyond one or two generations, as there occurs an explosion of strings of names that cannot practically identify and differentiate individuals. The inheritance of office and property can also introduce asymmetric principles. We in the United Kingdom are entirely familiar with the principle that the male gender takes precedence over birth order: Queen Elizabeth II would not have succeeded to the title had she had a younger brother. We take it for granted that titles and office more widely may be inherited by the eldest son. We readily take it for granted that property may be inherited asymmetrically – by primogeniture, for instance, and unequally between the sexes. As Gilmartin (1998) has pointed out, many classic narratives of the English novel are predicated on themes of inheritance and genealogy. Lost and found relationships and entitlements are among the stock narrative functions of nineteenth-century fiction. We have to be reminded, by anthropologists if necessary, that these conventions are only that, and are by no means universal. Even among European cultures, the practices and conventions are variable. In some contexts, ultimogeniture is the main principle of inheritance. Elsewhere, inheritance of property is strictly shared equally among all offspring (giving rise to highly fragmented divisions of land and other property).

There may be different systems of kinship classification and nomenclature. There are different classificatory principles that are possible. It is by no means necessary to identify one's kin according to the same principles of consanguinity. Indeed, when in this book we discuss our own research in terms of 'English' or Anglo-European kinship systems, we do not wish to imply that these are the only principles of family and kinship that are at work in contemporary British, European or American society. We fully recognize, on the contrary, that contemporary societies or nations are culturally plural and that cultural plurality extends to notions of relatedness. Indeed, a full appreciation of the diversity of kinship practices is vital for the work of contemporary genetics, genetic counselling and genetic medicine in many contexts. We certainly cannot engage in cross-cultural, comparative analysis always and simply by looking 'elsewhere'. The ethnic and cultural differences that are characteristic of contemporary global society, the diasporic flows of peoples, and the persistence of cultural heritage within ethnically plural societies mean that multiple systems of kinship are to be found within the same national borders, the same regions and indeed in the same local neighbourhoods. These diverse arrangements can have direct consequences for the study of everyday genetics. For instance, Alison Shaw (2000) has documented the significance of preferred cousin marriage among British populations of Pakistani origin.

In the course of this book, we shall be concerned with individuals and family networks from among white 'Anglo' British populations. This reflects the ethnography of the locales and the services we were working in. It does not reflect a blindness to the ethnic differences within contemporary British society, and certainly does not reflect an implicit assumption on our part that the arrangements discussed are the only arrangements that are practised in contemporary British society, or in contemporary Wales, where much of the fieldwork has been conducted.

In the light of renewed interest, and new biological possibilities, anthropologists themselves have been busy rethinking kinship. Moreover, formerly rather narrow definitions of the object of study have been redrawn. Broader and more fluid notions of 'relatedness' have in part taken over from earlier and more restricted analyses of kinship, marriage and the family. A number of anthropologists have, therefore, been rethinking the very nature of kinship studies, linking their renewed perspectives to new biological and medical interventions. Kinship is not derived, however, from a biological determinism. It is not a simple conceptual relationship. Social scientists do not assume that biology governs kinship, and do not therefore assume that new biological possibilities *determine* new social-science perspectives. It should be recognized that laboratory science, social science and medical science are part of an array of contemporary discourses in which the relationships and tensions between our biological selves and our social selves are subject to fresh scrutiny.

From a comparative, cross-cultural perspective, however, we can see that there is no necessary relationship between the cultural systems of kinship and our own beliefs concerning biological relatedness. Systems of kinship and descent are variable across cultures. Their variations have been among the enduring lessons of social and cultural anthropology, and it is important to restate them briefly here, as they will help to illuminate the specific analyses of kinship in contemporary Britain that we present later in this book.

Some of the classic anthropological literature has familiarized us with the notion of the 'virgin birth' (cf. Franklin, 1997; Leach, 1966). This does not refer to miraculous divine intervention, nor to any potential 'natural anomalies', much less to contemporary biomedical interventions. Rather, it refers to a well-documented belief system in which there is no role for the male in creating pregnancy and the physical child. Malinowski (1987 [1929]) famously described this among the Melanesian Trobriand Islanders. Sex between a couple has a role in this system in opening the way for the ancestral spirit, *baloma,* to enter the woman. However, the mother's husband – referred to as *tomakava,* 'stranger', or 'outsider' – is not recognized as the biological father of the child in any sense that corresponds to Western lay understandings of kinship, nor to biomedical understandings of procreation. This belief system is homologous with the Trobriand system of descent, which is matrilineal. In this system of descent – which has been documented widely – one's mother's husband (father) is not one's closest male relative. One's 'father' is an affine – that is a relation by marriage – rather than a member of one's kin group. The role of closest male relative is reserved for one's mother's brother. Descent and membership of a lineage counted through the female line.

Virgin birth is one system of monogenetic belief. There are parallel monogenetic systems that place all the emphasis on the role of the biological father, while recognizing the role of the mother as primarily a passive receptacle for the unborn child. In certain strongly patrilineal descent systems – in which descent is counted only through the male line – women are bypassed completely in procreation theories. In some Melanesian societies, such as the Madak or the Gimi, a child's body is thought to be made solely by the father's substance (Clay, 1977; Gillison, 1980). In Morocco and Egypt there are numerous monogenetic creation theories in which men are entirely responsible for the creation of children by ejaculating preformed fetuses into women, who in turn bring children to fruition (Inhorn, 1994). Carol Delaney (1986) reports that among Anatolian Turks men are granted a primary, active role in fashioning children, while women are accorded only a secondary and passive one. Men are described as 'planting the seed', while women are described as 'the field'. This asymmetry reflects broader cultural differences between the sexes. From elsewhere in Turkey, a similar model has been described (by Ilakó Bellé-Hann, 1999), in which women are identified as the 'baskets', while men are solely responsible for filling those baskets. In India, a parallel example has been described by Leela Dube (1986), where the relationship between the sexes in procreation is described in terms of 'the seed and the soil', also reflecting broader asymmetric relations between the sexes. These monogenetic ideas – or ideas like them – help to put into cross-cultural perspective the Western systems of thought that treat the social and biological classifications as coterminous.

Our aim here is not simply to review a diversity of beliefs and practices gratuitously. It is to remind our readers of, or to introduce them to, the actual and potential diversity of beliefs and practices concerning relations of kin, and of the role of the sexes in creating children. The 'natural facts' of relatedness and procreation are, therefore, quite different in different cultural settings. We do well to remind ourselves that there is no necessary relationship between kinship and what we take to be the 'natural facts' of biology. It could readily appear to be the case that the underlying facts of biological or genetic relatedness are self-evident. We take for granted, perhaps, that offspring 'take after' their parents, and that this is apparent even in the absence of a clear understanding of genetic transmission. One might assume, for instance, that close attention to the breeding of pedigree animals, plants or flowers would give rise to a clear appreciation of the general dynamics of Mendelian inheritance, independently of any awareness of Mendel himself or the subsequent history of genetic science. However, this is not automatically the case. In a remarkable piece of ethnographic work, Cassidy (2002) has demonstrated that British breeders of racehorses – who are obsessed with breeding and bloodlines – operate with monogenetic theories. In practice, breeders and bloodstock managers have quite asymmetrical beliefs. Although bloodlines are traced through both sides of a foal's pedigree, the main racing qualities are in practice believed to be inherited from the stallion (sire). The mare (dam) is regarded as having a more passive role. (This is reflected in the nomenclature that describes a foal as 'by' the sire and 'out of' the dam.) Qualities such as speed and courage are inherited through the male line of the pedigree. Cassidy also reports a variety of other practical beliefs in the world of horse racing which provide fascinating parallels between the world of animals (mediated by breeders) and that of humans.

In other words, there are multiple ways in which relationships given by the natural facts of biological relatedness have been constructed and given expression, across time and across cultures. As we have outlined already, we should make no simple assumptions concerning the primacy of biological relationships. We should certainly not assume that what is currently believed to be the case biologically, in accordance with biomedical science, directly maps onto the social categories and classifications that people use in their everyday lives to make sense of how they are related, and what that might mean in practice. Indeed, we want to insist that the natural phenomena of biology and procreation are themselves constituted out of the cultural and social categories that precede them.

Practical kinship – what relatedness means to the members of family networks – is a major theme of this book. We emphasize here by way of introduction the self-evident, but nevertheless important, observation that 'families' are not naturally-bounded entities. There are, as we have mentioned briefly, societies in which there is an ideology of precisely bounded 'lineages' that serve as well-defined corporate groups, although it would appear from most of the relevant ethnographies that these are models of social groups defined in kinship terms, and do not describe the range of practical arrangements that are in operation. Everyday reality is nearly always more complex and messy than such models and ideologies suggest. Under conditions of Anglo-European kinship, such bounded entities do not exist even in theory. Because we count relatedness through male and female lines of ancestry and descent, it is clear that kinship relations can ramify in all directions, and through multiple strands. (There are, of course, limits imposed by individuals or couples who have no offspring, so that potential lines of descent end.) Furthermore, family networks only make sense when considered from the point of view of a particular individual and her or his immediate relations: otherwise, we have large, proliferating networks. Strathern points out that in practice bilateral kinship networks do not extend indefinitely. The boundaries of kinship depend upon multiple, local and practical considerations:

> Social relations depend on multitudinous factors that truncate the potential of forever-ramifying biological relations. Biological relatedness – 'blood ties' – can thus be cut by failure to accord social recognition (someone is forgotten), just as social relationships can be cut by appeal to biological principles (dividing 'real' kin from others). So in practice one does not trace connexions for ever; conversely the most intimate group is also open to discovering contacts they never knew existed. Factors from diverse domains can affect the reach of an otherwise homogeneous network based on 'blood' or 'family'. (1996: 530)

In terms of everyday social realities, therefore, we have to think analytically about 'practical kinship'. That is, quite simply, who in practice is recognized as a relation, who is regarded as 'family' and where the boundaries of 'family' are placed. These are themselves flexible and permeable. We know that 'families' and the ties of kinship are constituted not through immutable facts of biological relationships, but through the everyday practical work of mutual recognition and interaction. We also know that the salience of these social arrangements often differs between individual family members. In other words, relations may not be recognized with equal force reciprocally, if at all. It is clear from all relevant research on 'the family', moreover, that the *work* of kinship is primarily women's work in Western societies (Leonardo, 1992). In practice, therefore, we probably ought to assume that families and representations of kinship exist in two forms: women's models, which are strongly delineated, and men's, which are weak and fuzzy.

The science of genetics and its applications in medical practice have given a renewed prominence to kinship and the inheritance of personal characteristics. Medical genetics and the wider consequences of the Human Genome Project have brought to general consciousness the biological bases of inheritance. These developments are visible in various ways.

There has been a dramatic rise in popular science concerning genetic inheritance. Human origins and evolution have become prominent topics in contemporary cultural discourse. The claims of evolutionary psychology are but one highly visible and controversial domain in which the genetic basis of human health and behaviour has become salient. Much of the popular science promotes reductionist views of genetics and the biological basis of behaviour (Hubbard and Wald, 1999). In such contexts, it is all too easy to read of 'the gene for' many things, as if single genes regulate complex phenomena of physical functioning, cultural understanding and social action. Notwithstanding the crude models of biology and of culture that are implicit in such representations, such constructions of genetics are widespread. They recur in the media coverage of genetics and genetic medicine – which is extensive – and 'the gene' is in itself a powerful cultural icon for the beginning of the twenty-first century (Keller, 2000). Human origins are now being written and rewritten in genetic terms. Evolutionary theory is being rewritten in terms of DNA, for instance – sometimes with startling effects so that we are constantly reminded that we are virtually identical to the chimpanzee, extremely similar to a fruit fly and quite similar to a banana (which shows that our 'genes' do not regulate things in simple ways). Current models of hominid evolution, which include the earliest origins of distinctively 'human' ancestral types and the temporal and spatial relationships between modern *Homo sapiens* and *Homo neanderthalensis*, are being represented in genetic terms.

Individual and collective identities are being expressed in genetic terms. Population genetics – in scientific and popular forms – are providing more and more occasions for the genetic identification of local populations, their historical origins and their spatial distribution. The popular television series and the resulting book *Blood of the Vikings* (BBC) are a case in point. They describe the search, through DNA testing, for the traces of 'Viking blood' in contemporary populations. In common with other such exercises, they suggest that the genetic markers of populations' origins, and for the interbreeding of populations are remarkably persistent, even over a span of many generations.

The inherited nature of many medical conditions has been increasingly asserted by biomedical research and its clinical applications. In the following chapter we shall discuss the genetic medicine and genetic counselling that underpin the experiences of the family members we interviewed. Here we note that the 'new' genetics are placing a renewed and special emphasis on families and relationships within kindred. Indeed, authors like Finkler have suggested that in the light of the new genetics, kinship has become increasingly medicalized (Finkler, 2000, 2001; Sachs, 2004). Medicalization is a remarkably vague concept that has been used to capture a number of phenomena. In general, it is used to refer to the transformation of social or moral problems into medically defined categories, with biological aetiologies and medical interventions (Conrad, 1992; Zola, 1972). It may also refer to the treatment of 'normal' physical processes – such as childbirth – as requiring management by a medical practitioner (Davis-Floyd, 1992, 1994). It can also refer to the redefinition of ordinary everyday experiences or emotions into medical or psychiatric conditions (Rhodes, 1995). The ever-expanding content of international classifications of disease is partial testimony to such tendencies (Bowker and Starr, 2000). When Finkler writes about the medicalization of kinship, it seems she is not describing the same phenomenon. There is no suggestion that kinship *per se* is treated as a medical phenomenon. Rather, Finkler means something much less restricted: 'Our kinship relations have been given a new dimension that stresses faulty genes' (2001 181). Finkler's own research is based on a group of symptomatic and asymptomatic women in families with familial breast cancer, and a series of adoptees seeking their birth parents and other kin. On the basis of these specific groups, she argues that: '... in the lived experience of those related to people afflicted with breast cancer, or of healthy adoptees who learn their birth parents' medical history, the medicalization of kinship leads healthy members in the afflicted family to redefine their reality by experiencing a new vulnerability that draws them into the biomedical domain' (Finkler, 2001: 183). In other words, what Finkler claims to identify is less the 'medicalization of kinship' than the 'geneticization of medicine', which is a relatively obvious and ongoing phenomenon in contemporary medical practice. Geneticization certainly does *not* necessarily imply that family and kinship are medicalized, in terms of the everyday constructions of social actors – even those who are members of families with inherited medical conditions. In fact, Finkler herself asserts that the true extent of prevailing genetically based explanations of inheritance among Americans is an empirical issue awaiting further study on a larger population (Finkler, 2001: 183). Finkler's (2001) contention that the 'medicalization' of family and kinship encompasses everyone, converting people into potential perpetual patients and causing their realities to encompass a future incessantly punctuated by worry cannot be generalized. She further asserts that 'the medicalization of family and kinship alters people's perceptions from "*if* I get breast or colon cancer" to "*when* I get breast or colon cancer"' (Finkler, 2001: 250).

As we shall show in Chapters 4 to 6, even when individuals are faced with a definite diagnosis for a genetic condition not 'everyone' is included and encompassed by this knowledge. The boundaries of disclosure constantly exclude selected members of kin for a whole spectrum of reasons. While our respondents' futures may well be conceptualized as one 'incessantly punctuated by worry' the shift from '*if* to *when* I get a particular inherited disease' is seldom marked and definite. As we shall show in Chapter 4 the surveillance and incessant worry of the future is almost always underscored by a sense of hope that perhaps '*it* may not happen after all' or the disease or mutation may even skip a generation.

Risks and Relations

The notion of risk has become pervasive in contemporary society and a mainstream topic for the social sciences. We have become familiar with risk-related discourse in many contexts. The concept of risk, Lorna Weir (1996: 383) argues, has become polysemic and the discursive shift needs to be discussed as a phenomenon rather than eliminated by definitional fiat. Thus, Ewald argues, 'nothing is a risk in itself; there is no risk in reality' and yet anything can be a risk depending on how one analyses the danger or considers the event. 'As Kant might have put it', Ewald further argues, 'the category of risk is a category of the understanding; it cannot be given in sensibility or intuition' (1991: 199). Ewald's notion of 'risk as evaluated danger' is, however, problematized differently by Castel (1991), who sees risk as autonomous from danger. He argues that 'risk does not arise from the presence of particular precise danger embodied in a concrete individual or groups but rather it is a combination of abstract factors which render more or less probable the occurrence of undesirable modes of behaviour' (Castel, 1991: 287). Accounts more directly focused on an idea of 'clinical risk' (Weir, 1996) analyse genetic risk as 'uncertainty' (Bharadwaj, 2002, Parsons and Clarke, 1993) while others are more focused on the embodiment of risk in late modernity and the production of a 'risky self' (Ogden, 1995).

The notion of clinical risk as developed by Weir and elaborated by Dean (1999) is an important element in this growing literature. Dean explains that clinical risk combines techniques of risk screening with both diagnostics and therapeutics. He argues that by 'mobilizing risk-screening techniques, and combining them with more traditional modes of face-to-face diagnosis, clinical risk seeks to attach risk to the bodies of individuals so they might become objects of more intensive surveillance and treatment' (Dean, 1999: 144). *Governmentality* perspectives such as these, while sharing a distinctly Foucauldian pedigree, nevertheless bear a close resemblance to accounts of *medicalization*.

Ulrich Beck (1992), on the other hand, has famously proposed that contemporary conditions of late modernity can be described as 'risk society'. Beck's formulation is intended to convey the sense that contemporary societies are increasingly preoccupied with managing the *consequences* of production, in terms of environmental damage, health risks and so on.

One of the major implications of 'risk society' is the inescapable sense that risks are shared, collective concerns. The most rampant individualism cannot escape the fact that risks to the environment, to health and so on are pooled to some degree. The same is true of risks in financial markets, where the most selfish pursuit of self-interest is limited by collective risks and responses to the market.

New developments in biomedical knowledge and practice have enhanced our widespread sense of risks. The rhetoric of late-twentieth- and early-twenty-first-century medicine is one of 'risks' (Gabe, 1995; Skolbekken, 1995). Risks to health derive from various sources. They include the exogenous risks derived from environmental phenomena, the personal risks derived from lifestyle and habit and, the inherited risks derived from one's genetic constitution. As with other risks, these have collective consequences. Certainly, the risks associated with inherited conditions are shared among biologically related kin.

Medical genetics identifies an ever-growing number of conditions that have a genetic component. The techniques of medical genetics have allowed clinicians and scientists to identify more and more 'genes' that either singly or in combination regulate medical conditions.

Even though genetic treatments are still not a reality for most conditions, the identification of the genetic basis of disease is important in many contexts. The provision of genetic counselling can help people who have a known genetic constitution to make decisions about their own reproductive behaviour – whether or not to conceive, or whether or not to carry affected foetuses to term (cf. Rapp, 2000).

Genetic risks and predispositions are inevitably shared. If a genetic test confirms, say, that a given individual has inherited a gene from one or both parents, then his or her siblings and offspring may also have inherited the same 'gene'. Consequently, the diagnosis of genetic risks and constitutions is never an individual matter. It is always in principle something that affects a wider network of people beyond the one individual who may have been tested (referred to as 'the proband'). Self-evidently, *genetics is a family matter*.

The work of geneticists and genetic counsellors is, therefore, not just a practice with and about individuals. Their work is directed at *families*. Risks are distributed among family networks. Consequently, genetic risks and predispositions go beyond the individual. A contemporary professional interest in genetic risk, therefore, necessarily directs analytic attention to the distribution of risks within social networks.

For the professional practitioner, the social distribution of risk implies a need for knowledge and understanding of genetic risks to be disseminated within family networks. In the real world of everyday social relations, this is by no means straightforward. The genetic counsellor may explain the determination of a genetic risk to an individual proband, or even to a small group of close kin. She or he cannot, however, control directly how such information is or is not transmitted among the extended social network of the kindred. There are, as we have already suggested, limits placed by everyday assumptions and practices as to who 'counts' as family. We have established that no cultural classification of family and kinship necessarily maps directly onto the biological relations as defined by genetic medicine. One certainly cannot assume that there are lines of family intimacy and communication that follow the biological 'facts' of genetic relatedness.

It is, apart from anything else, by no means the case that all individuals will want to talk with equal frankness – if at all – to all members of their kindred. Everything we know about families should prevent us from assuming that families are made up of individuals who communicate openly and freely about all the important practical and emotional aspects of their shared lives. Indeed, we know that this does not apply to couples and nuclear families, so there should be no assumption that wider family networks should be any more communicative.

Members of families may simply choose not to share information about genetic risk with one another. They may find it difficult to talk about such potentially important 'family matters' quite independently of any considerations of genetic knowledge and its implications for health and well-being. Feelings of shame and guilt may intervene, and medical conditions may be felt to be potentially discrediting and to require management and concealment rather than open discussion.

Furthermore, such genetic understanding is mediated through members' practical knowledge of genetics and the mechanisms of inheritance. The influence of 'lay' knowledge is certainly not restricted to the particularities of genetic medicine (cf. Lupton, 1994). There is now an extensive literature that documents the significance of everyday theorizing or interpretation concerning biomedical knowledge. People are frequently engaged in making sense of their own bodies and their own states of health. They do the same for other members of the household and significant others. We do not have to ascribe to such interpretations the same credence as to those entertained by experts such as life-scientists, geneticists, counsellors and nurses in order to recognize that they are socially significant in shaping how people receive, interpret and act on the sort of information given them by professionals.

While the tests and inferences of contemporary genetic science are very new, this does not mean that they emerge into a cultural vacuum. People have many ideas and belief systems concerning inheritance and its patterning. Popular ideas and observations that children may take after their parents and grandparents do not depend on the past fifty years of molecular biology, following the publication of the structure of DNA. The inter-generational inheritance of talents, appearance, character and predispositions is subject to ordinary, everyday systems of understanding.

Consequently, if and when a genetic practitioner transmits to an individual or family group a piece of news about their own and others' genetic risks, such information is likely to be refracted through their own frames of reference, which include their models of kinship and their understandings of how inheritance works. Such models and ideas do not have to be the equivalent of explicit, anthropological and scientific theories. Often they will be in the form of implicit, tacit knowledge, couched in practical everyday terms. It is, therefore, of the utmost importance for contemporary professionals that a degree of systematic understanding should be developed about how people think, talk and imagine family, kinship and inheritance.

It is, we suspect, easy to exaggerate the extent to which new biomedical practices intersect to transform contemporary kinship, and hence to consider that genetic medicine necessarily has a troubling and transformative effect on family arrangements and practical affairs among kindred members. It is easy to assume the impact genetic knowledge can have on everyday, practical understandings of inheritance, and hence to overestimate its impact on relationships and transactions between family members. We have already suggested that previous contributions to research in this general area too readily exaggerate the implications of new genetic technologies (e.g. Finkler, 2000). Equally, it is too easy to extrapolate from a relatively small number of new *possibilities* the implication that all, or the majority of, contemporary social actors experience such transformations. The various possibilities of new technologies and other social arrangements for reproduction, for instance, should not be extended to derive the conclusion that 'we' all experience 'postmodern kinship' or 'postmodern families'. While the shared cultural categories of contemporary Western societies may have become more permeable, and social relations more flexible, that certainly does not mean that the majority of individuals and families actually live their everyday lives under conditions of 'postmodern' relations. Empirical research like ours shows that the everyday realities of practical kinship and ordinary family life are less exotic than some social commentators – often in the absence of empirical evidence – would want us to believe.

Everything we have indicated already suggests that genetic counsellors, medical practitioners and other professionals certainly cannot identify the wider 'family' implications of their work simply by examining the biological 'facts' that they are dealing with (Atkinson et al., 2001). There are several reasons for this. First, as we have suggested already –and as we shall document at greater length later in this book – family and kinship are culturally variable matters. Not only are there clear cultural and ethnic differences in the models of kinship, but their translation into practical domestic relations and networks of mutual recognition is also variable. We certainly should not assume that all 'families' correspond to the same ideal type. In practice, families can assume a variety of shapes, and the relationships that are recognized among family members can vary markedly. It is not the case, therefore, that professional knowledge and practice can be informed simply by a basic reading of the anthropology of kinship and cross-cultural studies of the family. What is needed, in terms of fundamental research and in terms of professional practice, is a detailed acquaintance with the variable forms of family.

Understanding Inheritance

We have already indicated that there can be a wide range of everyday understandings about inheritance. Chronologically, these pre-date modern scientific ideas of genetics, and they certainly co-exist in contemporary society with the genetic understandings fostered by modern biomedicine.

In the course of this book, we shall be documenting a quite diverse array of beliefs and practices concerning the inter-generational transmission of physical and personal characteristics. We do not anticipate our detailed presentation here. Nevertheless, it is important to outline in general terms how we think about 'lay' and 'professional' knowledge in this, and related, areas.

We do *not* accord primacy to the knowledge of biomedicine in this or any other area. Equally, we do not privilege 'lay' knowledge. We do not analyse everyday belief systems because we need to celebrate them. Rather, we employ a principle of methodological symmetry in our analyses of risk and inheritance in society. That is, we assume *a priori* that a sociology of knowledge needs to pay equal attention to all forms of knowledge. Professional scientific or medical knowledge, marginalized or discredited knowledge and lay knowledge all need to be subject to the same kind of social analysis.

It is a methodological fallacy to assume that scientific or professional knowledge systems are self-evident, or that they are 'right' in some general sense, and therefore not susceptible to sociological analysis. It is equally fallacious to assume simply that everyday practical knowledge is a mistaken or imperfect version of scientific truth, and therefore in need of sociological explanation. We do not engage in sociological examination of scientific or medical knowledge simply in order to endorse official knowledge and explain away lay knowledge. Ours is not an exercise in 'public understanding of science' that is, implicitly, an analysis of the public misunderstanding of science. We do not subscribe to a deficit view of everyday knowledge. We believe that all and any socially shared and socially distributed systems of knowledge deserve careful attention.

This general sociological perspective requires a little further explanation here, as it can lead to a general misunderstanding. Indeed, various heated debates surrounding the so-called 'science wars' illustrate just how easy it is to misunderstand and misrepresent totally the analytic perspectives of the social sciences in the general domain of scientific knowledge. Oddly, equivalent analytic stances have not really given rise to 'medicine wars' between social scientists and medical practitioners: perhaps medical sociologists and anthropologists are less strident in their commentaries, and medical practitioners have more breadth of vision than their laboratory-science counterparts. In any event, we assume that we ought to pay serious attention to the forms and content of lay knowledge.

There is now a substantial and detailed literature on lay understandings of bio-medical phenomena in contemporary 'Western' societies – although in some contexts, 'other' and 'exotic' cultures seem to be more thoroughly documented than those of European and American societies. There is some debate as to just how lay knowledge should be conceptualized. There has been a tendency within the sociology of health and illness to grant ever greater legitimacy to lay knowledge, at least implicitly by virtue of the nomenclature employed. As Prior (2003) has recently noted, from lay 'beliefs', through lay 'knowledge', we now have analyses of lay 'expertize'. Prior himself is suspicious of the growing symmetry in these treatments, and argues that it remains necessary, as well as possible, to distinguish between expert knowledge and lay knowledge on a number of key criteria. We are in some sympathy with Prior's account and acknowledge that, in the most general terms, scientific and professional knowledge is more explicitly theorized and rendered more explicit. Lay knowledge is, however, more likely to be implicit or tacit and directed at practical ends rather than systematic and subject to critical reflection. However, Prior overstates these distinctions and differences. Not all professionals *use* knowledge in the most systematic and reflective ways. We know that in addition to what we might call expert knowledge, 'experts' also use a variety of practical modes of reasoning and action: they too have 'belief systems' (Atkinson, 1995). There are, for instance, multiple sources for medical knowledge and action. The knowledge of medical practitioners is derived in part from research and academic journals, certainly, and in that sense reflects highly articulated, explicit and theorized knowledge (which, of course, remains as provisional as any scientific knowledge). But it also includes what is more appropriately referred to as practical, recipe knowledge, reflecting a stock of personal experience, which is more tacitly held and less based on theorized knowledge. Professional authority derives from a mix of explicit knowledge and tacit experience. It is highly eclectic and syncretic. We cannot assume that it is always of a different order from the knowledge of lay persons. Equally, 'experts' are normally experts about something, and not everything. In medicine, for instance, geneticists have a quite different order of expert knowledge about their own field of specialization than do, say, general practitioners, who will in turn probably have greater expertise than general surgeons. The social category of 'expert' or 'professional' certainly does not guarantee a particular and coherent array of knowledge in practice. One of our respondents (a clinical consultant, Annabel) stands out as a good example of the tenuous nature of expertise. Referred to the genetic services in connection with her son's chromosomal syndrome, Annabel invoked lay explanations interspersed with her own everyday surveillance of her wider kindred (see Chapter 2).

Equally, lay knowledge can be internally differentiated. We do not need to elevate knowledge to a form of 'expertise' in its own right in order to recognize that some lay members of society can acquire highly developed and systematic knowledge about specific areas. Indeed, when sociologists of medicine have referred to lay experts and lay expertise, they have done so in the context of people – sometimes activists and advocates – who have developed knowledge that is comparable with that of the professional experts (Sexton, 2002). Indeed, it is not difficult to see how that is possible. An individual or a group who is concerned with understanding, representing and campaigning about a particular condition can read the available literature just as much as any other. An individual who is suffering from a given medical condition can not only read up on it, but can also relate the published findings to the phenomenology of her or his own symptoms. Individual 'lay' people, therefore, can, and do, develop a degree of 'expertise' in restricted domains – just as professionals do. Equally, a great deal of lay knowledge can be thought of as 'beliefs', in the commonsensical way that beliefs are transmitted and held in unreflecting ways, are based on sources like cultural tradition and are tacitly held. Beliefs are not normally based on systematic explorations of evidence. Consequently, we have no problem with identifying aspects of lay knowledge as 'beliefs' or 'belief systems'. Equally, however, the principle of symmetry requires that we identify some aspects of professional knowledge as 'belief systems'. A great deal of knowledge-in-action can be thought of as the application of beliefs, in which personal authority, tradition, local practices, personal styles and *ad hoc* justifications all play their part. In other words, there are no hard and fast divisions to be made between professional and lay knowledge. In the course of this book, we shall be concerned primarily with the knowledge and actions of lay members of society. As we have just indicated, this should not be taken to imply that we believe that lay understandings of genetics are necessarily in want of repair. We do not hold a deficit model of the public understanding of science and medicine. We are not committed to the careful exploration of everyday practical knowledge in order to derive ironic contrasts with a gold standard of received wisdom among scientists and clinicians. On the contrary, our starting point is an assumption – borne out in the research that is reported in the chapters that follow – that there is a rich cultural vein of lay ideas of inheritance to be explored.

Ours, then, is a study of how genetic information enters into the discourse of families, and a study of the interpretative frameworks that family members have developed to make sense of the general phenomena of inheritance. We look at the reported experiences and actions of families who share a genetic disease, or the risk of such a condition. Practical genetic knowledge is not, of course, confined to people who have a genetic disease 'in the family'. However, families affected by genetic conditions do provide the opportunity to examine more general belief systems as such matters are given heightened salience by the families' particular circumstances. It is also important for us to understand how such families specifically make sense of genetic information.

There are, therefore, practical and more general interests that inform our study. The practical significance of family studies in this context resides in the growing significance of genetically based medicine and genetic counselling. While therapeutic interventions based on genetic technologies remain a rather distant prospect for most conditions, there are increasingly large numbers of diagnostic and predictive tests for genetic diseases. Likewise, an increasing number of disorders are interpreted as having an inherited component. A good deal of contemporary work in medical genetics consists of classifying a condition, identifying the 'gene' responsible, assessing the pattern of inheritance, estimating the risk of an individual being a 'carrier' and/or of having the disease, and providing counselling on the basis of those assessments.

Our work therefore stands at the intersection of several key developments; in the social sciences and in biomedical knowledge itself. The so-called 'new genetics', both as scientific innovation and as medical practice, give rise to a special focus on the social phenomena of relatedness, defined in biological and social terms. Genetic medicine has developed at an extraordinary pace, as has genomic and post-genomic science more generally. Genetic medicine, which involves the identification of genetic diseases, locating their genetic bases, and the provision of genetic counselling to individuals and family networks, has significant implications for medical practice in general. Population screening for a number of common genetic conditions is becoming a key part of health policy. Ideas of genetic risk and susceptibility are becoming pervasive. Genetics is by no means the sole occupational preserve of specialists in genetics. Primary healthcare professionals are expected to be involved in the identification of individual and familial risks. The increasing identification of complex genetic risks and predispositions involves a widening range of medical specialisms, including cardiology, neurology, haematology and psychological medicine. It is easy to engage in sweeping and potentially premature speculations concerning the social impact of such innovations. It is, for instance, easy to assume that these innovations impinge on the consumers of health services, and that they necessarily transform the nature of medicine, personhood and patienthood. It is also dangerously easy to extrapolate from extreme cases, where the nature of genetic disease is stark (as in conditions like Huntington's disease), to claim radical and widespread transformations more generally. Our research has been predicated on the belief that detailed, empirical research on these issues is a necessary prerequisite to any such conclusions. Our work with families whose members have been investigated and counselled by genetic health professionals is informed by a belief that the social implications of new genetic technologies and genetic counselling have to be understood in the light of local, concrete experience and careful empirical research.

We shall, therefore, trace some of the complexities of families, kinship and genetic inheritance. We shall focus not just on the specific diseases that family members display and the medically defined risks they embody. We shall locate their experiences of medical genetics within a broader matrix of everyday beliefs and practices concerning inheritance and the inter-generational transmission of information about physical and personal characteristics. We shall see how the medically defined calculus of genetic risk is mapped onto an equally significant moral calculus of family relations.

–2–

Accomplishing Kinship

Introduction

Our book is about the intersection of family members and the world of genetic medicine. We conducted our research by observing the work of a medical genetics clinic, observing home visits by professional practitioners and interviewing members of families who were followed up after their clinic consultations. Our research is also about a different intersection – between those two domains of everyday experience and medical work, and the research activities of ourselves as social scientists. Authors such as Mishler (2000) have talked about the juxtaposition of two social worlds – that of medicine and that of the everyday lifeworld. However, such a dualism overlooks the fact that there is always the third element: that of research. In presenting the outcomes of our own study, we are conscious of the fact that the phenomena we report on are *constructed* through these engagements and intersecting sources of knowledge and experience. Another way of expressing this is to say that family relations and genetic constitutions are formed through several kinds of encounters. First, there are the encounters between lay individuals, families and professional practitioners. Second, there are the research encounters between family members and social scientists – notably in the conduct of research interviews and observational work. Moreover, the 'medical' world comprises more than one type of actor: medical practitioners, specialist nurses and laboratory scientists being among them.

As we have already made clear, 'families' and membership of families are by no means straightforward. Families and the relations of kinship are not naturally 'given' entities. Practical kinship is constituted through the kinds of relationships that members recognize, and that are activated from time to time. Particularly in the context of Anglo-European, somewhat diffuse, kinship systems, family relations are variable and 'families' are constructed through the performance of mutual recognition between members, the exchange of obligations and favours, everyday contact, childcare, family gatherings at calendar festivals and *rites de passage*, and the multiple occasioned ways in which relations between kin and affines are brought into being and sustained. There are, moreover, other settings in which relatedness is identified and constituted. The genetics service is one such setting where relations of kinship are identified and families constituted through the work of constructing the *pedigree* or family tree. We describe and discuss this aspect of genetic work, how genetic risks and diagnoses are inserted into the networks of past and present relatedness that constitute 'family' for the practical purposes of medical genetics.

This book is not intended to be a comprehensive account of genetic medicine. It is, however, imperative that we provide some background to the practice of genetic medicine and the delivery of genetic counselling, before documenting some of their consequences and implications for individuals and their families. In this chapter we draw attention to some of the salient features of contemporary genetics. Our intention is not to review all of genetic medicine. Here we offer an introduction to the sort of genetic services and conditions that inform our sociological analyses. We are more concerned with general principles and the social processes involved in genetic services, than with the particularities of many genetic conditions. By way of background, we provide some introductory discussion of contemporary genetics and their implications for medical practice. As with many aspects of this general field of work, we avoid exaggerated claims either *pro* or *contra* biomedical innovations.

The experiences of the family members we have met need to be set against the backdrop of contemporary genetic science and genetic medicine. Moreover, it is important to understand particular experiences because they will help us to illuminate the sort of encounters that are likely to become much more common in the foreseeable future, as medicine and health care become increasingly influenced by genetics. The prospect of increased genetic screening and surveillance has recently been emphasized in the United Kingdom by the Department of Health in its White Paper on genetic services (Department of Health, 2003). The White Paper projects general population screening for a number of common genetic conditions in the near future, as well as more widespread genetic screening in the longer term. As a point of departure we consider one way in which families are constructed in the course of our study: that is, the research encounter between family members and social scientists.

The Ethnography

This study is set within a broader perspective that reflects our more extensive ethnographic involvement with a clinical genetics service within a major UK teaching hospital. It represents a significant joint research venture between social scientists and medical geneticists. Over a period of 5 years, we have been involved with the department at a number of levels, observing the work of a number of clinical teams, following their clinical caseload and the everyday mundane work of the clinic.

Featherstone carried out an ethnography of two clinical genetic teams and their patients, following them over a period of 18 months. Travelling to a large number of regional clinics, sitting in on clinical consultations and, following the everyday caseload of the teams and the wider department meant that a wide variety of conditions were observed (in total sixty-two consultations were observed). The individuals and families observed were all at various stages in the process of diagnosis, classification and disclosure. Additionally, the work and caseloads of genetic specialist nurses and specialist registrars were followed so that a number of their home visits with patients and their families could be observed (twenty-two families were observed within their homes). From this sample, nineteen families were also interviewed.

Featherstone attended a large number of clinical team and departmental meetings, as well as meetings with other specialists such as paediatricians and laboratory staff, in order to observe the everyday work of diagnosis (in total thirty-five meetings were observed). Other collaborations and encounters between the clinicians and other professionals were also observed. Additionally, Featherstone had the opportunity to gather data in a wide range of less formal and decidedly informal settings where cases and the work of the clinic were discussed, such as in the car on the drive to and from a clinic, over coffee and in bars and restaurants.

Once Featherstone had met the individuals or family groups within the clinical setting, their consent was obtained to visit them at home to talk to them about their experiences. Initially the study had been planned to follow a specific sample of patients, but the clinical setting quickly revealed that individuals and families could not be separated into neat categories.

We had planned to follow those who had received a diagnosis or been referred for a familial genetic condition that had, by its very nature, implications for other family members. However, the identification of such individuals does not occur in a straightforward way. The clinic is sometimes unable to state categorically that a condition has occurred for the first time or, is unrelated to other problems 'in the family', or to provide complete reassurance that the condition will not occur in the next generation. In addition, as we shall show, even when individuals and families have received reassurance from the clinic that their condition is not or is unlikely to be familial, this does not prevent them from seeing a wider pattern of inheritance in the family or from believing that the condition is likely to occur again.

The study planned to follow a series of retrospective and prospective family case studies, using snowball sampling to interview members of each kindred to follow the flow of genetic information through the kinship network. However, it became clear that families could not be categorized as 'retrospective' and having achieved 'disclosure'. Nor did families start from a position of referral with no prior knowledge or ideas of what their diagnosis might be or who was at risk. Instead, all the families we met were at different stages in the 'messy' process of understanding the implications of their diagnosis or potential diagnosis, assessing who may be affected and making decisions about what to do with this information.

It was initially usually hard to establish the stage of diagnosis and disclosure involved. Several observations of clinical consultations were followed by in-depth conversations with family members within the privacy of their own homes and only then did their positions become clearer. The process of genetic counselling, diagnosis and disclosure can take a number of years, with a series of individuals or family groups attending the clinic, and the involvement of different specialisms, technologies and tests.

In addition, the clinical team often made assumptions about families, presenting disclosure as a straightforward linear process. Interestingly, the clinical team focused their concern on individuals who were explicit about their decision not to disclose genetic information to family members who might be at risk. However, within this setting, most individuals agreed to disclose or reported that they had informed those at risk, and few admitted that they found this process problematic. The clinicians involved were given specific details of the project and its focus on the issue of disclosure and communication of genetic information. This had a number of effects; the clinicians sometimes appeared to be anxious about the research process, but at other times were enthusiastic, suggesting various 'good' families attending the clinic in which 'everyone knows' about the familial condition. We found, often in stark contrast to the clinical perception, that these 'good' families had complex understandings and beliefs about inheritance that meant that genetic information was not distributed to family members unproblematically.

The forty-one individuals we refer to in the following chapters are members of nineteen families and have all been diagnosed with, or referred to the genetic services for, a potential genetic condition. We will now describe these individuals, their families and their genetic conditions. The conditions and their modes of inheritance are described in more detail in the Appendix.

Veronica, Lindsey, Maggie and Suzanne

Four sisters, Veronica, Lindsey, Maggie and Suzanne (all in their late forties and fifties), and five of the next generation of women in their family (all in their twenties) were interviewed. This family is affected by an extremely rare degenerative disorder that does not follow the classical patterns of Mendelian inheritance, but instead follows matrilineal inheritance because the underlying genetic alteration is located in the mitochondrial genome instead of the nuclear chromosomes. For the women within this family, the early symptoms have tended to be fatigue and muscular aches and pains, leading to increased disability. Mitochondria are transmitted solely from the mother to her children, so the condition affects both males and females but is transmitted only through females, with all the children of affected women inheriting the altered mitochondria and most going on to develop the condition, but none of the children of affected men.

Patty and Philip

Patty is in her early forties. Divorced and looking after the home, she is a carrier of FRAXE and has an 8-year-old son who has been diagnosed with the condition. Her two daughters, one in her late teens and the other (Theresa) 20 years old, also have some learning disabilities, although undiagnosed. Her brother Philip, an engineer, lives in England; he is married and has no children. Their other brother lives in Australia and has three school age children. Fragile X syndrome type E (FRAXE) is a chromosomal condition, is not associated with any particular facial appearance, and usually causes only a mild to moderate degree of learning difficulty. It most commonly affects males more than females and is transmitted through families in a sex-linked fashion, from a man to his daughters and from a woman to half of her children of either sex. Molecular and cytogenetic tests are available for this condition and to identify carrier status.

Julia, Chris, Mary and John

Julia and Chris have a 5-year-old son who has also been diagnosed with FRAXE. Julia's brother lives nearby and her parents, Mary and John, are retired and live in the next village. She also has a sister, a nurse, who lives in Canada.

Isobel

Isobel is in her early thirties and is worried that there may be a familial risk of inherited cardiomyopathy in her family. She is a widow, following the sudden death of her husband, Richard, the year before we met her. She lives with her 2-year-old son and her 12-year-old daughter (from a previous relationship) and works as a nurse in a local hospital. She is attending the clinic because Richard and his father both died from cardiomyopathy and she is concerned that her son may also be at risk. Dilated cardiomyopathy (DCM) and hypertrophic cardiomyopathy (HCM) are the two major categories of cardiomyopathy and can be inherited, most typically as autosomal dominant traits passed from an affected parent to half their children of either sex. One complicating factor is that cardiomyopathy may be present in some family members without causing any clear physical problems while it may lead to sudden death in others at a young age. This condition is usually established clinically using cardiac echo or at post-mortem examination, although in some cases, molecular tests may be available.

Joanna and David

Joanna and David are a professional couple in their mid thirties, with two sons, 7 and 9 years old. Their 7-year-old son has been diagnosed with XYY. This means that he has an additional Y chromosome. XYY is a condition associated with increased growth (tall stature) and a higher incidence of mild learning and behaviour difficulties. A cytogenetic test is available to establish this condition.

Kate and Mark

Kate and Mark attend the clinic to establish their risk of having a child affected by cystic fibrosis. Mark's sister died of the condition in her early twenties and he grew up believing he was a carrier of the condition. Mark has a son from a previous relationship who is not affected, but they believe he may be a carrier. This is an autosomal recessive disorder affecting the transport of chloride ions across epithelial membranes in the body – such as the linings of the airways, the sweat glands and the pancreas. The frequency of healthy carriers of CF in the UK – those who carry a single altered copy of the gene – is about one person in twenty-five; about one child in 2,500 receives a double dose of the altered gene and is affected. Although most affected individuals are detected clinically or through newborn screening, a genetic test is available for this condition and can be used to identify healthy carriers, who will not develop the condition but who may transmit it to their children.

Jill

Jill is in her mid fifties and has three sons in their twenties; the eldest is living and working in London and the younger two are at university. She has been diagnosed with neurofibromatosis and is concerned about the risk to her sons. She also believes there is a strong history of cancer in her family. Neurofibromatosis (NF) is one of the commonest autosomal dominant disorders worldwide, largely because the large gene which can give rise to the disorder has a high mutation rate. NF1 leads to the development of coffee-coloured (café au lait) skin marks in early childhood and, from late childhood, the development of numerous benign tumours on the skin, the neurofibromas. About one third of cases have some degree of learning difficulty, usually mild, and about a third have some significant medical complication including malignancies, brain tumours, hypertension, epilepsy, scoliosis and other bone or joint problems. Although diagnosis is made clinically, molecular tests are becoming available for this condition.

Tamsin

Tamsin is in her mid twenties. She has also been diagnosed with neurofibromatosis and is concerned about the risk to her 2-year-old son. She is also worried that there may be some other familial conditions because her older sister died of skin cancer in her late twenties and her mother had multiple sclerosis (MS). She told her aunt about her diagnoses and discovered that her cousin also has the condition.

Nick

Nick is in his early fifties. His wife and two of her close relatives died suddenly from the rupture of blood vessel aneurysms within the brain – a form of stroke. He is extremely worried and concerned that his three children, in their late teens and early twenties, will suffer a similar fate. However, he is unable to discuss the condition with his family and seeks help from the clinical team. There are several different types of arterial aneurysm, with different causes and a range of possible consequences. A number of inherited disorders are associated with these weaknesses in the arterial wall, but they can occur for other reasons too – for instance, they can be associated with high blood pressure and high blood cholesterol. Thus, it is important to ensure that an accurate diagnosis has been established in the index case – perhaps through a lumbar puncture, a brain CT scan or post-mortem examination. For other family members, risk assessment is made on the basis of the pedigree.

Nicola and Mike

Nicola and Mike are a professional couple in their mid fifties who are concerned that their three sons (all in their late twenties or early thirties) may be at risk of aortic aneurysms. Nicola's father and two of his brothers died of this condition. There are a number of inherited (and non-inherited) conditions in which the strength of the arterial wall may be reduced and aortic dissection can occur as a cause of sudden death. Diagnosis is established in the index case clinically, often through a CT scan or at post-mortem examination; risk assessment for other family members is made on the basis of the pedigree.

Carla

Carla, a woman in her mid twenties, has recently been diagnosed with polycystic kidney disease and has a 4-year-old daughter, who is also at risk of the condition. She has a number of other relatives, including her father and two aunts, who are also affected. Although she has been diagnosed, she does not want her condition to be monitored by the clinical team and is not sure whether she wants her daughter to be tested. She attends the clinic with her mother. Polycystic kidney disease (PKD) is an autosomal dominant disorder affecting 1 in 1,000 of the population. It leads to the formation and enlargement of cysts in the cortex of the kidneys and is a common cause of chronic renal failure, often requiring dialysis or transplantation. Overt symptoms do not usually arise until well into adult life, but cysts may be detected much earlier (often from the teenage years and occasionally even in infancy) and diagnosis is made clinically if cysts are detected using a renal ultrasound. Later morbidity results from renal failure, cardiovascular disease and cerebrovascular disease, including subarachnoid haemorrhage from intracranial aneurysms. Complications can be delayed and reduced but not abolished if hypertension is detected and treated promptly and if urinary infections are managed effectively. Although molecular testing is not routinely available for this condition, two genes have been identified where mutations are associated with PKD and molecular genetic testing is available in some families.

Claudia

Claudia is a professional woman in her mid forties. She is also affected by PKD and, a few years ago, had a kidney transplant. She has two daughters in their late teens and she is concerned that they may be at risk.

Anthony and Rosie

Anthony and Rosie are a couple in their late twenties who are affected by a translocation. Anthony is a carrier of a Robertsonian translocation that has caused Rosie to have a series of miscarriages. They are currently undergoing pre-implantation genetic diagnosis (PGD). Anthony's father has passed on the condition and one of Anthony's sisters has a daughter who is affected by the translocation and has severe learning disabilities. His other two sisters and their children appear unaffected; however, as these children are reaching maturity they too may be at risk of having children who are affected. A Robertsonian translocation occurs when two chromosomes fuse together at the centromeres (the junction of the chromosome's short and long arms and the regions at which the chromosomes attach to the cell's chromosomal locomotor apparatus at cell division). While the carrier of a balanced

Robertsonian translocation will be unaffected by it, they will have an increased chance of having a fetus or child affected by severe disability because of problems with chromosome segregation at meiosis, the cell division leading to the production of eggs or sperm. Cytogenetic testing is available for this condition.

Lucy and Sally

Lucy and Sally are two sisters in their late thirties. Lucy has two young sons, one of whom has been diagnosed with Charcot Marie Tooth disease (CMT); Sally has two teenage daughters. They are concerned that they and their other children may also be affected by the condition. Charcot Marie Tooth disease is a progressive condition affecting the peripheral nerves as they carry impulses from the spinal cord to the muscles and from the sensory organs in the skin and other tissues to the spinal cord and the brain. The condition usually progresses very slowly but in some affected individuals it may eventually lead to severe physical disability. Although molecular testing is available for some types of this condition, diagnosis is usually made clinically and on the basis of electrophysiological tests.

Connie and Andrew

Connie and Andrew are a couple in their early twenties, and their 1-year-old daughter has been diagnosed with hemihypertrophy. Hemihypertrophy is a type of asymmetry of physical growth involving a relative enlargement of one side of the body. Diagnosis is established through a clinical assessment. This condition may affect the whole of one side of the body or just a part or parts of it, such as the face and tongue, or one or both limbs; it can be quite severe. Hemihypertrophy is associated with a risk of Wilm's tumour (a malignant tumour of the kidney that occurs in childhood) and children with hemihypertrophy may be offered regular ultrasound scans for the early detection of a Wilm's tumour.

Matt and Gabrielle

Matt is in his fifties. He is severely affected by Becker muscular dystrophy (BMD) and is wheelchair bound. He has a brother who is similarly affected and a sister who is unaffected. He is married and has one daughter, Gabrielle, in her late twenties; she too is married with one daughter (7 years old). Becker muscular dystrophy is a sex-linked disorder affecting skeletal muscle and cardiac muscle. The first muscles to become weak due to BMD are often the limb girdle muscles, those that move the limbs on the pelvis and the shoulder girdle and which are essential for standing up from the sitting position and for walking up stairs or up a slope.

There is a great variation in the age of onset and rate of progression of the condition. Men are affected more severely than women, and often at an earlier age. Women who carry the altered gene on one of their two copies of the X chromosome will occasionally go on to develop a degree of weakness or cardiac problems but at a later age than affected men. Diagnosis in an index case is made on the basis of clinical measures, a serum creatine kinase test, molecular genetic tests and sometimes a muscle biopsy. Further diagnoses within a kindred are usually made on the basis of creatine kinase and molecular genetic tests only, without the need for a muscle biopsy.

Sarah

Sarah is in her mid forties. Her youngest son is affected by severe autistic spectrum disorder and her older son in his late teens is concerned that he may be at risk of having a child who is similarly affected. She has two daughters from a previous relationship. Autism is the term used to describe a pattern of behaviour in which young children withdraw from social relationships and become focused on themselves and on the things around them. There is a wide range of severity of autism, and it is clearly not a single, distinct condition. The underlying causes of this range of disorders are unclear, but autism certainly can cluster in families and genetic factors appear to make an important contribution amongst other possible causal factors. This condition is established clinically and may incorporate a psychological scoring system. Risk for other family members is usually made through an assessment of the pedigree.

Annabel

Annabel is a hospital consultant in her early forties, married with two young sons. Her eldest son, who is 6 years old, has been diagnosed with an unspecified dysmorphic condition that has caused learning disabilities. Many children with unusual physical features and developmental delay remain undiagnosed despite undergoing careful physical examinations and all the relevant investigations.

Sue and Tom

Sue and Tom have three children. Their daughter (11 years old) has been diagnosed with a genetic syndrome that has caused some mild learning disabilities. They believe Tom and his family are similarly affected.

Alan and Dawn

Alan and Dawn are a couple in their early thirties. Alan and a large number of his kin have Best's macular dystrophy and they are worried about their risk of having a child who is affected. Best's macular dystrophy causes degeneration of the eye and affects the macula – the small portion of the retina that gives us central vision and our awareness of colour. This condition is identified through ophthalmological examination and is a progressive disorder inherited as an autosomal dominant trait.

Although some family members were only interviewed once (usually for two to three hours), the probands were usually interviewed again, telephoned for updates and interviewed with other family members. Contact varied; some families were interviewed in small groups over short periods of time, while others were interviewed in larger groups over a number of years. Once the proband who attended the clinic had been interviewed, their permission to interview other family members was sought. Often permission was not obtained, because the proband had either not informed others sufficiently about the condition or there were other practical barriers. However, when on occasions Featherstone was introduced to other family members, the importance of caution whilst broaching the research topic became apparent and crucial. A proband would often present their family in a way which led us to believe that information had flowed freely and unproblematically and that their kin knew about the condition and their personal risks. However, it became clear through the course of the interviews that although many of the family members knew there was 'something in the family' or that a relative was ill, they were not necessarily aware that the condition was familial or that they too were at risk. Additionally, Featherstone often felt that some probands saw the interview process as a way of disclosing risk information, particularly if other members of their kindred were present during the interviews. Such occasions reinforced the need to be cautious about discussing the genetic or familial nature of the condition. This was particularly the case when mothers and daughters were interviewed together. These occasions often became emotionally charged encounters, with mothers voicing their concern for their daughters or using the interviews as an opportunity to point out the signs of the condition or its onset in others. For the daughters it was often a chance to look for reassurance or deny that they were at risk.

The observation of the clinical consultations (each consultation usually lasting one hour) and clinical meetings yielded near-verbatim notes. The interviews were audiotaped and transcribed verbatim. Consent was obtained from all family members present in the clinic or the home setting, with the exception of very young children or children with learning disabilities which meant that it would have been unrealistic or unduly invasive to seek consent. In such cases, consent was obtained from parents. The Multi-centre Research Ethics Committee (MREC) approved this project and all names and places have been changed to preserve anonymity.

Our main research questions were: how does lay reasoning about genetic risk inform disclosure to others? How do individuals construct and define networks of disclosure among members of their kin? We recognize that the work of family and kinship is accomplished through self-presentation and narrative accounts that are occasioned performances for a number of different audiences. For example, the clinical team, other family members and the researchers were each presented with different narrations and performances of 'family' and 'family communication'.

Thus, such interview data should not be treated as providing proxy data about actual events or as equivalent to observational data of family life. Moreover, even if we were to observe family life *in situ*, we would not necessarily be able to derive direct evidence about kinship. Our approach is to apply the well-established principle that interview data should be treated as narrative accounts of family relatedness and inheritance. We would also like to stress that interviews elicit both biographical and autobiographical accounts. These narratives and reflections have particular kinds of *functions* and have their own *forms*, which must be examined in order to consider what kind of biographical and social work they accomplish. We thus recognize the force of narrative analysis in making sense of interview materials (cf. Bauman, 1986; Mishler, 2000; Plummer, 2001; Riessman, 1993). We do not, however, believe that interview accounts, such as the ones we present here, are entirely devoid of any referential value beyond the occasion of their own telling. We believe that no individual 'family' or 'family relations' exist independently of the kinds of accounts and performances that actors engage in and produce on multiple occasions. We would not, therefore, seek to privilege one kind of family talk or family enactment over all others, as constituting reality. We recognize that our interviews constitute one discursive site in which families and their genetic constitutions are brought into accountable being (Atkinson and Coffey, 2002).

We have thus based our analysis on a number of propositions. Family and kinship are accomplished, or performed, and are constructed through the biographical and autobiographical work people do. Their biographical work takes many forms, including family stories and reminiscences, photograph albums, family social events, letters and so on. Interview narratives can be thought of as, in principle, among the repertoire of possible performances. These are not performances about 'families' or 'relatedness' that exist independently of the biographical work. In a fundamental sense, they constitute or produce the relationships and the families. These narratives are performances of memory and are reflexive: they generate the topics they describe. To analyse these biographical accounts we examine the narrative forms that accomplish this work. These include the construction of the life-course, age and generational differences; the performance of moral character and personality types; and the embedding of the self in accounts of relatedness, through the performance of memory and emotion.

In order to understand how the biological 'facts' of genetics and biomedical knowledge are aligned with the social 'facts' of relatedness, families and persons, we need to understand the biomedical background and, the professional role of the clinic and the laboratory in achieving the work of genetic relations. Recent accounts of innovations such as the Human Genome Project and the popularization of genetic science can readily convey the impression that one can simply 'test' DNA and read from the resulting sequences of bases a wide range of information about individuals, their relatedness and their actual or potential health status. The assembly of a predictive or diagnostic assessment for an individual, or for the members of a kindred, is not a straightforward matter. In the first place, there is a variety of biological tests that can be deployed for different conditions and investigations. Second, laboratory testing of DNA and other traces is not the whole story. Geneticists also construct and examine the *pedigree* or family tree and the medical histories of family members in order to decide on appropriate diagnostic and predictive tests and to calculate risk values.

In the context of new genetic services and the exponential growth in both the scope and the volume of genetic testing, it is imperative that we understand how the experience of genetic testing, of genetic knowledge and of interventions based on this are interpreted by individuals and other family members. Family groups may be identified as sharing a genetic condition, being affected by a genetic condition, being 'carriers' of genetic disease, or having a 'risk' or 'susceptibility' to one or more conditions. However, the terms that we have just introduced – such as testing, risk and even disease – need to be understood within the context of new genetic technologies and techniques, and placed within the framework of contemporary genetic medicine. We also need to locate our understandings against a backdrop of wider social and cultural concerns – such as the claim that medicine is becoming increasingly geneticized and that new genetic knowledge is transforming the way we think about persons as actors constituted by biological and social practices.

Drawing Up the Pedigree

Geneticists – clinicians and scientists – construct 'pedigrees' of their patients. These are representations of biological relatedness. Graphic versions of these pedigrees use conventional modes of representation and are generated by standardized computer software. Nukaga and Cambrioso (1997) have explicated the conventional production of pedigrees and the visual construction of familial disease. Such devices share features of genealogical work familiar to social scientists through the anthropological tradition established by Rivers and subsequently incorporated as a taken-for-granted mode of representation (Bouquet, 1995, 1996). In constructing a pedigree, geneticists bring into a particular form and a particular situated reality the 'family' relations inscribed in the family tree. The pedigree is a particular kind of representation. It does not transparently represent an independent family entity. Because we are so familiar with it as an idea and as iconography, it is too easy to overlook its contrived and conventional nature and the fact that it derives from historically specific models of human and animal 'breeding' (Klapisch-Zuber, 1996; Ritvo, 1987, 1995).

The pedigree is initially constructed during the first meeting between the professional and the individual and will focus on the proband, whose diagnosis brings the disorder to attention within the family and is a vital resource in exploring potential familial patterns of inherited medical conditions. After referral, but prior to most clinic appointments, the genetic counsellor or specialist nurse contacts the individual and their family to arrange a meeting, usually a home visit prior to their clinic appointment. The main purpose of this meeting is to create a family tree. Alternatively, if an individual comes to the clinic 'cold', the first part of the consultation will involve taking a pedigree. A report of the initial meeting and the pedigree or family tree is placed in the medical records held by the clinical genetic service. The pedigree can then be inspected by the clinical team and more widely by other specialists for patterns of symptoms, diagnoses and causes of death through the generations, in order to identify possible familial conditions.

The clinician usually refers to the process of constructing a pedigree as 'taking a family tree'; however, occasionally they also refer to 'taking a pedigree', which can lead to some astonishment among families because of its association with animal breeding, for example, as one mother (Joanna), for example exclaimed 'my son is a dog!' The pedigree focuses on the proband and, radiates out to other family members to include details about partner(s), parents, grandparents and children, typically encompassing up to four generations. For each generation details of siblings and their children are included. During this process, both the clinician and the individual routinely use everyday kinship terms such as 'aunt' and 'cousin' to identify members of the kin and to locate them within the often complex relationships described. For each individual included, the clinician routinely requests details about their health status in relation to the specific genetic referral. In addition, they ask about pregnancy history and health problems, with broad questions about family members such as 'Are they fit and well as far as you know?' or 'Any problems with children or their development?' The clinician routinely requests date of birth, marital status, location and, employment history for all those named as kin as well as cause of death if applicable. Each family member is represented by a symbol on the family tree.

The clinician and the individual construct the family together and this is often a chance for the individual (or other relatives) to recount family stories that may suggest where the condition started or which family members are similarly affected. These stories are incorporated within the pedigree. For example, one mother, Annabel (a clinical consultant), whose son has been referred with a chromosomal syndrome that causes learning disabilities, recounts to the genetic specialist nurse during the making of the pedigree how she has scrutinized her family for similar problems. The clinician prompts her to recall other family members who may have similar 'problems'. She recalls a half-brother who is a 'family secret' and whom they believe is 'not quite right' and a cousin who is 'a bit odd'. However, she rejects a genetic classification, because family stories suggest her cousin's problems were caused by his 'upbringing'. She adds 'he's a bit slow but from family talk it sounded as though he was a bit under-stimulated as a child. So environment.' She also recounts family stories that situate her mother's family within the pedigree. They were a 'well-to-do landed family' and Annabel's mother 'traded down' when she married. Thus, not only the health status of particular family members, but wider judgments and beliefs about the kin and their genes become incorporated into the pedigree.

This 'face to face' encounter often takes place in the individual's home and this means that not only clinical information is obtained, but other knowledge is also acquired. For example, when discussing the kin the clinical team often incorporate their own stories and judgments about families including other social problems, relationship histories or the levels of cleanliness of their homes. They draw on their social knowledge and recollections about the kin and their relationships.

Thus, two frames of reference intersect, the social world of family relations and the biological realm of genetically related individuals. Genetic scientists and clinicians alike base their everyday work on bringing knowledge about families and representations of pedigrees into conjunction. The meetings between scientists and clinicians and the clinical team meetings are prime occasions for such work. In the course of those meetings, family and kinship are occasioned products. The social and the biological are assembled out of the shards of information available to the participants.

One of the important outcomes of the clinical and laboratory meetings is the successful allocation of blood samples to families and the ability to draw up a meaningful pedigree. As we have suggested already, the pedigree – the representation of biological relationships among kin – links the world of the laboratory gaze and that of the clinical gaze. It links the social worlds of the scientist and the clinician. In this work setting, therefore, the pedigree is a 'boundary object'. Boundary objects are produced in more than one 'social world' and facilitate the negotiation of shared understanding or concerted action across those worlds. As Star and Griesemer put it:

> Boundary objects both inhabit several intersecting worlds ... and satisfy the informational requirements of each of them. Boundary objects are objects that are both plastic enough to adapt to local needs and constraints of the several parties employing them, yet robust enough to maintain a common identity across sites. They are weakly structured in common use, and become strongly structured in individual-site use. They have different meanings in different social worlds but their structure is common enough to more than one world to make them recognizable, a means of translation. (1989: 393)

Such boundary objects are therefore objects of use by different occupational groups, specialisms and the like, and are used to articulate the work and the meanings of the respective groups (see also Fujimura, 1992). The pedigree is a boundary object in two senses. First, it inhabits the epistemic space between the laboratory scientists and the genetic clinicians. Second, it simultaneously occupies the domain of biomedical knowledge on the one hand, and the world of everyday relations on the other.

First, then, the pedigree straddles the work of two specialisms, the clinical and the laboratory, which are both concerned with assembling patterns of relatedness linking family members' shared biological characteristics, although its status as such may be obscured by the close proximity of the specialist groups. Of course, in one sense, the clinicians and the genetic scientists may be held to occupy the same social world (and this is a reminder that the boundaries of social worlds' must be viewed relatively and not absolutely). On the other hand, the knowledge, skills and expertise of the respective groups are different, and are brought to bear on different objects. Second, the pedigree is a boundary object in that it spans the mundane experience of family life and practical kinship on the one hand, and the world of biomedical knowledge of biological relatedness, inherited disease, medical diagnoses and causes of death on the other. The ordinary social relations of everyday kinship are refracted through the narratives, recollections and constructions of probands. They capture the enunciated 'facts' of social kinship. Through the conventions of representation and the computerized graphics, the potentially fuzzy and complex relations of 'families' are translated into 'standardized packages' (Fujimura, 1992). Standardized packages have functions similar to boundary objects, in that they allow phenomena to be decontextualized and re-contextualized. In that sense, then, pedigrees facilitate the creation of 'standard' kinship and standardized relatedness. As a physical, graphic embodiment of those constructions, the pedigree is also an *immutable mobile* (Latour, 1987), in that it 'fixes' the varied possibilities of mutual recognition that constitute practical kinship relations into canonical patterns, while being detached from the particularities of practical reasoning. Moreover, the pedigree becomes an impersonal representation of 'the family', in that it has no 'ego' of origin; although in its creation the initial proband is the narrating subject of the family tree, in the depersonalized and decontextualized biomedical pedigree there is no such personal authorship ascribed or implied.

The pedigree is also used to interpret the results of specific genetic tests. Test results are 'fitted' into the overall familial pattern that is established in the pedigree. The pedigree itself may also be modified in the light of test results, or at least the accuracy of the information may be called into question. A clear case of such modification arises when biological paternity is called into question. This is an obvious, but by no means trivial, instance where the social and the biological need to be reconciled.

The social and the biological also intersect in the clinic, focused on work with the pedigree, in that clinicians and scientists can bring to bear two different registers of knowledge about their patients. The family-in-the-laboratory is constructed through successive iterations of biological testing and the tracing of shared physical traits. The family-in-the-clinic may also be known to clinicians on the basis of long-term engagement with the family – successive consultations with different members of the family, sometimes drawn from more than one generation. The first knowledge register constitutes the domain of biomedical knowledge, in which the family is constituted out of biologically derived evidence. Here scientists and clinicians alike may face a complicated puzzle: 'bits' are missing and they feel they do not have the whole story. In the case of doubtful paternity, the biologically defined pedigree and the socially recognized relations of kinship may be in direct conflict. The facts of the case need to be reconciled, while the social niceties of family and kinship may need preservation.

In practice, the identification of a person with a pedigree, and the specification of kin and affines may be problematic and may rest on a series of ad hoc and local judgments on the part of the professionals. The scientists and the clinicians bring together contrasting professional expertise and two contrasting bodies of knowledge about the individuals concerned. The clinician has knowledge acquired from a face-to-face encounter, while the scientist's knowledge is based on a name and the identification of an individual's genetic make-up. The individual, as part of a family and as part of a pedigree, is the object of the ensuing discourse. The construction of those social and biological categories is not always unambiguous: scientists and clinicians make ad hoc decisions and interpretations in the course of the review meeting. The fieldnotes and transcripts hint at the variety of ways in which family and kinship are invoked and assembled by participants. They draw, for instance, on social knowledge and recollections about families, their members and their relationships. Within this professional setting, they also use everyday 'English' kinship terms (such as aunt and cousin) in their attempts to locate and identify individuals.

It is clear from our observations in the clinic and at clinical genetic team meetings that individual cases are identified and placed in families based on the team members' shared knowledge and recollections. In the absence of a pedigree, 'the family' is reconstructed and called to mind. 'Scientific' knowledge of individuals and their genetic constitution has to be supplemented with the sort of general, social acquaintance with families that clinicians recall from previous clinical encounters; as a genetic scientist said with great delight during one team meeting, 'It's such a comfort when names ring a bell with someone.'

Medical genetics thus depends upon the intersection of two frames of reference. The first is the essentially social world of family relations; the second is the essentially biological realm of DNA testing and genetically related individuals. Indeed, it is abundantly clear from our fieldwork that the construction of the biological findings is often dependent on the geneticists' collective memory for families. That understanding of families represents them not only as social entities, but also as a collection of DNA that can be represented on a pedigree, stored in a freezer or even dispersed by post. They can thus be translated from the social, everyday frame of reference into the decontextualized representations of the pedigree and the genetic tests that may be performed. The results of genetic tests are mapped onto family trees to create a composite entity in which kinship and biology are brought into conjunction.

The goal of the scientist is to provide genetic information in a way that is sometimes referred to as 'making a family informative'. To do that they need genetic material from the 'index case'. If the gene has not been mapped or a deletion found, they need the family to provide the missing pieces in the jigsaw puzzle. The scientist needs to find differences between the various copies of the gene or chromosome present in a family group so they can trace the transmission of genetic material between the generations. The key issue in this process of mapping is not whether a person is alive or dead but whether they have donated, or will donate, some genetic material that can be made informative. The contribution of genetic material from family members enables the scientist to build up a more comprehensive picture of a particular individual's genetic make-up.

Genetic Testing

The very idea of genetics, and genetic medicine, contains within it a diverse range of understandings and interventions. One core element of genetic medicine is genetic *testing*. Genetic testing itself represents a broad category of investigations intended to define an individual's genetic constitution. It refers to the examination of an individual's entire set of chromosomes or, to be more precise, focused examination of one or more specific genes to look for variants that may have functional consequences, including an association with medically defined disorders. Some of these important genetic variations may be inherited through the family, passed from one generation to the next, although the patterns of inheritance and the manifestation of disease are often not as straightforward as this suggests. Genetic changes can arise as spontaneous events in the production of gametes – egg or sperm – so that the associated disorders may be 'genetic' in origin, but not inherited, and thus not manifest in the parents or in earlier generations. Equally, some genetic changes may occur during growth and development – arising within an individual and giving rise to tumours, including cancers and other malignancies, or perhaps to malformations, if the mutation occurs early in the course of development. Consequently, the equation of 'genetic' with 'familial' or 'inherited' conditions is not a simple one. Equally, not all genetic conditions can be accounted for at the level of single genes; a number of genes may be involved – they may be located next to each other on a chromosome, so that a chromosomal anomaly affects them all, or there may have been independent changes in the DNA sequence of several different genes, which together lead to health problems.

Furthermore, there are different ways in which a particular genetic make-up (the genotype) can contribute to a particular outcome for an individual (the phenotype). In some instances it is possible to tell with near certainty that a particular genetic constitution will lead inexorably to the manifestation of a disease or syndrome. In other cases, the inheritance of one or more genes that are associated with a disease will not necessarily lead to the manifestation of that disease in the individual. The genetic basis may increase one's *risk* or *susceptibility* for developing or manifesting the disease, but does not automatically foreshadow the certain onset of that condition. In other cases again, it may be impossible to predict with any degree of certainty either the age of onset or the degree of severity for a particular condition. The genetic constitution of an individual family member is not only an issue in terms of her or his own health and well-being. Where a disease-related gene is known or suspected within a family, the individuals may also have the status of *carriers*. They may be liable to pass on a gene to their own offspring, even when they do not manifest the disease themselves.

As a consequence of these different biomedical possibilities, we can identify different kinds of genetic investigation that are carried out within genetic services, and which have a number of different implications for individuals or families. Broadly speaking, these are conventionally defined in terms of *diagnostic, predictive* and *carrier* testing. As the term implies, diagnostic testing is used to try to identify the causal basis for a manifest, symptomatic condition. For example, if a patient's symptoms of lethargy and arthritic pain are identified, and genetic haemochromatosis (GH) is in the differential diagnosis as one possible cause, then a diagnostic genetic test may 'fix' the diagnosis as GH. However, a clinical diagnosis will occur only on the basis of frank symptoms. In that sense, a genetic diagnostic test is much like any other laboratory test that may be employed to investigate the underlying cause(s) of manifest disease. This may be seen as an oversimplification because the identification of a genetic basis will have potential consequences for offspring or other family members, but those potential consequences are present whether the diagnosis of a genetic disorder is achieved through genetic or non-genetic investigations; non-genetic tests have been used for many years to identify inherited diseases, existing long before DNA was recognized. In contrast to a diagnostic test, predictive testing has a future orientation and it can be carried out on asymptomatic people in order to identify whether they have a genetic constitution that will lead to the manifestation of a disease or that will give them an increased risk of developing symptomatic disease. In the former case, the outcome of the test will be a confirmation (or otherwise) that the patient will become symptomatic – although the time of onset and its severity may not be entirely predictable. In the latter case, the outcome of a genetic test will be the estimation of the patient's risk of or predisposition for developing the disease.

The results of genetic testing can clearly vary greatly, with many different potential consequences for individuals and members of their families. They may range from the confirmation of disease caused by a new, spontaneous mutation in a child, to the prediction of the inevitable onset of disease (for example, in someone at risk of cancer), to the generation of risk values which will have implications for other individuals in the family – the risk being relevant to their own personal health or the health of their future children. Equally clearly, the consequences of such biomedical work will vary, depending on the condition, the individual tested (the proband) and the family concerned. There may be a wide variety of decisions to be made and reflected upon. These can include decisions about reproduction, about lifestyle, about monitoring for early signs of a disease, and about disease prevention (where that may be feasible).

The Work of the Clinic

In the service under study, genetic work is dispersed between consultants of clinical genetics, genetic specialist nurses, other genetic associates, such as genetic counsellors, trainees in clinical genetics (specialist registrars or SpRs), other clinicians (GPs and other clinical specialists) and the family. In the current service, clinical work is also distributed between the home visit, the clinical consultation and the regular team meetings. As we have described, following referral the majority of families receive a home visit prior to their clinic appointment. The purpose of this visit is to take a history, create a family tree, and collect relevant materials (e.g. photographs). In addition, the nurse obtains permission to trace and acquire medical records for relevant family members, including test results and autopsy reports. At this stage, there is no examination of the proband.

The process of referral and diagnosis can take a number of years and for some individuals and families there may never be a conclusive diagnosis of the cause of their condition or assessment of their risk of inheriting and developing the condition. Despite recent technical developments, many genetic abnormalities cannot be identified through either molecular or cytogenic tests. As we have argued elsewhere (Featherstone et al., 2005), despite the developments of genetic technology, diagnoses are still made based on the long-standing mechanisms of clinical perception, which draw upon the experience and expertise of the specialist clinical geneticist.

The following case is an example of a referral where there is a concern that a condition affecting one member of a family may have risk implications for other family members. Anna is attending the clinic for the first time. At the initial clinical consultation, it is usual for both the consultant and the genetic specialist nurse who conducted the home visit to be present. Anna is in her early forties; she is a civil servant and arrives at the clinic carrying a briefcase stuffed with reports and paperwork. Before the start of the clinic appointment, the genetic specialist nurse describes the home visit. She tells us that Anna's mother has developed what may be early onset Alzheimer's and that Anna is concerned that she too may be at risk of developing this condition.

Typically, as in this case, at the start of the clinic appointment, the consultant discusses the route of referral and takes a history. The consultant begins by asking questions to confirm the condition affecting Anna's mother. For this condition, the age of onset is an important factor in assessing the familial risk. Anna reports that although her mother received her diagnosis at the age of 64, she had been experiencing symptoms for two years prior to that. The consultant uses the pedigree of the family (obtained at the home visit by the genetic specialist nurse) to prompt her enquiries and moves on to ask about the wider family, particularly Anna's maternal grandfather, who is reported to have had similar symptoms. Anna and her brother remember their grandfather showing some signs of dementia in his seventies. The consultant then asks about the health of Anna's two maternal aunts and an uncle and Anna confirms they were unaffected; however, her father and paternal grandmother had Parkinson's disease. The consultant seeks to clarify the distinction between these two diagnoses within the kindred.

> *Consultant*: I had a letter from your GP and he asked if I could see you with regard to the family history of Alzheimer's. What I understand, your mother has developed Alzheimer's and some concerns have been raised because it was below 60 when she first showed signs. Can you tell me about your mother.
>
> *Anna*: She's 74 but was diagnosed when she was 64 but it was probably two years before that but we didn't pick it up. We thought she was just tired and depressed. We just thought she was worn out.
>
> *Consultant*: Was it her GP who diagnosed it?
>
> *Anna*: Yes, she kept going back with the same thing. I think it was also a case of denial. It's a hell of a diagnosis to get from a GP.
>
> *Consultant*: In the notes, it says she had a bit of a tremor in her hands.
>
> *Anna*: Yes, I'm not sure what that's down to. Its not there all the time – sometimes she can pick a cup up, sometimes she can't.

Consultant: But no ones thought it was Parkinson's or anything?

Anna: No, my dad has Parkinson's.

Consultant: Which nursing home is she in?

Anna: _____

Consultant: How long has she been there?

Anna: 5 months.

Consultant: How old is she?

Anna: 74.

Consultant: So far she's been examined by her GP and Dr M___.

Anna: Dr M___ and she saw Dr G___ when she was first diagnosed. She's been diagnosed for quite a while and then she started fainting so I asked Dr M___ to see her. All the investigations were normal. He didn't pick anything up. He said leave well alone, don't interfere.

Consultant: Has it got better?

Anna: That stopped after a few months but she definitely deteriorated after that. That happened about a year and a half ago. It's been strange, she deteriorates and then plateaus out.

Consultant: How's her health otherwise?

Anna: The only thing she's got is folic acid. She's got energy and walks.

Consultant: So it is your mother's father. Can you remember what happened to him?

Anna: I think I was too young. I tried to ask a lot of questions but I remember as a young child he was very active but then he started wandering and being aggressive. He died when he was 81. He might have been about 70 but my brothers can remember him being like that.

Consultant: So your mother has two sisters and a brother and they don't have anything.

Anna: No.

Consultant: So at the moment it's just your grandfather and mother. Your grandmother had Parkinson's and your father has Parkinson's. When did his start?

Anna: In his late sixties.

The consultant moves on to ask about Anna and her siblings. Anna describes her anxiety that her poor memory is an early sign of the onset of Alzheimer's. Once the family history has been taken, the consultant usually carries out a detailed physical examination of the affected individual and/or other family members present who may also be at risk and the consultant may take photographs of any features that appear distinctive or relevant to the potential diagnosis. Any test results, the causes of the condition, its progression and the risk of recurrence (if known) are discussed after this process of examination. In this case, the consultant is reassuring; she believes the condition cannot occur at Anna's relatively young age and onset within the family appears to occur over the age of 70. However, she acknowledges that the mother's Alzheimer may have started earlier, at around 60 years of age, which would be consistent with the familial form of the condition. As is commonly the case, there is no predictive test for this condition and the consultant suggests the only possible option would be to store a sample of Anna's mother's DNA. As technology improves, a test that can establish the family's risk may become available. Typically, as in this case, molecular tests are not available to establish the personal and familial risk of recurrence for this condition. The clinical team commonly take or discuss taking a blood sample or a skin biopsy to store, as they are sure technologies will improve in the future. The consultant continues to provide reassurance and to stress to Anna that there is no 'significant risk' of her mother's Alzheimer's being familial.

Consultant: You yourself are well and healthy?

Anna: Yes.

Consultant: How old?

Anna: 44. I know my memory is atrocious but I don't know whether its stress at work or …

Consultant: I think if it is familial you are far too young for symptoms, so it is important to remember that. Also you've got three brothers and a sister [she looks at family tree]. Who's looking after [son]?

Anna: He's 20!

[they laugh – from the family tree it looks as though he is 2 years old.]

Consultant: What I see in your history, we have your mother and one grandfather. We don't know but it is likely to have developed it over the age of 70. Senile dementia over 60 is unlikely to be familial Alzheimer's. There is no other family history, all over 70 and doing fine, so there's no family history of Alzheimer's. If she had developed it in her seventies we wouldn't be here. So there is a slight concern her Alzheimer's started earlier. At the moment there are no specific tests for Alzheimer's. The genes that have been found can only be applied to a few families. But what might be useful would be to store a DNA sample of your mother so that if any test does become available we can do a test on your mothers DNA and that might give me an indication.

Typical of the individuals attending the service, Anna is not completely reassured. The risk of recurrence has not been completely ruled out by the consultant and Anna expresses her fear that the condition will occur again within her family. She has traced the pattern of inheritance of the condition and believes others within her kinship will be affected in the future. This is a common discourse expressed by individuals and families attending the clinic.

Anna: Could it start younger?

Consultant: Yes, but I wouldn't have too many concerns and its not strong enough to say it's a familial condition. If anyone has a relative with it then there is a risk but I don't think there's enough evidence that this is an Alzheimer's family with a significant risk. [Adds that tests might be available in the future.] So at the moment you have a slightly increased risk but I can't see any evidence that you are at higher risk.

So I want to be reassuring at the moment. Your family history does not suggest you are likely to be at risk of developing Alzheimer's. By that I mean between 60 to 70 you have a slightly raised risk of it just like the rest of us. [Suggests storing a sample of her mothers blood.] Do you have any questions because we have been doing all the talking?

Genetic Specialist Nurse: That was the main thing.

Anna: I look at my mother and you look at the future and he [son] is an only child.

Consultant: I can entirely understand it and your questions are entirely reasonable and we do explore this. If you or any of your siblings get any problems early, in your early sixties then your risk for your son would change, whereas if it's seventies and eighties then it would be the same. [Again suggests storing a sample of her mother's blood]. We're not good at dealing with grey zones. I'd err on the side of positive. [Reiterates low risk and the option of storing mother's blood.]

[Anna leaves. Throughout the consultation she looked very anxious and tense.]

Two months later, Anna revisits the clinic; she has been in contact with the genetics specialist nurse and appears to be highly anxious. She has not discussed the possibility of storing a sample of her mother's DNA with her family. She tells us that she cannot discuss this issue with her father because she believes at present he is unaware of the familial implications of her mother's condition and any discussion of blood samples could lead him to worry about his children and grandchildren. The consultant stresses that the risk of the condition being familial is 'borderline' given the information they have about the onset of the condition in Anna's mother and maternal grandfather. She suggests that although they are unable to classify the risk, to best way to improve their chances of doing so in the future would be to store a sample of Anna's mother's brain post-mortem. Anna does not think this would be in line with her mother's wishes and believes this option would be particularly hard to discuss with her father. As is typical in most consultations, the consultant provides reassurance and acknowledge Anna's anxieties.

Genetic Specialist Nurse: She was very upset on the phone.

[Anna arrives looking very tired and anxious. Throughout the consultation she sits very still and looks extremely tense.]

Genetic Specialist Nurse: You said your mother's doing a bit better at the moment.

Consultant: Good.

Anna: [Talks about her mother's symptoms: what she can and can't do. Sometimes she feels her mother is there, sometimes she feels she's gone.]

Consultant: And you didn't feel comfortable asking your father?

Anna: No, I don't think he realized the implications. He's not well and I think he's then worrying about his children and grandchildren. I don't want him to worry.

Consultant: If we go back to our previous discussion, it is borderline that it runs in the family. One of the most important things is to establish as closely as possible what has happened to your mother. The best thing is to wait for a post-mortem and look at her brain. There are lots of things that can affect the brain which are not genetic and it is helpful to rule them out. I know it's difficult to think about but it's where we can answer the main one of the questions. So we can think that we could have a post-mortem. It might be that you can discuss that with your father. It might be difficult.

Anna: I think it would be harder. I'd rather ask him about the blood sample than a post-mortem.

Consultant: Yes, but is also more helpful. It's something to consider but its not urgent. I doubt that there's anything else out there. I have seen other patients with this recently although they had a higher risk. There is support out there and people find it helpful and she got a lot of information and did a lot of thinking. I don't know. I could ask her if you wanted to get in touch it might be helpful. I do sympathize. There is a lot going on: there's your mother, protecting your father, worrying about the familial aspect of what is undoubtedly a terrible disease. So far the only tests available are where its clearly in the family and your mother is borderline. I'm looking into whether anything else is available. I know they will tell me that looking at the brain is the best way to find out.

Anna goes on to describe the burden of this knowledge; the potential risk has dev-astating implications for her family members. Throughout this consultation she looks extremely anxious, tense and close to tears, sitting very still and clasping her hands. She describes her practical character assessment (see Chapter 5) of her rel-atives to identify who she believes can and cannot 'cope' with this knowledge. To obtain a blood sample from her mother, Anna would have to discuss her concerns with her father and she fears that were she to do so, he and her brothers may start to realize that there may be familial implications to her mother's condition. The consultant suggests that this may not be a bad thing and this leads Anna to recall a recent comment made by one of her brothers who appears to share her anxieties. He believes he is the most likely to be affected by the condition and has told his wife that if he is affected he does not want to become a burden to her. The con-sultant and the genetic specialist nurse urge Anna to talk to her father and siblings about her fears and suggest her mother's GP could be an appropriate mediator to help her to discuss this issue with her family. Although the clinical team reiterate that a blood test will be the only possible way of clarifying the familial risk, this test will only be available with improvements in technology. The team suggest that they will get in touch with Anna in the future to check whether she needs any further support.

Anna: Knowing my mother, I don't think she'd agree to it. Her personality wouldn't have gone for it. She wasn't that way inclined. I don't mind the blood test because I know she wouldn't have objected, but not a post-mortem. We didn't tell her about her illness. We thought about it and struggled with it but we didn't.

Consultant: That would give you the best answer. Then the DNA would leave us with something. Just to have it stored if anything becomes available in the future.

Anna: What's the problem with consent? Is it that blood is being taken or what its being used for?

Consultant: [Outlines the issues.] Your mother's legal guardian would have to give consent. It would be difficult to do a blood test if he [father] didn't know. You could put it that there are lots of tests available and you may be able to find the cause in the future.

Anna: I've thought about that. He would consent to a blood sample for anybody's sake and I think it would be easier for him if he didn't think it was anything to do with us.

Consultant: [*Runs through how storage of blood sample could help in the future to find out the cause of Anna's mother's condition.*] Which is the truth but you could leave out the implications for the family.

Anna: Yes, he does ask a lot of questions about the disease but he doesn't ask about [the familial aspect].

[*The consultant suggests using the consent form and focusing any discussion of the future test on finding out the cause of the mothers Alzheimer's.*]

Anna: Yes, that's better. I think about it, if we take blood and it gets back to my father that could be a big thing for him [...] I think that might also start my brothers questioning things.

Consultant: Is that a bad thing?

Anna: Well, it is starting. My brother never mentioned anything and he did recently. We talked about my mum and he said 'I think I'll be the one affected, I've told ___ [his wife] I don't want you to have the burden for looking after me.'

Consultant: They might be quite relieved that this is going on.

Anna: My eldest sister and younger brother have mentioned it. My two older brothers have no idea. They haven't said anything. That's left it open for us to talk about it. I'm not sure if they are asking for information or telling me.

Consultant: You could ask them.

Genetic Specialist Nurse: It might be that they are discussing it with their partners. You can explain that it's for the future rather than diagnosis or treatment and the limitations of it now.

Consultant: Purely for storage, we wouldn't do anything with it now [...] Did your mother ever have a brain scan, an MRI?

Anna: When the GP diagnosed her she had a scan a while before but I don't know what that showed. It was never discussed. My mother had signs for a long time before. We didn't pick up on it.

Consultant: So I would say we'll go along with that. Taking blood might be considered.

Anna: If I do say to my father [discuss the blood test].

Consultant: You might want to discuss with the home how best to do that.

Genetic Specialist Nurse: Sometimes that's the easiest.

Consultant: It may be useful to meet [new GP attached to the home] and you can give him the letters from us and tell him about our discussions and that might be a useful option.

Anna: That's probably not a bad idea. Up till November we had the family doctor. [She adds that she hasn't met her mother's new GP at the home. She is unsure of her role, and is not sure whether she should she be taking a more active role in her mother's care or if would that be stepping on her father's toes.]

Consultant: So that might be helpful and he could get in touch with [Genetic Specialist Nurse] if he wanted to discuss it further. Also it's not an emergency. We have time […] Your brother has given a huge indication that he is also worried about it. [Talks about her other patients with a familial type of this condition.] You are probably quite aware of the support out there but I'll perhaps get in touch with her.

Anna: My father went.

Consultant: Well, we're back to asking if you want to explore that further. I've seen two families where it's not so borderline. There's no rush.

Genetic Specialist Nurse: Is there no other blood test needed?

Anna: No.

Genetic Specialist Nurse: I was just thinking if she needs any other test they could take for that as well.

Anna: I'll have a word with him. That's a good idea.

Consultant: He's also a good idea for future support.

[*consultation ends.*]

Thus, typically, Anna's concerns over the risk to her and other family members inheriting this condition are not resolved. Although the clinical team are reassuring, they are unable to completely rule out the possibility that this condition may occur again within the kindred. As for most individuals and families, assessing the risk is a long and drawn out process.

Genetic Counselling and Disclosure

As we can see in the example above, the work of the genetic service is very largely concerned with *counselling* individuals and families. Affected or at-risk individuals may seek information and advice about the outcomes of testing, the options available to them, how to make sense of genetic information, and how to manage the personal and family consequences.

In the course of this book, we are not primarily concerned with the dynamics of genetic counselling *per se*. They have been the subject matter of major sociological and discursive analyses in their own right (Armstrong et al., 2000; Richards, 1999a; Sarangi and Clarke, 2002a, 2002b; Sarangi et al., 2003). Here we want to emphasize a number of issues that have implications for our own research with and about families with genetic conditions. Genetic counselling is a source of 'information' about the underlying genetic basis of diseases and syndromes. Indeed, one of the prime functions of genetic counselling is imparting relevant information – such as risk values – to those who come seeking information. In addition geneticists and counsellors normally practice non-directive counselling. While the blanket application of the notion of non-directiveness may be problematic from an analytic perspective, it does mean that 'forced disclosure' of genetic information to other members of a proband's family is generally not practiced. Geneticists do not themselves directly transmit the genetic constitution and risks of a given individual to other members of their 'family'. While individuals and couples are encouraged and may choose to share their understandings, concerns and genetic status with other family members, this is in no sense required. It would be truly exceptional for the genetics professionals to reveal information about one individual to others without their consent.

In an idealized model, one can envisage a proband being given genetic information in the course of one or more counselling sessions, and electing to share that information openly with other family relations so that the family becomes a small system of open and well-informed communication about shared risks, carrier status and predicted outcomes. On the basis of such shared information, all members of the kindred would be in a position to seek further genetic counselling on their own behalf, and to make well-informed choices and decisions concerning reproduction, lifestyle and so on. In practice, things are not so straightforward and no genetics practitioner would be so naïve as to entertain explicitly the model we have just sketched as a faithful representation of ordinary, mundane reality, although it seems implicitly to inform some professional writing and practice. In the families we have worked with, we can certainly not assume that we are dealing with unproblematic 'information' that is shared equally and explicitly with all possibly relevant family members. We shall elaborate on this theme in the course of the chapters that follow. Here we wish to highlight three things. First, it is highly misleading to think in terms of 'information' as if it consisted of discrete packages of knowledge that are received and understood equally by all probands. On the contrary, our own research and that of several other authors demonstrate very clearly that 'information' such as a 'risk value' is interpreted in ways that differ between individuals. It can also differ significantly from (and between) genetic scientists and health professionals (Bharadwaj, 2002; Richards, 1996b; Shaw, 2000). Second, there can be no assumptions that in the everyday world family members 'share' information in an explicit fashion, if at all. It is nearer the truth to think in terms of fragmentary disclosure, partial disclosure, or even 'family secrets'. The entirely 'open' family may be an ideal, but it is rarely reflected in our own research experience. Third, what is shared within families, or between small numbers of family members – or indeed, what is kept secret, or preserved at the level of suspicion and innuendo – is not necessarily the packets of 'information' that are transmitted in clinics and counselling sessions. On the contrary, as we have already indicated, there are processes of translation and interpretation that are brought to bear on genetic information. Background cultural assumptions about inheritance and local assumptions about one's family and kin all interact with professional advice and information.

As we have already suggested, the very idea of 'family' is not altogether straightforward. We can add to this the further complexities of lay understandings of genetic information, the outcomes of predictive tests, the consequences of carrier status, the genetic bases of disease – indeed, the entire range of work that is performed in the course of genetic counselling and the monitoring of individuals and families by genetic services. Within the clinic, and between the clinic and the laboratory, there are, therefore, multiple kinds and sources of evidence that are assembled and brought to bear. In that process, families and individuals are constructed, and the various aspects of family and laboratory evidence are brought together.

The dispersal of the 'patient' into fragmentary scraps of tissue, representations and information calls to mind the usage imported by Fox (1993) of the postmodernist notion of the 'body without organs'. The body so constituted and conceptualized is not the unitary physical embodiment of a 'patient', thought of as the corporeal presence of an individual or self. The body of the contemporary clinic – whether described as 'late modern' or 'postmodern' – is distributed in time and space. It is an object of discourse. It is 'anatomized' not by the gaze of the lone practitioner at the bedside or in the consulting room, but by the routine work of a diverse range of specialties. This dismembered body is thus dispersed through the complexity of the clinic – its laboratories, procedure rooms and professional encounters. It is constituted through the practices of the clinic's specialists, and by their specialised talk. The body is an object of professional discourse and thus the work of the geneticist is part of the production of the 'body without organs'. The geneticist shares in the fragmentation of the 'patient' into shards of information (Atkinson, 1995).

Genetic information is pieced or slotted together in order to construct pictures of families in pedigrees. We have seen that the pedigree may usefully be thought of as a boundary object that links two discursively distinct domains or registers. On the one hand, there is the domain of kinship and of social relationships. It is the province of meaning that is familiar to lay people in our culture, and is couched in terms of Anglo-American kinship terms. Common-sense terms such as aunt or cousin are current here. Consanguinity and affinal relations are established through everyday practices, such as naming and residence. Kinship is not only a domain of everyday practical reasoning; it is also one of the professional domains that are explored by the geneticists themselves. This is the world of clinical practice: of genetic counselling, for instance. Clinicians supply and speculate on such personal information. In the professional encounters we have been considering here, they fill in a great deal of information about a family on the basis of diverse kinds of knowledge. They may recognize families, recalling names and places of residence and approximate dates of birth. They supply anecdotal evidence concerning the size of a particular family and the number of cases in a family.

On the other hand, there is the domain of shared genetic material constituted in terms of biological relations. The laboratory scientist, of course, rarely meets any individuals. His or her discourse is informed by the specimens that are available for testing and by the pedigree of biological relatedness. His or her discourse is guided by the principles of biomedicine. It is grounded not in the social or cultural realm of the family, but in the realm of invariant biological facts and the calculation of probabilities. Interestingly, probabilistic statements concerning the likelihood of genetic inheritance contrast with the categorical affirmation (or denials) of *family* membership. It is to these aspects we now turn.

The Production of Kinship

In the routine negotiations between clinicians and scientists, then, the occasioned identification of individuals and their kin brings together the two domains of the family and the clinic, underscored by two discursive registers. The close relationship between biomedical assumptions and 'our' Anglo-American bilateral kinship systems and categories should not blind us to the distinctiveness of those two contrasted domains. The assembly of family and kinship is a locally managed affair within the genetics team of scientists and clinicians. Such local work is in turn predicated upon more widely shared assumptions concerning the taken-for-granted relationships between family, kinship and biological relatedness.

In contrasting the domain of kinship and the domain of biological relatedness, we have not sought to imply that the one is simply cultural and the other simply natural. We reiterate therefore that the biological is as inescapably a social product as the cultural. We do not mean to imply that there is a prior realm of biological facts onto which culturally defined kinship terms are mapped. Rather, our research is one of the few empirical studies that has addressed the simultaneous professional constructions of the biological and the social. The congruence of Anglo-American bilateral kinship terminology and the biomedical definition of kinship readily 'naturalizes' both domains. It is easy to assume that the social categories merely reflect the 'facts' of nature. We imply, on the other hand, no such priority for the biological categories: the 'facts' of biological inheritance and genetics are artifacts, just as thoroughly as are the representations of family trees and anthropologists' kinship diagrams.

Indeed, rather than assuming that modern Anglo-American kinship is explicable in terms of a biological base, it may prove more fruitful to speculate that modern biological understandings of genetics and inheritance owe much to the culturally arbitrary fact that European, and North American kinship systems are bilateral. Had they been markedly different – matrilineal, say – then one cannot guarantee that biological inheritance would have had the social history it has, nor that bio-medical scientists would have conceptualized genetics in the way that they have. The contemporary congruence of our concepts of nature and kinship must not blind us to the contingent nature of that relationship, nor to the fact that geneticists (among others) achieve that congruence through their everyday routines of scientific and clinical work.

We have introduced some of the ways in which 'families' are construed in the clinic. The clinic is here defined not just as the physical location of the hospital genetics service, nor solely in terms of encounters between practitioners and their patients. Rather, we mean the entire constellation of occasions, work and talk through which individuals and family members are brought under the aegis of medical genetics – whether in the home, in the genetic counselling encounter, in the laboratory, or with the genetics team. We have emphasized that families are constructed in particular ways, are made up of the results of scientific tests, of social relationships and of the distribution of genetic 'values', such as risk assessments.

Through observation of the work of clinical geneticists we examine how family and kinship are constructed and transformed by the technologies of the clinic to make a genetic diagnosis. Within the clinical consultations, the clinical team constructs the notion of family and the individuals referred to the clinic. Within the clinic, families are assembled, examined, assessed and diagnosed, and their patterns are identified and classified. We show how the family is surveyed and put together in particular ways by clinical staff. Family information is used to aid diagnosis and construct an ethical framework of appropriate responses. The clinic is also the site where individuals present their families in particular ways. For example, as we will show, many of the families we spoke to had presented themselves within the clinic as being part of a kindred who communicated well and where risk information had been (or would be) disclosed unproblematically.

Our own perspective also constructed the family in a particular way, with a focus on genetic risk information and, in turn, we received a presentation of 'family' in a particular way. We often found that the presentation and beliefs about the disclosure of risk information varied among family members. As Margaret Voysey (1975) demonstrated in her study of families who have children with disabilities, family members' construct their own versions of 'ordinary' family life, and the moral categories of family relations.

–3–

Routes and Journeys: Beliefs about Inheritance and Routes of Transmission

Introduction

If we are to make sense of the reception and interpretation of genetic information in everyday life we need to acquire a systematic understanding of how inheritance (genetic and otherwise) is understood. We certainly cannot assume that members of contemporary industrial/post-industrial society share the same knowledge and beliefs with scientists, medical practitioners and other professionals. It cannot be assumed that the beliefs of British or other European – American populations are entirely governed by contemporary biomedical understandings of procreation and inheritance. Despite the existence of a number of programmatic statements on this topic, there are relatively few intensive anthropological or sociological studies of genetic belief in contemporary Britain.

In addressing our own south Wales materials, we shall try to examine the extent to which recognizably 'lay' theories of inheritance and relatedness co-exist with (biomedically) received notions of 'genetic relatedness'. In so doing we shall argue that new biomedical knowledge and practice have not generated wholesale changes in popular understandings of kinship and inheritance. For instance it would be quite wrong to assume that the conceptualization of such phenomena among 'Western' (Euro-American) populations is a reflection of prevailing biomedical orthodoxy. We need to be mindful of the cultural and historical contexts in which kinship and inheritance have been formulated more or less independently of scientific or medical knowledge (cf. Coster, 1993; Finch and Mason, 2000; Firth, 2004; Holy, 1997; MacEowen, 2004; Stone, 2004). We do not mean to imply, therefore, that the inspection of popular beliefs and practices reflects a 'deficit model' of public understanding of science. Our intent is not to examine whether or how well our informants 'understand' the biological basis of their familial conditions or the more general scientific understanding of inheritance. To do so would be to assign primary importance to the biomedical domain and to regard all other cultural domains as more or less adequate reflections of it. On the other hand, we wish to avoid the danger of constructing ironic contrasts between the scientific and lay frames of reference in order to 'orientalize' the latter. In describing popular or lay concepts in these sorts of areas of everyday life, it is too easy to seem to stress the exotic, the quaint or the antique. It is dangerously easy – notwithstanding explicit accounts to the contrary – to construct a *volkisch* portrayal of a traditional, pre-modern cultural repertoire. While we insist that there are sets of ideas that exist with relative autonomy from biomedical science, we do not imply that we are uncovering some elementary cultural forms. We do not simply seek out 'uncontaminated' ideas as if they represented a world untrammelled by contemporary science.

The so-called 'lay beliefs' are dialectically produced as a consequence of a sustained engagement with the clinical domain where biomedical ideas of relatedness and inheritance penetrate other (non-biomedical) models of relatedness. We do not disregard that popular ideas about genetics have become an inextricable part of late modernity but, as existing research has shown, very often such conceptions are produced in relation to the wider discursive practices as they emerge in the media accounts that abound in the everyday worlds of Euro-Americans (Nelkin and Lindee, 1995; Dijck, 1998). Dijck argues that an ever-increasing portion of popular science- including documentaries and television series on The Human Genome Project – is distributed through channels of popular culture (Dijck, 1998: 25). Meanwhile Nelkin has shown how powerful media imageries produce ideas about genetic relatedness. Referring to the ever-increasing popular interest in biological relationships in accounts of adoption and in stories about adoptees in search of their biological roots, Nelkin draws attention to the example of *Esquire* magazine which featured an image a man surrounded by the powerful roots of a large tree, each root represented as the ladder of the double helix (Nelkin and Lindee, 1995: 66). Such notions of genetic roots, instantiated through graphic imagery, compound an understanding underscored by, rapidly globalizing forces of mass media rather than personal experience of genetic conditions or their clinical diagnosis.

It would be quite misleading to assume that there exists a single 'lay' belief system among British populations. Even if we ignore the possible effects of different cultural heritage among UK populations (such as 'ethnic minorities') we do not find a single belief system within our Welsh families. Rather, a variety of discursive registers intersect and co-exist in our respondents' accounts of relatedness and inheritance. The cultural themes that we have identified include beliefs about what traits are transmitted and how. For example, we examine beliefs about the *routes* of transmission, such as inheritance through the 'sides' of the family or through gendered lines of descent and the *modes* of transmission, such as blood (cf. Fox, 1996; Goody, 2004; Strathern, 1992b). Not only genetic conditions but traits which include personal characteristics, emotions, practical skills, moral qualities and social standing are believed to be transmitted within families.

However, we are not suggesting that there is a literal belief within a kinship in such routes and substances. Rather these are well-established idioms used to express the principles of inheritance employed by our respondents rather than those employed within biomedical theories of inheritance.

Blood: The Point of Departure

Blood is often construed as the 'substance' and the location in which personal traits and diseases reside. The notion of substance whilst culturally variable and malleable can show considerable similarities in the way it brings together procreation, relatedness and personhood (Carsten, 2000, 2004). Within the domain of English kinship for instance substance is often metaphorized as blood (Strathern, 1992b). This notion has cross-cultural resonance. In many parts of India, for example, one's caste purity is thought to be situated in one's blood. Many times this notion of blood goes far beyond an 'ethnophysiological' view of human biology. For instance Ostor, Fruzzetti and Barnett (1982) have shown in their case study of the South Indian Tamil, that multiple understandings of blood, and the ethnomedical belief about the movement of blood in the body and its transformation into other body substances are the very basis of constructing a rich metaphor in daily speech. Ostor et al. argue that the transmission of blood purity from parent to child underlies the entire ideology of south Indian caste system. In such a system the child is formed from his or her parents' blood and inherits the purity contained in that blood. In the same study Ostor et al. compare this conception of blood with that found in East Indian Bengali culture. Here the term *kul* is used to refer to blood purity, quality, highness and nobility that must be preserved and handed down from one generation to the next. The wife of a man is a vehicle through which he establishes his line: he transmits his blood to the children through her (cf. Atkinson et al., 2003).

In south Wales, on the other hand, when talking about inheritance, a number of respondents described having 'bad blood' within the family or discussed the purity (or not) of their blood. A trait or disease was often described as coming into the family from a certain source or via an incident that was believed to have caused changes in the blood. Suzanne refers to 'bad blood' in making sense of the origins of a condition within her family. Stories are passed down through families, in this case from mother to daughter, and used to rationalize why family members are affected by a condition. In Suzanne's case, family stories suggest that the condition is caused by bad blood on both sides of the family.

> *Suzanne*: Like they wouldn't have remembered the auntie but I remember her. My
> mother always used to say it's the bad blood on both her parents' side. She always
> said that.

In many cases these stories are linked to concerns about how a disease is transmitted though the family. Jenny (Suzanne's niece) makes sense of the condition in her family by referring to health problems she believes she has inherited from both her mother (a skin condition) and father (high blood pressure) and attributing these problems to 'bad blood'. However, in doing this, she makes no reference to the debilitating late-onset condition she is likely to have inherited from her mother; this appears to be more generally referred to within the kindred as the 'bad family blood'. In her, so far, this bad blood has expressed itself or 'come out' in her skin, but it may express itself in other ways in the future. She struggles to make sense of how differences can occur within her kin because her sister appears unaffected by health problems so far.

> *Jenny:* So I can't see how they, why they check my fingernails and my hair because you can see under the skin they said if I was having it, before it come out on the skin. So I can't see how me and my sister are connected. And then there's like my father then, got high blood pressure, they'd say 'Oh bad family blood line.'

Blood is also described explicitly as a mode of inheritance. For example, two sisters, Veronica (Jenny's mother) and Lindsey, describe why they grew up believing Veronica may be free of the condition. She had a blood transfusion shortly after birth and this was linked to her identity within the family, marking her as different and 'no longer one of us'. There was also an expectation that the male police officer's blood she received had additional potency and protective factors and would provide her with strength and good health:

> *Lindsey:* And I used to say to her 'Oh she's not one of us because we don't have that, she's not one of us', didn't I? I used to be always arguing.
> *Veronica:* And a student nurse took my napkin, or took my napkin off and put the pin in my belly button, pulled it out and I haemorrhaged about 1½ or 2 pints. And I had, I'm rhesus negative and I had, they got in touch with the police training place and I had a lot of policemen's blood and I used to say 'Well, there you are, I'm not going to be, I'm going to be strong', and I'm bloody weak as can be (laughs).

Journeys: Routes, Transmissions and Flows

If within the domain of English kinship substance is often metaphorized as blood, the connections created by the transmission of substance are equally metaphorized as flow (Strathern, 1992b).The majority of individuals and families in our Welsh study similarly believed they could trace the genetic condition through their kindred and identify patterns of transmission. Conditions were often described as being passed 'down the line' through the generations of a family and sources and routes of transmission were traced. Strathern rightly argues that in popular belief the parts that an individual person gets from either their mother or their father may be thought of as parts of other ancestors that show in descending generations (Strathern, 1992b: 80).

An important focus for most of these individuals and families was the recognition and identification of characteristics such as personality characteristics, physical features, skills and talents they could trace through their kindred. These traits were often believed to be inherited in association with the conditions, providing families with a shorthand for diagnosing individuals.

For example, Philip believes he can trace the genetic condition affecting his sister and her son. Because his sister has a personality trait which he associates with his mother's side of the family, he believes she has also inherited the condition from this side. The family trait of 'nervousness' in this case brings with it the inheritance of FRAXE, a genetic condition causing learning disabilities.

> *Philip*: I mean Patty [sister] I think I'd have to speak to her. Because she's gone through a lot of problems. She's had a lot of health problems. She's got the same sort of thing as the [maternal surname] family, which is my mother's family. You know my father's [paternal surname]. She's got that nervousness. Her mother was nervous, a possible carrier if it can affect that but like me has overcome it, no question about that. But may be not overcome it quite so dramatically as I have because she doesn't have that side, because her father is more nervous as well.

Parents often attended the clinic with clear beliefs about who else in their family was affected by a condition. Two sisters, Lucy and Sally, discuss the diagnosis of Charcot Marie Tooth. Although Lucy has a young son who has been diagnosed with the condition, the sisters can also see the condition in a large number of other family members. They believe that they, their other sister and a number of their children are also affected; they all have the 'clumsiness'. Sally is particularly worried about one of her teenage daughters and, similarly, Lucy believes another of her sons is affected and showing symptoms similar to those of his brother. Because their mother is not clumsy, they dismiss her as the source of the condition, but fix on their father, who 'has slight walking problems'.

> *KF*: You're worried about her [daughter]?
> *Sally*: Yes, she doesn't have the usual symptoms, but then she's unique in a lot of ways!
> *KF*: And your daughter, she's fine?
> *Lucy*: She seems fine to me and my sister has got one borderline dyspraxic and a son with ADH [...]
> *Sally*: I have two daughters, 18 and 17. I've noticed nothing with the eldest but the youngest, I don't see it so much now but she was always very clumsy, terrible problems with her walking. It was always hard to tell how much she'd hurt herself. [*Sally goes on to discuss her daughter's learning problems: 'no concentration span', 'not*

interested in school' 'not good socially'. She describes how her teenage daughter leads a separate life within the house and stays in her room much of the time]. [...]

KF: Do you have any similar problems?

Lucy: Always clumsy, always had a funny gait, pins and needles, curled toes and tight tendons [*Lucy adds that geneticists have said she has CMT but no test has been done.*] [*Her 11 year-old son has severe CMT and was diagnosed when he was 6 years old*]. Very exaggerated gait, always falling over, he can't use his whole foot. Poor spatial awareness. It started in his legs but it's now in his hands and arms. He has to hold his arms across himself now. He has no idea how hot or cold things are, and no idea where his feet are anymore [...] We're all clumsy and get pains in our legs. [Other sister] had the clumsiness, every single one of us does, all the children. We've all got one who's praxic. [Other sister] has always had funny feet.

KF: How about your parents?

SG: It's hard to tell. We don't see our dad much. He has slight walking problems. [...] Mum's not clumsy, but the arthritis is bad. Dad is an only child, so there are no strong family problems because there aren't any.

What is Inherited

The descriptions of 'family traits' believed to be transmitted between kin were often vague, such as 'the way we deal with things' (David). Similarly, Sue and Tom believe they can trace 'It' through Tom's family to their daughter. Sue can trace the condition that has caused her daughter's learning disabilities from her husband's family because she believes they all lack social skills; although the pattern of inheritance is mainly through the male members, she also sees it in some of the women. Her husband, Tom, agrees, that there is 'bad behaviour' in his family, as this extract from their clinical consultation shows.

Consultant: There are a number of people in your family (*referring to Tom*) with learning difficulties?

Tom: Yes, me included!

Genetic Specialist Nurse: One of the nephews has ataxia. When you showed me that we wondered if he had it, not assessed but milder. But otherwise it's the learning difficulties and the family trait.

Sue: It, whatever It might be!

Consultant: What is It?

Tom: Bad behaviour in our family.

Sue: Lacking social understanding, social skills.

Tom: Lacking understanding of people's feelings.

Consultant: Who has It?

Sue: It's more in the males but the females do have it.

Tom: Do I have it?

Sue: No, only in a mild way, but some of them are a nightmare! (*Gives example:*

cousin parks in private driveway and doesn't understand when his car is towed away.) His dad's a nightmare. He tried to sue his own daughter. They don't seem to understand the way other people understand the world.

Tom: He was always clumsy. I'm clumsy as well. [They discuss his dyslexia.]

Consultant: (*To Sue*) And your family?

Sue: No. Its all new to me really.

Character traits, particularly emotional qualities such as shyness and low self-esteem, were often described as being passed on through generations of the family. Philip, as we have already shown, can see the transmission of such traits within his family. He describes family members, particularly the women in the family, as being quiet, having low self-esteem and poor social skills, taking anti-depressants and having few friends. He believes this 'nervousness' is passed down through the women's side of the family and has bypassed him.

> *Philip*: So if you look at that the logic of her family, who are all basically nervous. I mean she's one of is it six, six children that's right. She's the only, there's three of them left, there was three brothers and three sisters. Two sisters have died and three brothers, one of the brothers has died the other two are still alive. But they all have this, they had all this sort of nervousness and without question all of them and I think my mother is one of the worst, actually the worst, but varying degrees of nervousness, unsureness do you understand what I'm saying? ... Again this nervous side, nervousness on my mother's side. Do you see where I'm coming from? Whereas my father's side were much more stable, much more sort of logical, will take the situations – we all get stressed from situations – but be able to take it. If my mum's side gets into a stressful situation, they sort of go to pieces. And I think that's probably ... the Syndrome X [FRAXE].

Traditional masculine skills are often described as being inherited from fathers or transmitted through the male line. Isobel believes her young son has inherited the practical skills of home improvement and car maintenance from his father. Even though he is only 2 years old, she envisages a future when he will be helping in the home: 'He's going to be wonderful to have around'.

> *Isobel*: Because [husband] was very good at DIY and cars and very practical so it's going to be handy ... I mean he's going to be like his dad when he gets older. I can see it now. He's going to be wonderful to have around ... [husband was] very practical, very practical. He did all the bathroom upstairs, could do anything, turn his hand to anything and [son] is going to be like that. He can do everything for me then.

Identifying the Origin of the Condition

Part of the process of working out the pattern of transmission is identifying where the condition originated in the family. This is often achieved by naming an individual who is believed to be the source and tracing the condition through to others in later generations.

Jill is concerned that neurofibromatosis has been transmitted by her mother; she additionally associates some of her mother's physical traits – red hair and freckles – with the inheritance of the condition. Based on this association, she is unconcerned about her own personal prognosis and traces the condition to the next generation. One of her three sons becomes her focus of concern because he 'follows' her mother and has similar physical traits, the red hair and the freckles. In contrast, she is less concerned about her other two sons because they do not physically resemble their grandmother. She additionally considers the route of transmission, not only in present but in future generations. Following the genetic diagnosis, she has become increasingly concerned about her son and her granddaughter and sees the condition potentially affecting future generations.

> Jill: I've sort of told them that there is something genetically wrong with [brother] and it could pass down through the family but that's as much as we know at the moment about it. So I need to keep those updated on it I think as well. But my main worry was I've got to admit thinking that it might come from my mother because he's the one that follows my mother. That was my main worry because he's the one who's got all the sort of freckles and the big spots, the other two haven't got it as badly ... I think then you start worrying because you think, well you hear of so many genetic diseases don't you and I think you start worrying more when they say genetics you start worrying a bit more, for your own family as well the boys and we've got a granddaughter and you keep thinking how far down the line is it going to come.

Naming Practices

An important aspect of beliefs about inheritance is the recognition of traits and their attribution to individuals or groups within the kin. Often an individual's behaviour is explained or rationalized as coming from or reflecting a wider pattern within the kin and becomes a 'family trait'. The process of tracing the pattern of inheritance of a known genetic condition was often linked to the identification of other features or traits within a kinship.

When Mary describes the condition FRAXE that causes learning disabilities and has affected one of her grandsons, she expresses strong beliefs about who is the source of this condition and the path of transmission. She traces the condition to her husband's family and describes how, when one of her daughters, Julia was young, she could see that this daughter had inherited traits from her husband's mother. When disciplining Julie she recalled threatening to 'hit the Richard's [father's surname]' out of her. She fails to identify similar traits in her two other children but believes Julia inherited her cheekiness and the ability to 'stir up trouble' from her father's kin and recalls telling her daughter that she was like her mother-in-law. She now looks at Julia's son (who has the genetic syndrome FRAXE) and makes a connection; she believes both these personality traits and the condition have been transmitted by her husband's side of the family to their daughter and grandson. By sharing the same personality and temperament, Julie and her son must also share the condition; as Mary says to Julia, 'He's like you'. The identification of familial similarities is associated with issues of blame and responsibility: the pattern of inheritance Mary has identified absolves her of any role in the transmission of this condition.

> *Mary*: I was really dominant you know as a parent and the only time, I used to say to Julia 'The only time you're happy is when you're making a row. You're like my mother-in-law.' I used to say. But she was, if she could stir up a little bit of trouble and she'd sit there and enjoy it you know. And even though she didn't I don't think she realized it at the time you know and I used to say to her 'I'll hit the Richard's [husband's surname] out of you' ... And people used to say to me if I had one like her I wouldn't have any more ... but the other children they were, I couldn't say that they took after anybody, not acted in that way you know only Julia, poor old Julia. There we are. I used to say, Julia used to say about [affected child] being like Jekyll and Hyde just to annoy me because I think it's a terrible thing to say to a child and I used to say 'Yeah he's like you.' If you look at him sideways he's up in the air you know he's very quick-tempered. So I see [affected child] like him in that respect you know so, and I wouldn't say that in front of him mind.

When inheritance was discussed, traits, features and medical conditions were commonly associated with 'sides' of the kindred and a 'side' was often identified and referred to as the source and route of transmission. Joanna rationalizes her son's problems (he has a genetic syndrome called XYY which causes mild behavioural and learning disabilities) by referring to other male members of her family. Within her family there is a strong belief that all the men have inherited certain personality traits. This has become a family joke and when displaying these characteristics the men are described as 'being a Pierce [paternal surname]'.

Beliefs about Transmission

The discussions of inheritance often incorporate a belief in gendered modes of transmission. Traits are believed to be transmitted from male to male or female to female. Isobel believes that her son has inherited both his personality traits and his physical features from his father, but little from her. This belief is strengthened because she notes that his behaviour and mannerisms have not had a chance to be influenced by his father, who died when her son was only nine months old. Thus, these traits must 'come from within' and Isobel fears that her son's inheritance will also include the genetic condition that led to his father's sudden death.

> *Isobel*: His features, he's very much like his dad in ways and in features. His characteristics are the same as his father. He's built like his dad. I mean there's very little of me in Sam [son].
>
> *KF*: You can just see Richard [father] in his …?
>
> *Isobel*: Yeah, everything, everything is his father. And because he hasn't got a father as a role model because he was only 9 months old when his father died, I don't think he was quite that, but he hasn't had his father to look to and follow the mannerisms from so that has come from within, that's come from –
>
> *KF*: Yes.
>
> *Isobel*: You know genetics. He's just got the same interests as what his dad had and he's just like a smaller version.
>
> *KF*: Yes.
>
> *Isobel*: I mean, he's going to be like his dad when he gets older.

Similarly, Tamsin believes her son has inherited personality traits from his father. However, in contrast to Isobel, because of this she hopes that her young son will not be affected by her genetic condition (neurofibromatosis) as she hopes her husband's genes will dominate. The following field notes were taken during a home visit with a genetic special nurse.

> Tamsin's GP has diagnosed neurofibromatosis and she tells us that she is mainly concerned about how the condition will affect her, especially in terms of her life expectancy and whether her son could also be affected. Her sister died of skin sarcoma one and a half years ago at the age of 27 and she is concerned that this may be related, even though her GP has said this is 'unlikely'. Her symptoms include the café au lait marks and 'lumps' on her body. Previously, a lump that had been 'bothering' her was removed and she currently has one lump on a finger. She adds that she is concerned about her and her family's life expectancy. Tamsin is particularly worried that her son has the condition. However, she adds that she hopes he hasn't inherited the condition from her because 'He's tended to follow my husband in a lot of ways'.

Complex rationalizations of the way in which traits or conditions are inherited or express themselves within an individual were often described. As we have seen, traits and characteristics were often depicted as being transmitted by named individuals or through male or female lines or 'sides' of the family. However, the inheritance of traits does not mean that they automatically express themselves within an individual; rather inheritance was often described as a dynamic process, with traits undergoing a struggle to express themselves within a member of the kin. Thus, only the strongest or dominant traits and features prevail.

For example, although Philip suggests we are all a mixture or blend of our mother and father's genes, he also describes a complex process by which these 'genes' interact. He believes that within him, his father's side is the stronger and thus exerts a powerful influence on his personality. In contrast, he describes his mother's side as too 'weak' to express itself within him. The strength of his father's traits has protected him from the genetic condition present within his mother's family. He additionally describes the way in which the trait of intelligence he has inherited from his father has exerted a 'calming influence', which has balanced out the 'aggressive' traits he inherited from his mother.

> *Philip*: My mother's side would not have done that. It was far too weak. I'm being honest here. I believe that my father's side is the commanding influence that is, because it's all, it's all strengths, which is the stronger. We've all got split personalities to a certain extent. We've got a nice side, we've got a calmer side, we've all got an aggressive streak, we've all got a nice side. It's what makes you rational, what actually guides you. It's obviously got to be a combination of your mother and father's genes ... but I've always believed, and that's my father in me, because my mother in me is very tough, actually the family on my mother's side, very aggressive. Certainly nobody would dare take them on. So I've got that and it's been handy the odd time, but most of the time kept under wraps. Now that's my father's side that keeps me under wraps. My father's side has had the calming influence on me and I believe the more intellectual side.

In a similar way, Sarah has strong beliefs about how one of her teenage sons came to be severely affected by autistic spectrum disorder. The clinical genetics consultant agrees with her that her son may have a familial form of the condition. In the light of this, Sarah explains her theory; she believes her son is affected because she and her husband are too similar. They are both trained scientists and she maintains this did not provide their sons with a broad enough spectrum of inherited traits. In contrast, she believes her daughters have been protected from developing the condition because they have a different father who is very different from her. He has a very practical personality which provided their daughters with diversity in their 'gene pool'. Based on this theory, Sarah advises her unaffected son to avoid a partner who is too similar: 'just don't marry a scientist!'

> *Consultant*: It seems to be there are a number of people especially in your father's family who have a mild form of autism. It's not unusual to have this type of pattern in other family members [...] It's not easy to tell you what your chances of having a child with similar problems is. We can't say what the genetic mechanism is. It's also very variable. It seems to be something that is coming through the father's line.

Sarah: We are similar personality-wise. We're not broad enough. [*Sarah explains at length that both she and her husband trained as scientists and that she believes that because they are so similar the children have inherited these autistic traits*]

Consultant: We can't exclude it. It might be a possibility. But it's very difficult to put a specific figure on it. I suggest when you [to son] think about starting a family you come back and see us. It's an area where things are happening.

Sarah: I said just don't marry a scientist!

(*They discuss whether mum has similar traits. They reassure her. She thinks she also has some similar personality problems.*)

Sarah: The girl's father is very different, very practical, never had an intellectual thought in his life. The girls there was more of a variety in the gene pool with them.

There was often a belief that genetic conditions or traits gain additional strength and vigour when they are transmitted through a succession of family members and generations. Thus, it was thought that current and future generations were more likely to be affected by genetic conditions than past generations and the symptoms and effects of these conditions were likely to become increasingly severe.

Nicola and Mike are concerned that although the family history of aortic aneurysms in Nicola's family has not affected their generation it will go on to affect their three sons. They ask the consultant if the condition could 'skip' a generation, bypassing Nicola to affect the next generation of men. They also hold on to the hope that the effects of the condition will be reduced by Mike's 'influence'. They assume the condition only affects men within their kindred; however, the clinician explains that if the condition is familial it is dominant and places their sons' risk at 50 per cent.

Consultant: So in the present generation everyone is ok, so in the previous –

Nicola: My father is one of five, three all died of the same thing. One of my cousins died of the same thing. We don't see this side of the family as much. We see my mothers family more.

Consultant: So basically three uncles in all?

Nicola: The sister was ok. I'm not sure what he [4th uncle] died of but it could be the same thing. I know my mother's side of the family more than my father's. This [her family tree] goes back to 1764. I've left it too late to ask my mother, she gets confused.

Consultant: Interesting, it looks like it could be transmitted by males but P [4th uncle] puts a query on that.

Nicola: [Cousin] gave me your number so I don't know if you've seen them. They said it only affects males.

Consultant: It wouldn't be from me, but you can see how it looks like that [from the family tree].

Nicola: What about passing it on to my sons?

Mike: Would it skip a generation?

> *Consultant*: Its difficult to say. That's why it would be helpful to know about [4th uncle]. Most of these type of conditions are dominant (*explains 50 per cent chance of inheritance*). So I think it will be a step by step process. I'll examine you and send you to [cardiology] and an MRI. If everything is normal we can discuss the chances for you and your sons.
>
> *Nicola*: And grandchildren.
>
> *Consultant*: We will reassess the risk for all the next generations. So if there are no indications then the chances for grandchildren and children will be –
>
> *Woman*: will it be watered down by my husband, half from each? Will his influence mean they are less likely?
>
> (*Consultant explains mode of inheritance and the risk for the sons.*)
>
> *Consultant*: But overall there won't be a diluting factor.

This is a vivid example of how the everyday idioms of explanations from the two domains of understanding are brought together within the clinical setting. Here we see the patient and the clinician searching for ways of negotiating a common perspective to explain and understand the genetic complexity of the condition within this kin group.

Fate, Destiny and Chance

There was a strong belief in biological destiny. The majority of these individuals spoke fatalistically about the genetic conditions affecting them and suggested that the conditions were 'written in the genes'; if a trait or condition was within the body at a genetic and molecular level its expression to some extent was inevitable.

Isobel describes her fear that her young son will die suddenly from the cardiac condition that led to the death of his father and grandfather. She notes that both appeared to be healthy and fit when they died and from this she concludes that 'there was nothing you could do' to prevent it – this was their fate. She acknowledges that at the time of her husband's death, she held him in some way responsible for leaving her a widow with a young son; she now believes 'he didn't have a choice'. Even though a diagnosis that the condition is familial has not yet been confirmed, Isobel is sure this cannot be a random occurrence and thus she worries that her young son will share the same fate. She watches him and waits, believing 'there's nothing anyone can do'.

> *Isobel*: Because there is nothing wrong with [son] at the moment, but there was nothing wrong with [husband] or his father either so, but obviously there was because they both died young men. Even though they're physically okay and all the tests that [husband] had were okay there was something definitely wrong … Yeah I've always thought, always thought that there was a link. I said to her I always knew that [husband] was going to go. I know that [husband] wouldn't go on. I knew that

he was going to die young. How I don't know but I always knew, always had a gut feeling, always. Yeah because, like I said to you earlier, to me anybody who's fit and healthy, in their twenties, everything to live for, who's happy with their life doesn't drop dead for no reason you know. And, like I said to you, when he died I was, I was very angry and I blamed him and he should've fought and, but, like I said to you, he didn't have a choice. He didn't have a choice, he was either taken or there was something that, that is so sudden and so severe that death is imminent really. There's nothing anybody can do.

However, there was also a belief that individuals could exercise some level of control over their risk through modifying their lifestyles. Such behaviour modification was not only protective in relation to conditions commonly believed to be multi-factorial such as heart disease, but also relevant to the familial conditions identified in these kin. Philip is aware that he may be a carrier of the condition that causes learning disabilities and affects his nephew; he believes he is also mildly affected by the condition because he too struggled to achieve at school. However, he is also concerned about other conditions he believes are familial, such as heart disease, because these too are 'written in the genes'. Because his father died of a heart attack in his seventies he worries that he will share this destiny and he tries to counteract this with exercise. However, he believes there are limits to the effects of such health interventions and is still strongly fatalistic:

> *Philip*: I do try, and work a bit on that. The trouble is I think, oh well, my dad died of a heart attack, probably because his cholesterol was a bit high but he was 77 and he lived a pretty good healthy life. I think you've got to sort of say, well, you don't want to lead a completely clinical life or else you'd never do anything. And again I believe, I don't know how you feel about it but I believe a lot of it is written in the genes. I think you can abuse yourself … I think a lot of it is written in the genes. I mean you can control it but you can't stop it.

Such fatalistic beliefs were also tempered with beliefs in luck and chance. Many believed that their risk of inheriting a condition or of passing it on to the next generation was dictated by chance; family members were either lucky or unlucky recipients in a genetic lottery.

Rosie believes she should have a very low risk of passing a Robertsonian translocation on to a child. However, the extremely high number of miscarriages she has had suggests a higher rate of inheritance within her pregnancies (a translocation in a foetus can lead to miscarriage). She believes that although other family members also have 'a chance' of inheriting the condition, their 'pure luck' means they have not passed it on to their children. In contrast, she and her husband appear to be unlucky and have a higher risk of passing it on.

Rosie: They have a chance but [nephew] was completely free. He had a test back: nothing. So with a bit of luck the other two are … the chance of passing it on is, I know it's, oh yes I do for a woman to have a child it's 4 per cent and pass it on as a carrier or worse and 1 per cent for a male. There is a difference between the sexes. Basically that's why I should have 1 per cent chance.

Similarly, Patty describes herself as being extremely unlucky in life, particularly in contrast to her two siblings. Her son is affected by a condition that causes learning disabilities, her two daughters also have learning disabilities and she may be mildly affected. In contrast, her two siblings and their children appear to be unaffected. She deals with this fatalistically.

Patty: I don't really want to feel sorry for myself. I wouldn't because I don't think that achieves anything. Okay may be I was dealt a bit of a rough set of cards at the start so maybe we all are sometimes, you know. I think you've just got to get on with it haven't you.

In tracing the routes and journeys in the narratives of our respondents, we have tended to remain focused on the multilayered and florid accounts of their beliefs in inheritance and routes of transmissions. We see these accounts in no way as a reflection of respondents' actual 'level of understanding' of the transmission and reception of genetic traits or as indicative of some kind of false understanding of the scientific 'facts' of inheritance but rather as sense-making, meaning-generating devices in the lives of individuals and kin groups grappling with multiple consequences of genetic diseases.

–4–

Mutual Surveillance

Introduction

The focus of this chapter is to examine the ways in which individuals and families use tools of inspection and surveillance in order to visualize the future trajectory of the conditions within their kindred. It has recently been suggested that techniques of surveillance are necessarily related to practices of self-surveillance (Vaz and Bruno, 2003). Self-surveillance is understood as the attention one pays to one's own behaviour when facing the observational gaze of others whose opinion is deemed relevant. Additionally self-surveillance and its implications have been conceptualized in relation to social regulation and identity formation (Armstrong, 1995). Such a conceptualization excludes the diverse ways in which individuals pay attention to their actions and thoughts when constituting themselves as subjects of their conduct (Vaz and Bruno, 2003: 273) and the diverse ways in which embodied experience can impact upon self-surveillance (Howson, 1998). The increasing relevance of the concept of risk in the realm of health-related behaviour has further activated such self-surveillance, in that both individuals and others are increasingly subject to a surveying gaze that is both reflexive and objectifying. Howson (1998) argues that Foucault's (1979) critique of the idea of centralized knowledge and juridical power was accomplished through discussing a shift towards self-surveillance from surveillance. Deborah Lupton (1999) has shown that a central aspect of governmentality in neo-liberal societies is the idealized figure of the autonomous, self-regulated citizen. However, the notion of mutual surveillance is seldom evoked or expressly discussed in documenting shifts towards either self-surveillance or self-regulation. Whilst emphasis on self-regulation (and self-surveillance) is strongly evident in discourses on health and risk emerging from public health institutions (Lupton, 1995), the focus on surveillance in the context of biomedicine and medical genetics must also confront the objectifying and reflexive consequences of the technologies and practices that produce vivid illustrations of mutual surveillance.

This is not to suggest that the emergence of surveillance of the self and other family members is in some way connected to the emergence of molecular genetics and risky genetic prognostications. As argued earlier, knowledge of disease running in the families and corresponding mutual as well as self-surveillance within families have existed independently of medical definitions and even pre-date molecular genetics (Richards, 1996a, 2000). In this chapter, therefore, we describe how everyday beliefs about inheritance and the specific genetic conditions affecting families lead to the inspection of one's self and other family members. That is, how family members look for patterns within the kindred (past, contemporary and future generations) that indicate whether certain members are particularly likely (or unlikely) to be affected by or carriers of a condition. Families can thus become sites in which members of different generations inspect one another. Older generations look for signs of emergent illness in younger generations; members of younger generations may equally look at older kin in order to gauge what their own fate may be. These patterns of mutual surveillance follow lines of practical kinship and relatedness, and do not necessarily follow the biomedical definitions of inheritance patterns: for instance, all members of a younger generation may be inspected, irrespective of whether they are equally at risk of inheritance.

Surveillance is a tool used by these individuals and families to piece together their past and present in order to visualize the future. This act of visualizing or imagining can on occasions 'encompass a future that is incessantly punctuated by worry' (Finkler, 2001). However, such imagined futures are not just part of the process of worrying about the future consequences of a condition, but rather an integral part of a wider search for answers. This search for answers, however, does not place individuals and families in the medicalized domain but rather in a terrain of uncertainty. All the individuals and families in our research expressed a strong desire to identify where the condition originated in the family, the pattern of transmission, how it manifests in the present and what consequences, if any, this will have for the future. In this respect, they collapsed various temporal dimensions in their search for plausible, probable answers.

Examining the Past

All of the families held multiple and often complex theories of where the condition had originated and how it was transmitted though their kindred. Surveillance was commonly used as a means of identifying the pattern of inheritance within previous generations to help predict who was likely to be affected (and who to worry about) in the future. A number of studies have identified the processes of monitoring family members who are believed to be particularly at risk (cf. Cox and McKellin, 1999; Kessler and Bloch, 1989).

All held extremely strong views about where the condition had originated in the family and it was clear that accounts had been constructed through the process of surveillance. Surveillance was often motivated by the need to assign responsibility or accountability and to apportion or accept blame. For example, Anthony says of his father: 'he's introduced it' and has passed on the condition to him and his siblings. Feelings of guilt were also common, and Tamsin, a young mother, is convinced she has passed on neurofibromatosis to her young son: 'I know this has come from me.'

There were frequent discussions about which 'side' of the family introduced the condition (as we have described in more detail in Chapter 3). Once there was a diagnosis or a suspicion that there may be a pattern of genetic problems emerging within the kindred, the wider process of sifting through the family (past and present) and the adjudication of what traits were or were not 'genetic' began. If the genetic nature of the diagnosis was disclosed to wider family members, they too began to reflect on their family history and additional accounts began to surface about other members who may show signs or have traits that may indicate similar underlying genetic problems. These collective memories drew on family anecdotes and often provided complex rationalizations to associate a range of traits with the condition. Two families with sons diagnosed with a genetic syndrome that causes learning disabilities debate the various theories that have emerged within their kindred to explain where the condition may have originated.

Julia. her husband, Chris, (their young son has been diagnosed with a genetic syndrome, FRAXE) and Julia's mother, Mary, describe a number of stories that have led to complex theories about whom in their family they believe is affected by FRAXE and where it originated. Julia believes she has passed on the condition to her son because she links the condition to family stories about her own birth and early development which suggest she may have had intracranial pressure. Additionally, all three have screened the family and focus their gaze on an uncle and niece related to Julia's father who they think may be the source of the condition. They associate the niece's 'nervous disability' with the child's learning disabilities. An alternative family theory is also considered. Julia thinks that her mother may have transmitted it to her and her affected son because her maternal uncle also appeared to have some learning disabilities. However, this theory is debated and Mary has a different interpretation of her brother's problems. She recounts the family story that he suffered brain damage because of physical abuse. She additionally puts forward a third theory by placing a question mark over the status of relatives who live in Australia who she believes have the 'look' and the personality traits she associates with the condition. Despite the differing theories, they come to agree that it originates with Julia's paternal grandmother. Julia and Chris agree that Julia's father's side of the family is the source and they believe any signs of the condition they had identified in Mary are caused by environmental factors, in particular, her 'upbringing'. Her mother and sister's memories confirm this theory for Julia; they remember her paternal grandmother and believe it started there. Interestingly, at no point in this debate are the child's paternal family considered.

> *Chris*: Well, it was just looking at Dad's brother, wasn't it really, and one of the nieces and [...]
>
> *Mary*: Yes, I know but they reckon she [niece] had nervous disability, whatever that is. I just don't know.
>
> *Julia*: Yeah, but the thing is. I mean, I'm saying that's what they think she might've had. It's the same as when I was born they turned round and said I had pressure on the brain ...
>
> *Mary*: But, you know, the one sister she comes to stop with me and her brother came from Australia so, you know, they're and when you see them they're pretty gabby sort of thing, you know, they talk. But of course, I mean, we don't see anything. The only thing was my brother. They used to call him retarded but he wasn't retarded. My father beat him so badly, damaged his brain, but of course nothing was done in those days.
>
> *Julia*: Oh, well yeah, I mean, as soon as they said it was a genetic problem I thought to might ... right obviously it's going to come from my side. And, I mean, we'd more or less gone down the path of we know where it comes from like. I mean, we're 99 per cent certain it comes from my father and we're certain it comes from his mother. [...] I mean, I didn't know my grandmother. She died when I was 18 months old but my mother and my sister remembers her. My sister was saying about it last week. We were talking about it and she said that she most probably thinks it comes from my grandmother.
>
> *Chris*: Still the strain is there [...] but you see your father's got it and I don't think your mother has got it but I can't say till they've had the test but it's not something that your mother's. How can you put it? I think it's her background her, her upbringing that's slightly different.

Thus, we can see from an account such as this the ways in which family narratives are constructed. They are multiple, shifting and can be contested by others. All three family members above provide a number of complex and competing theories that variously identify where the condition originated, who is at risk and the path of transmission.

Similarly, Patty and her brother Philip discuss where (FRAXE) may have originated within their family. From their ongoing surveillance of other family members they conclude that the syndrome comes from their mother's side of the family because 'they've all got speech impediments'. They both present rationalizations of why they think the condition has been transmitted by their mother's 'side' of the family. Patty catalogues the various problems in their mother's family and lists the members who she thinks may have had similar problems in the past, particularly a cousin who appeared to be 'slow' and a cousin's child with an unspecified 'problem'. Philip has scrutinized their family by researching the family tree and can find no evidence to suggest a pattern of disability within their father's 'side' of the family. He believes the provenance of their father's family rules out the condition. They were from London and all had successful careers – good evidence, he believes, that they were unlikely to be responsible for introducing the condition.

> *Patty:* Well, I think it could be on my mother's. My brother said that as well. My brother said he thinks it could be my mother's side, more than my father's side because nobody, he knows on my father's side, either than I can think of either. Although my brother has gone more in-depth with the family you see because he's done a family tree.
>
> *Philip:* Well, they've all got a speech impediment. I've never really had a speech impediment. I've got to be honest. I mean, my problems are mainly related to my mother's side. I mean, I think this particular thing comes from my mother's side … The reason I think that is because I've done family trees and I've got it all on computer, a lot of it.

Surveillance of the family and the search for patterns of inheritance often led to a belief that a genetic condition or family trait was transmitted through only male or only female members of the family. This identification of gendered routes of transmission was both a way of explaining the presence of certain traits among a large number of the kindred and used to predict who will be affected in the future.

For example, within one kindred a 7-year-old boy has recently been diagnosed with a genetic syndrome (XYY) that causes mild learning disabilities. His parents, Joanna and David, appear to have expected the diagnosis and XYY is accounted for as a family trait within the kindred. They describe how a large number of the men in the family have very similar and conspicuous personality traits and these are expected to affect the next generation of boys. They have been aware of this pattern for many years and it has become a familiar family story. The couple respond to the diagnosis by saying their son is just displaying a typical 'male characteristic' of his father's family; it is the way they all 'deal with things'.

> *David:* It's just a family trait, yes.
>
> *Joanna:* And just left it at that really.
>
> *David:* Because my nephew has been diagnosed with Aspergers as well. You could say it was just a male characteristic of our family, the way we deal with things.

Examining the Present

All the families and individuals we spoke to looked for signs of the genetic condition in their kin in a number of ways. Many believed they were family experts who could see 'it' in certain members of their kin by identifying traits they believed were either early signs or predictors of the onset or carrier status of the condition.

The scrutiny of children and the identification and assessment of their development were a common feature of this process of surveillance. Sometimes, others (most commonly family members, friends, health professionals and teachers) brought potential health or development problems to the attention of the family. For example, they provided suggestions or hints that a child's development was delayed or identified features that they thought may be outside the normal range. Often the physical and intellectual development of the subsequent generation was scrutinized and compared with that of previous generations. A number of comments from others suggesting that 'something is not right' usually led parents to seek further medical assessment of their child.

For example, Julia reports that her mother, Mary, continually scrutinized her son's development, comparing him with other children in the family and noting his failure to reach certain developmental milestones. Julia admits that, despite protesting that each child develops at their own pace, she was prompted by her mother's comments to seek further clinical investigations of her son's development, which led to him receiving a diagnosis of FRAXE.

> *Julia*: Er, well, I didn't. When all this thing was, it was mostly my mother who said 'Oh yes he should be doing this.' She was comparing with the other grandchildren. And I said 'Well, you can't compare with any grandchildren because basically all people progress at different rates.' [...] And then so she was saying he should be doing this. He went to a speech therapist, and then we had the test and found out he was ill.

Similarly, Annabel was aware that her son had some developmental delay; however, she was happy to 'deal with what you've got' rather than seek a diagnosis. Annabel reports that, she was prompted to seek a genetic diagnosis by her family and her sister was particularly insistent that he may have a genetic syndrome. Both Annabel and her sister are clinical consultants and they use the term FLK (Funny Looking Kid), a term widely used within the clinical domain to refer to a child who has dysmorphic features that may be associated with a genetic syndrome that causes learning disabilities. In contrast, Annabel's parents focus their concern on external factors, particularly the school.

> *Annabel*: I wasn't that concerned; you deal with what you've got. But it would be where is he on the continuum. You do get mixed messages. My sister thinks he's a FLK and thinks we're not doing enough for him. (*Annabel goes on to state that this message was passed on to her by her mother.*) We're very happy with him. We are worried about secondary school. In the short term he's got to leave school at 7.

KF: How about your parents?

Annabel: Initially nothing. My mother is an ex-teacher so she is hypercritical of the school. So I'm more relaxed about it. They are worried about what we are going to do when he is 7. My mother's view is that his behaviour is coming from the social. He's with all these children with behavioural problems and he's easily led. That's a concern when he gets older. Will he be picked on and seen as slightly odd. I'm worried about his potential vulnerability.

Seeing 'It'

Often those who surveyed their wider family for signs of the condition believed they could 'see' the disease in undiagnosed members of their kindred. By recognizing the early signs of disease, they believed they could predict who was most likely to develop the condition in the future.

Family members were often thought to be at risk if they had the 'look' associated with the condition. Julia's son has been diagnosed with a syndrome causing learning disabilities and she believes she can trace the path of the condition through the family and see the 'look', the outward expression of the disease, in other members of the kindred. Her mother, Mary, agrees that the condition is latent at present but will express itself either within Julia's cousin or in her children; she can see it in them. The wider family may not recognize such knowledge, but these family 'experts' have the experience to see the subtle signs or the 'look' they believe is associated with the condition.

> *Julia*: Well, no. My uncle in _____ he's very slow. I've got a cousin up in ____ even though she – I mean she's got beautiful writing and everything if you look at her. Even her daughter. I mean, looking at it now you can see where it is.
>
> *KF*: Oh, really. You think so?
>
> *Julia*: Yes, I mean, you look at my cousin and I'm not saying she looks thick or nothing but you can. We've always wondered why they look – I can't explain it.
>
> *KF*: Yes.
>
> *Julia*: It's just that you can actually see where it is now. I mean like my sister and my brother. My sister thinks that she might be carrying [...]
>
> *Mary*: She always looked as though she, she had something, you know, but I mean I couldn't put my finger on it, you know.

Family members also look for signs in those diagnosed with the condition that can be associated with the presence of the genetic material causing the condition. Most commonly, features such as personality types, skills, intelligence or physical traits are identified and associated with disease inheritance. These are used to assess family members; if family members have these features, it is assumed they will have also inherited the genetic material causing the condition.

For example, since his nephew was diagnosed with a genetic syndrome that causes learning disabilities, Philip has looked back over his family, searching for clues to identify who is most likely to be affected. He attempts to establish the pattern of inheritance so that he can identify who is currently affected and predict who is likely to be in the future. He links the condition to relatives on his mother's side of the family because he believes they displayed the trait of 'nervousness' which he associates with the expression of the syndrome. In contrast, he believes relatives on his father's 'side' were much more 'stable' and 'logical'. In light of this assessment, he judges that he has the personality type that originates from his father's side of the family and thus is unlikely to be at risk of inheriting the condition or passing it on to his children (see p. 63).

Both Jill and Tamsin have surveyed their families and formed strong beliefs about the patterns of disease transmission within their kindred. They have both identified additional traits that they believe are associated with susceptibility to the genetic condition neurofibromatosis. They use these to predict who within the following generation is most likely to be protected from or at risk of this condition. Interestingly, while Tamsin identifies traits she believes will protect her son, Jill has identified features that she believes place one of her three sons at a particularly high risk of inheriting the condition.

Tamsin has recently been diagnosed with neurofibromatosis and is extremely concerned that her 2-year-old son will also inherit the condition. This concern is heightened by other distressing events in the family; she links her sister's death in her twenties from skin cancer with her condition (neurofibromatosis affects the skin by causing *café au lait* marks and benign tumours). The apparent pattern of serious skin conditions within her family leads her to worry about her son. However, her concern and anxiety about this risk are tempered by the belief that rather than resembling her, her son takes after and 'follows' his father. She rationalizes that because her son's physical features and personality are similar to those of his father, his father's genes must dominate and thus provide protection from the condition. (See the field notes on p. 66.)

Similarly, Jill has surveyed her family and identified a pattern of inheritance whereby a range of skin problems and other physical features are associated with susceptibility to neurofibromatosis. This has led her to develop strong beliefs about who is most likely to be affected. She believes the condition 'comes from' her mother and her side of the family who have similar physical features; she associates the transmission of the condition with freckles, birth marks and red hair. Jill has three sons in their twenties; however, as we have seen in the previous chapter, the focus of her concern is her youngest son who she believes is most susceptible to the condition because he has inherited red hair and freckles. In contrast, she does not consider her two other sons to be at so great a risk because they do not share these features. Rather than discussing the condition in any detail with her sons Jill plans to survey and monitor her youngest son closely for any signs of the condition.

> *Jill*: I'd like to know just to keep a check on my, because my mother is and I've got one son who's a redhead so that's my main worry that if that is the actual line that it comes from, the redheads, because my mother's family were all redheads as well ... Because my son is absolutely plastered with freckles in the summer time so that would be my main worry would be him where the other two are more my colour but _____ is a proper redhead. He's like my mother so that's the only thing I worry about.

Through this process of surveillance, genetic conditions become related to a range of other traits such as physical resemblance, personality types, skills and talents. Those who 'take after' the affected individual are believed to be more likely to be affected. For example, Isobel believes that her son must have the same condition that killed his father because he closely resembles him in terms of his physical features, mannerisms and personality; as she says, 'everything is his father'. As 'a smaller version' of his father, she believes he has not only inherited his father's traits but also the condition because both these traits and the disease 'come from within'. (See dialogue on p. 66.)

Sometimes surveillance within families has been going on for so long that family narratives about inheritance have been developed over a number of years and in some cases over generations. Usually these theories are well rehearsed within the kindred, often to the extent that they have become family jokes or stories. Joanna and David believe their child is 'very much his father's son'. His diagnosis is interpreted within the context of the wider pattern of communication problems that have been identified within the men in the family, and more specifically David. The couple's rationalization of the men's behavioural traits normalizes the genetic condition; to them it is not a serious problem to be medicalized because there are generations of men in the family who have all adapted well and have overcome their problems. Certain personality traits are expected and all the men are scrutinized for signs.

> *David*: I mean, he shows a lot of what we'd I suppose call family traits really because he's as stubborn and awkward as I can be at times.
> *Joanna*: I mean, he's very much his father's son, isn't he really? I mean, you're your father's son and your father's is, a whole line of them.

However, even though traits such as these are to some extent to be expected, once her son receives a genetic diagnosis, Joanna spends considerable time and energy scrutinizing the wider kindred to establish who would also receive this genetic classification and establishing to what degree the condition may be present. The couple examine the family tree and consider who is 'healthy' or who may have similar problems. Both Joanna and David focus their attention and concern on one nephew who is the same age as their affected child; they have monitored him closely and believe he fits the clinical diagnosis.

> *Joanna*: Oh well, you know. Now to be honest with you, from what I've read from XYY I would actually say [nephew] fits the category a lot better. He's very, very tall, very, very loud, very, very aggressive.
> *David*: Yes.
> *Joanna*: I mean, not over, well not in a nice way.
> *David*: Very forceful is a nice way to put it.
> *Joanna*: Yes.

Surveillance of the Wider Family

Receiving a genetic diagnosis from the clinical genetics service appears to lead to the retrospective surveillance and scrutiny of previous generations of the kindred. This is part of the process of searching for answers; individuals want to know why *they* are affected by the condition and how it came to affect *their* family. Their need to answer these questions is often so strong that even if a thorough scrutiny of family members they know reveals nothing significant, they shift their focus onto sections of the wider family where there is little or no contact. Thus, family stories about the health status and indeed any other traits or details of distant kin, however vague, become essential to individuals rationalizations of how they came to be affected by the condition.

Patty and her brother Philip, as we have already seen, believe they have identified the pattern of inheritance of FRAXE and have clear ideas about who is or is not likely to be affected in their wider family. They discuss their cousins who all live in different parts of the country and with whom they now have little or no contact. They agree that two of their cousins are unaffected, but they believe a third is likely to be affected because he has 'educational problems' and a fourth has a child who they suspect has an unspecified 'problem'. Thus, they make clear classifications of who is or is not likely to be affected by the condition, even though they have had only limited contact. Philip recounts their assessment of the family:

> *Philip*: My cousin ___ there's no problem with him and my cousin ___ there's no problem with him. I'm talking about my mum's side now because I think that's where the problem is. My cousin ___ no problem with him. I'm talking about anything affecting them, then I've got to go a cousin then now, possibly my uncle's children. Like I say, one of them has got, she's got a boy who's about 21 now and he has a problem but it's – I don't quite know. Without really talking about it I'm not quite

sure. He's a bit slow. ___ has got some problems. Now my uncle's son ___ has got educational problems ...

Since receiving her diagnosis of polycystic kidney disease, Claudia has scrutinized her family for signs of where the condition has come from. She is the first case in her family (as far as she knows) and her two teenage daughters are at risk of inheriting the condition. She finds it inexplicable that she is the first to be affected in the family, but fails to identify anyone who may have had the condition in previous generations. However, Claudia has no information about one part of her family, her paternal grandparents,   and fixes upon this section as the likely 'suspect', with her paternal grandfather as the source of the condition.

> *Claudia*: Well, the only thing I could think of is that I have no knowledge of my father's mother's family and at 36 she wouldn't have developed symptoms, would she, of polycystic or necessarily have developed them ... yes again, you see, I know my mother's family quite thoroughly. I know right up to sort of sixth cousins and nobody has had any problems with kidneys ... so the only suspect is my paternal grandfather.

Scrutiny of the family does not necessarily remain focussed on the known symptoms or signs of the condition affecting them, but can also include a wide range of features and characteristics that may appear to be unusual or 'abnormal' in some way. Often a genetic diagnosis leads to the telling of family stories from the past about individuals who may have been outside the norm in some way because they had behavioural or intellectual disabilities or physical abnormalities or malformations and these may (however vaguely) or may not be related to the diagnosis. For example, a young couple, Connie and Andrew, recount how since their daughter's diagnosis of hemihypertrophy (an asymmetry of physical growth, particularly affecting one side of the body or face), both they and their parents have scrutinized their family histories for signs of similar problems or malformations. The family stories prompted by this diagnosis suggest a maternal uncle who had a 'club foot'. Family members past and present are scrutinized and traits thought to be outside the norm are brought to the fore.

Surveillance of the Self

Surveillance is not just an outward gaze. These individuals also constantly scrutinized themselves for signs of the conditions affecting their families. They often reported spending considerable time scrutinizing their bodies, comparing themselves with others, going over their personal histories and tracing their past development in order to find (or rule out) similarities in their health with the natural history, symptoms and development of the conditions.

This is also part of a process of making sense of their own lives in relation to this information; once a familial condition had been identified, family members often scrutinized their past and present behaviour, health and development for signs that indicated they may be affected to various degrees or may have passed on the condition to their children. Julia and Patty examine both themselves and their siblings for signs of the genetic syndrome (FRAXE) that has caused learning disabilities in their sons. They both believe that this syndrome has also affected their own abilities, skills and behaviour and looking back at their lives believe they see signs of the condition in their childhoods. Julia believes that her brother and sister were more intelligent than her, while Patty notes that both she and her brother (Philip) had problems at school; both conclude that they too have been affected and have passed the condition on to their sons. Even though other family members have provided reassurance, they remain convinced, displaying similar levels of guilt and producing similar accounts of how their children came to be affected.

> *Julia*: The thing is I'm not academically – You know, like as far as [sister] is concerned because I mean they're a lot brighter than what I am. I'm terrible.
>
> *Mary*: I'm not going to answer that because your school reports are only a little bit worse than what theirs were.
>
> *Julia*: Yeah, but the difference was, I mean, the thing is that [sister] is obviously a lot brighter than me because she's a nurse and my brother is a lot brighter than me.
>
> *Mary*: Yeah, but, I mean, I couldn't walk in there and do the job you're doing.

> *Patty*: I mean, me and my brother both said that as we were growing up we felt it was hard to take things in, you know, like educationally, you know, and our minds could easily just wander off out to space and you just turned a deaf ear to everything else that was going on around you. You know, so your concentration was gone, you know … when I mentioned it to my fiancé, he said, well, that happens to a good number of people. He said that they just drift off, they're not interested in the lessons, he said. So he said that may not be a problem.

Individuals' surveillance of their own bodies and development can not only inform beliefs about how conditions are transmitted through their families, but is also part of the process of predicting the future. There was a common belief that patterns of health, behaviour and development repeat themselves within families and appear through subsequent generations. For example, Patty believes that because both she and her brother 'overcame' the various problems they had as children, the boys in the next generation of her family will similarly progress and overcome their genetic condition.

Patty and Philip have scrutinized their past in the context of the new genetic diagnosis her son has received. Patty believes that she and her two siblings were a bit 'slow' at school, had problems 'understanding things' and found schoolwork difficult; however, as they got older they found things 'became easier'. Similarly, her brother connects their early educational problems, which he later 'overcame', with his nephew's condition. They both read patterns in the family and use them to predict an improved developmental trajectory for her son, believing he too will grow out of his educational problems. Thus, they search for patterns not only to help them make sense of the past and the present but also to predict the future.

> *Philip*: Very anxious, very nervous, my mother has difficulty retaining things. She's not stupid we're not talking about that, but she certainly has, if she has to. I had it when I was younger and may be that was something to do with the condition. Maybe because when I used to go to exams I was hopeless. I used to get fearful, even though I might've swotted. I eventually I think overcame it but I've still got a bit of that sort of thing. I don't like exams, but it became easier.

Similarly, David has also spent a lot of time since his son's diagnosis looking to the past, both to explain the present and to predict the future. He reflects on his own childhood 'problems' and believes he can see similarities with his son's development. Despite his son's genetic diagnosis, he clings to the hope that, like him, his son will grow out of and transcend his condition to lead a 'normal' life.

> *David*: So we don't have any difficulty with it really, you know. Hopefully he will. I mean, I keep, I keep reflecting back to my childhood and by the time I was 9 or 10 I grew out of a lot of problems. I mean, basically you learn to work around them and he's quite a bright lad as well so he's learned to cope with most of it. The only areas we're concentrating on sort of therapy-wise is just his communication skills and dealing with group situations. I mean, he doesn't like being in crowds. I mean, I'm exactly the same and just taking step-by-step a little bit at a time and he's gradually dealing with things.

Examining the Future

Within families where there is a known genetic condition, there is often a complex process of mutual surveillance. Those affected spoke of monitoring the development of their conditions, comparing their progress with those who are at different stages of disease progression and looking for early signs of disease among those who may be at risk. Similarly, those who may be at risk of developing a condition discussed watching the progression of the disease in other family members and looking for signs of disease onset in themselves and others. They additionally witnessed the emotional consequences of predictive testing and of receiving a diagnosis and the burden of carers. Thus, family members observe not just the physical effects of the disease, but also the practical and emotional problems the diagnosis brings not only to the individual but also to the wider family. Both the affected and unaffected watch the progression of the condition within family members from its onset and development through to disability and (in some cases) death. Jill reports that the high and 'frightening' incidence of cancer in her family means that it is a common topic when members of her family meet. They constantly scrutinize each other for 'signs' of the disease and a common topic of conversation is a 'who's next'. When Jill became ill with no clear diagnosis, she became extremely anxious; she had seen the early signs of onset of the condition and believed she was following the trajectory of the pattern of illness and subsequent death within her kindred.

> *Jill*: Yes, we do. Because it's so bad you do. I mean, that is the main topic of conversation half the time in the family when we do get together because it is so bad everybody does talk about it. You've got to talk about it I think because it's so frightening because it's so bad. [...] Yeah, we all. It's quite out in the open. We have some conversation in the family. They've just grown up with it I suppose because it's so bad. It's very rarely a year goes by when somebody doesn't die of cancer in the family so it is the topic most of the time unfortunately. But I think some families do get hit by it don't they, same as anything else I suppose. Some families get cystic fibrosis so you get on with your life isn't it and hope for the best ... Look out for any signs. That's why I was so upset when they did nothing down the surgery because knowing the family history and to just you know giving me antibiotics. Because after a year if it had been a cancer I wouldn't have a chance anyway.

Surprisingly, receiving a conclusive test result from the clinic removing the risk of developing or passing on a genetic condition does not automatically stop this process of surveillance and worry. Mark reports that he grew up believing he was a carrier for cystic fibrosis and that his children could be at risk of inheriting the condition. Because of this, he and his fiancée, Kate, have sought testing to assess their risk of passing this condition on, and to their surprise, they discover he is not a carrier. However, this does not completely reassure them. They still believe there may be some risk to his child from a previous relationship and to any child they may have in the future. Despite reassurances from the clinical staff they 'can't help wondering' whether the condition may still be there. They decide not to disclose the test result to Mark's family, particularly his mother, who continues to believe his children are at risk.

> *Kate*: Well, they had your mum's name and maiden name. I've got to be honest I can't, you know. I mean [nurse] was very efficient and very nice and I'm sure that the result is right but I can't help wondering if there was a bureaucratic error or you know.
> *Mark*: Right, we did sort of mention that, didn't we, but she was 'Oh no, no, we've been through a certain,' you know.
> *Kate*: I mean, it is right. I know it's right but you can't help. I mean, after you've labelled them carriers for so many years you can't help wondering.

Mark: Yes, the fact that we entered into – The fact that you went then was down to the thought that I was carrying.

Kate: Yes, and I can't – I suppose if I'm honest I can't – I do wonder for [his son from a previous relationship], you know, and if we had a child then I do, I do, I know it wouldn't be a sufferer because I haven't got that genetic make-up but I can't help wondering if it will be a carrier.

Similarly, Matt, who has muscular dystrophy, is aware of the biomedical model of inheritance of the condition, according to which his sister and daughter cannot develop the condition (this is a sex-linked disorder which mainly affects men, although women who carry the altered gene can sometimes develop mild muscle weakness later in life). Yet, this does not prevent him from inspecting his daughter for signs of the condition or his daughter from mentioning potential signs to him. He worries that her reported health problems (however mild) may be the onset of the condition. This is particularly the case if these health problems could be associated with symptoms of the condition, in this case muscle problems. For example, he reports his concern when his daughter tells him that she has muscle pains in her leg; his anxiety that these symptoms represent the onset of the condition appears to be shared by his daughter and he acknowledges that, although unspoken, the condition is always on their minds. However, although he has these concerns about his daughter's health, he is reassured that she has additional qualities that will protect her; she is not only very fit and healthy but also wealthy.

Matt: I think it's always at the back of both of our minds, you know, that there's – Although you know they said that she wasn't a carrier, it can always be at the back of your mind somewhere you know. Because you get some people it manifests, manifesting you know like a lot of mothers of Duchenne they get slight symptoms like enlarged calves and that you know, manifesting signs of disease but probably not even noticeable, you know. But I think because they've said that she wasn't a carrier in the first place I think you know obviously you have to trust what they say, but even so, it's still at the back of your mind, you know, there's always that nagging little doubt, you know.

Observing the ways in which others cope with their diagnoses and the effects of conditions has a powerful influence on following generations' decisions about seeking diagnosis and treatment. A young woman, Carla, has polycystic kidney disease and is adamant that she does not want her condition monitored by medical staff, who recommend regular check-ups. She feels that, despite the potential benefits to her health, this process would generate further anxiety by reminding her of the disease and the inevitability of the gradual deterioration of her health. She has seen other family members experience the process of diagnosis and monitoring and has witnessed the wider negative effects it has had on their lives and life choices; she does not want to be affected in the same way.

> *Carla*: I'd rather not let them tell me constantly every 6 months 'They're getting worse, they're getting worse,' because the whole family sort of goes through that stage of, like 3 years before, oh, your kidney functions are getting worse and worse. Oh, I'd rather not know. I'd rather it just hit me one day and then, you know what I mean, that is me isn't it … it's just I don't want a prolonged wait like all the family have had and then you see the family, once they know oh my God it's coming, they sort of sit back, give up work, sit back and wait for it and I'm like.
> *Mother*: Oh no, no, don't want you to do that.
> *Carla*: I'm not doing that.

Who is at Risk

The process of surveillance has profound implications for the disclosure of genetic information. Within all these kindred, beliefs about the origin of the condition and the mechanisms of transmission exert a powerful influence over who is informed. The process of looking for patterns within the kindred in order to predict who is likely to be affected in the future is highly problematic. This process rarely maps the biomedical models of inheritance and thus individuals using their own assessments of who is at risk are likely to either worry about the 'wrong' family members or fail to recognize the risk posed to others. Thus, those at risk are often not informed.

We can see that beliefs within the families about the patterns of inheritance exert a powerful influence on who becomes the focus of concern. Isobel describes her concern about the men in her family inheriting a fatal cardiac condition. She lives in a high state of anxiety and fear of the possibility that her 2-year-old son will inherit the condition that killed her husband and her father-in-law. In contrast, she shows no concern for the women in the family (her husband has a sister who according to the biomedical model may be at risk) and acknowledges that if she had a daughter rather than a son, she may not be concerned.

> *Isobel*: I don't worry about anybody else in the family because [son] is the only male descendent now from [husband] that we know of anyway, you know … I don't think I worried so much if it had been a girl.

Similarly, Tamsin has scrutinized her family for health problems that might be connected with her condition, neurofibromatosis. She is searching for an explanation of how she came to be affected and trying to predict who is likely to be affected in the future. She is concerned that her sister's death in her twenties from skin cancer and her mother's multiple sclerosis may also be associated with the condition. The condition is rarely discussed within the wider family; however, when Tamsin did confide in her aunt, she discovered that her cousin also has the condition. Rather than disclosing the potential risk to other family members, Tamsin makes judgements about who is at risk and who needs to be informed.

Based on the surveillance of her family for physical signs of the condition (in this case small benign tumours on the skin and *café au lait* marks), Tamsin believes that the condition originated from her maternal grandmother because she remembers her having 'lumps' and that her father is not at risk. She remarks that although her father does have a 'lump' he does not have other features (the *café au lait* markings) of the condition. Interestingly, Tamsin remains adamant that her father is unaffected, even when the genetic specialist nurse informs her during a clinical consultation that her father is likely to be affected and visibly marks the symbol representing her father on the family tree as an affected family member. Tamsin appears to ignore this information and focuses on the potential risk for her young son.

Tamsin states that when her GP told her the diagnosis 'I Panicked … I was upset for a couple of days worrying about [son]: I just thought they [café au lait] were birthmarks.' She has talked to her aunt about the condition who then told her that her cousin had the condition and had a large lump removed. However, she has not mention her condition to her father because 'he doesn't have it'. Despite the nurse saying a number of times during the consultation that 'your dad is likely to be affected' this woman repeatedly states that although he had some lumps he didn't have the café au lait markings [implying that he doesn't have it]. The nurse replies that these markings are not always obvious, especially if you have a darker skin tone. During the taking of the family tree, the father's status is discussed and the nurse shades her father in as a carrier. The woman is sitting very close to her and can see this and has been told what the shading meant. The nurse shades in the woman, her father and her cousin. They discuss the questions she has. She wants to know when she can have the lump on her hand removed and would also like to discuss her concerns about her son and the nurse agrees that at the clinic her son should be 'looked over' for signs of the condition.

Many of these individuals had strong and profound beliefs that the genetic condition would inevitably affect other family members. According to Matt; it was only a matter of time before muscular dystrophy affected someone within his wider family.

Matt: Well, they seem to think so, like I say, and there's no family history. There's no other sign of other parts of the family with it. So whether it is a mutation as they say or whether, you know, it's skipped generations. But if it had skipped generations it's bound to have shown up somewhere in the family but there again I don't know the family. I haven't seen any of them for years.

Thus, these families are ever-vigilant, scrutinizing their immediate and wider family for potential cases or to identify patterns in the past and the present to help detect which individuals or branches of the family are most at risk in the future. We go on to show in greater detail how these practices of surveillance have profound consequences for beliefs about who is, or is not, at risk of developing or transmitting the conditions. Within the next chapter, we will show how processes of surveillance inform disclosure in a number of important ways. We will argue that beliefs about practical psychology (which family members are variously believed to be able, or unable, to cope with information about conditions) and the wider discourse of practical morality (the beliefs, advice and directives family members provide about the appropriate responses) become important features informing genetic information and disclosure.

–5–

Practical Ethics and Disclosure

Introduction

It is important to point out that 'ethics' are not solely the concern of counsellors and other professionals, but also for family members. The actual process of practical ethical decision-making carried out by family members is complex, especially in regard to the disclosure and exchange of information about the risk of transmitting or manifesting genetic disease. This chapter discusses how surveillance is linked to beliefs about who is, or is not, at risk of developing or transmitting a condition and describes how surveillance can affect decisions about to whom (and when) information is disclosed. Disclosure is associated with beliefs about practical psychology, leading to assumptions about family members who are variously believed to be able or unable to cope with certain information. We also discuss the discourse of practical morality within the kindred: the beliefs, advice and directives family members provide about the appropriate responses (for example, behaviour modification and life choices) to genetic information. Whilst existing research suggests that communication within families about genetic risk is influenced by both pre-existing familial and cultural factors and individuals' responses to risk information (Forrest et al., 2003), the data in our research emphasizes that members of families with a known genetic condition are potentially engaged in everyday bioethical decision-making.

A starting point for this research was the premise that the identification of a genetic condition or a risk in one individual (a proband) necessarily has implications for other members of the kindred. Equally, the conduct of family studies by genetic scientists and practitioners creates a professionalized context within which the distribution of knowledge and belief among family members is of considerable moment (Deftos, 1998; Green et al., 1997; Leung et al., 2000). Consequently, family members who are given genetic information can readily face practical problems of *disclosure* in the family. Additionally, if a patient or individual does not want information about his/her personal genetic risk or health status communicated to other family members, the resultant potential health implications for the family can become seriously 'risky' (cf. Leung et al., 2000).

Whilst such a context presents a moral and ethical quandary for physicians, it also calls into question whether ethical issues of confidentiality and disclosure are matters restricted to the issue of individual privacy or whether there is a moral duty towards siblings and the wider familial unit. Weijer (2000) for instance, emphasized a fundamental distinction between strangers and family, arguing that 'family members are not strangers to one another; rather they share an indissoluble bond'. Here the family is placed squarely in a domain where a set of moral rules for strangers, such as the right to patient confidentiality, are deemed inappropriate when invoked within the close confines of the family. This argument is problematic as it draws on a simplistic notion of family and what and who constitute it. Finkler (2001) similarly romanticizes the geneticized family as one brought closer together through practical aspects of collecting and sharing genetic information and in confronting actual and possible genetic illness. Intra-familial communication in such a context is assumed to be free-flowing, unhindered by the need for secrecy and confidentiality. In fact it is too easy to assume that processes and patterns of disclosure are relatively straightforward. Our research suggests quite the opposite. Indeed, it is even questionable whether the term 'disclosure' itself is altogether helpful.

Here we come to one of the key messages of our own research. Some formulations of the consequences of genetic work pose the general issue in terms of 'the disclosure of genetic information among family members'. We have already made it clear that family members do not have or share 'information' in any simple sense. They express complex, sometimes inconsistent, beliefs concerning inheritance and genetics. They interpret and explain 'genetic' information in the light of frameworks of everyday, practical knowledge. It makes little sense to think in terms of 'disclosure', which implies the once-and-for-all sharing of discrete parcels of 'information'. In practice, we see that the processes are much more diffuse, and much more embedded in the everyday realities of practical kinship. Indeed, what counts as 'family', among whom knowledge may or may not be shared, is contingent. It depends upon the gendered practical kinship-work that members (usually women) perform in defining and maintaining relatedness among those who are potentially identifiable as relations. Existing research in the area suggests that disclosure of genetic information is a gendered activity, with the benefits and burdens of this task falling mainly on women (d'Agincourt-Canning, 2001; Hallowell, 1999). In other words, we identify the family as a complex gendered domain where communication, disclosure and information interpenetrate and circulate. This makes the contours of the familial unit fuzzy as individuals define, limit and draw boundaries around the family through partial disclosures that include and exclude family members contextually.

Disclosure

From our observational work and discussion with the clinical teams it was clear that, assumptions were often made about the nature of disclosure within families and what 'family' consists of in the context of genetic information. The notion often implied the unproblematic transfer of information about the potential risk of inheriting a genetic condition. However, we found the experience of disclosure within families to be much more complex. For example, the disclosure of genetic information is not likely to constitute a single episode where information is unproblematically provided to a willing recipient. Rather it is a process with no clear boundaries and always partial in nature. Even when apparently 'complete' disclosure is reported within a kindred, it still has clear limitations and it is debatable whether the term 'disclosure' is an appropriate term to use or a realistic goal to expect families to achieve.

When Rosie and Anthony were initially introduced to the study, the clinical team believed that 'full disclosure' had taken place. Family members also described a process of disclosure that appeared to be both comprehensive and complete. When the clinic identified that a child's severe physical and learning disabilities had been caused by a translocation all the adult members of the immediate family (the parents of the affected child, their siblings, their partners and the child's grandparents) attended the clinic together. As a group, they had given blood samples to be tested, received their test results and been informed about the condition, the risks for future pregnancies and the mechanism of inheritance.

> *Rosie*: We all went down there. Even I went down obviously. We were sitting there and we were just discussing it as a family weren't we, as a group … after the individual sort of discussion he did come out then and discussed it as a group. And we all sat. We were all sitting there in a group and then the second time we went down for the results and [parents of the affected child] came out of the room with [consultant] because [consultant] had told them that everybody of the family were carriers. So they knew when they came out with [consultant] and then we sat down and he said 'Right this is it you're all carriers basically you know.' It was just a blood thing you know. Yeah but it was, it was a group discussion we were all down there waiting for the results and you all your test done and I think I had a test then as well.

This process of disclosure within the immediate family had been translated subsequently into everyday terms of reference and understanding. Rosie recalls that they were informed they were all 'carriers' and she translates this some years later as the condition being a 'blood thing'.

Thus, two generations of this large group of adult family members were informed simultaneously by clinical services of their risk and potential diagnosis in the context of genetic testing. Yet this apparently comprehensive approach to disclosure of risk information did not mean that the process was complete or that information would be passed on to the next generation unproblematically. This immediate family still encounterd a common dilemma that affects all of the families in the process of disclosure and communication: who needs to be informed, who is at risk and who has the right to inform or be informed.

When we meet Rosie and Anthony for the purposes of this research, almost ten years have passed since this initial process of disclosure and the next generation are reaching adulthood with no knowledge of the genetic condition in the family or their potential risk. After the initial flurry of interest at the time of detection, the condition is no longer discussed by most of the kindred; two of the siblings have children who are unaffected and thus they have come to believe that these children are not at risk. Disclosure seems to be fixed in time and although information had initially travelled across this generation of siblings, it does not pass easily through to the next generation.

However, Rosie and Anthony are affected. Anthony carries the translocation and as a result Rosie has had a number of miscarriages. They are now going through pre-implantation genetic diagnosis to ensure they have a child who is not affected by the condition. The wider kindred, although apparently aware of Rosie and Anthony's problems, do not broach the subject with them and this couple also try to be discreet; they fear the subject will upset other family members. For example, they do not refer to the condition or their treatment in the presence of Anthony's father because they are aware that he has passed the translocation on to his son and they believe any further discussion will upset him. Thus, even though they are aware of the genetic condition, they do not discuss the problems and decisions they face more widely within their kin.

In such cases, further disclosure and rediscovery of a genetic condition amongst the wider family is often prompted by an event that will lead to another family member being at risk of inheriting the condition. In Rosie and Anthony's immediate family, their nephew (cousin of the affected child) and his girlfriend are expecting a baby and they appear to be unaware that this child might be at risk. His parents also fail to make the connection that he may be a carrier and it is left to their sister-in-law (Rosie) to remind them. Rosie admits that she is anxious about this role and chooses to communicate this information indirectly through her mother-in-law.

> *Rosie*: And, like I say, we look into it now so we know exactly what happens and, you know, we've told everybody else what happens, especially when [nephew] found out [about the pregnancy], you know, it was like well you'd better go and have a check and I don't think they realized. They were like oh yes you know he's going to have to get that checked out.
> *Anthony*: Yes.
> *Rosie*: And it wasn't exactly planned was it so.

Anthony: No.

Rosie: No, that's what I mean but I don't think [sister-in-law] unless your Mum hadn't said 'What about this?' she would've, you know, she'd forgot type of thing because it, it didn't happen to her children so they were okay but again she didn't realize about the carrier thing, you know … In that group meeting that we went to we were told that even though they look fine it could be carrier but, you know, it's, over the years it just gets pushed back doesn't it?[…]Like I said, until they're in a steady relationship or whatever and they know yeah okay we want to do this let's get tested. It's the testing part I think they. Once they're in a relationship they all need to be tested.

Rosie is highly motivated and has a strong belief that all who are at risk of being a carrier should be informed. Acts of disclosure are also provided with a sub-text of responsibilities: Rosie is clear that all of the next generation within the kindred should be tested for the translocation once they reach a potentially 'risky' life stage – for instance, when they begin serious relationships. She is the only family member who still has links with the clinical service.

The Burden of Knowledge

The burden of knowledge was a recurring theme for individuals in our research. There was a palpable sense of awareness that genetic risk information not only could have far-reaching and potentially devastating consequences for them, but would also implicate other family members in very direct ways. Not surprisingly, they all expressed high levels of anxiety in dealing with the moral, ethical and practical dilemmas they faced in disclosing such information. To a large extent these concerns defined, structured and constructed the boundaries of disclosure. Many discussed their concerns about what they should do with this knowledge in the face of practical problems of testing, the moral burden of who to tell and decisions about when is the most appropriate point in time to disclose.

Carla has polycystic kidney disease (PKD), a degenerative condition that can lead to kidney failure. She describes her constant anxiety that her 4-year-old daughter is at risk of inheriting the condition. She frequently discusses her concerns with her mother and holds conflicting beliefs about how she should respond: should she have the child tested to identify whether she is at risk of developing the condition or let her decide whether to be tested when she gets older? PKD is a condition that does not usually cause overt disease until individuals are in their forties or fifties. However, both Carla and her mother describe how they continually discuss and survey the health of the child, looking for signs of the condition. This pattern of surveillance and worry has been going on for many years; a large number of Carla's kindred, including her father, are affected by the condition and for the last year, since Carla was diagnosed, her daughter has been her focus of concern. This is likely to continue as the child grows up until she is tested and then beyond with the next generation.

> *Carla*: See so you could be telling me now if we had the test she's got it and then I'm worrying when she's old enough she could just be a carrier.
> *Mother*: She was panicking about it. She just worries too much.
> *Carla*: Oh, I'm dreadful.
> *Mother*: She just worries too much – it's only natural isn't it. I said 'Don't worry, don't worry.' I come off the phone and I was worried.
> *Carla*: I'm a panicker.

These individuals were aware that as well as holding important knowledge about their own health, they also held important genetic knowledge about other family members – often in relation to potentially debilitating conditions that have serious health consequences. These individuals often said that they believed this knowledge was just too terrible to share. So rather than disclosing, they chose to hide the genetic nature of their conditions, the potential risk to others and their concern and anxiety.

Family Structure and the Problems of Communication

Individuals and families in our research often observed that the process of disclosure was particularly complex for them because they believed their family did not fit the stereotype of the classic 'nuclear family' and was unusual in some way. They often assumed that the problems of communication they faced either would not occur or would be easier for others with families who fitted an ideal type. These individuals and families faced a complex issue that had to be negotiated: how far should information extend through the kindred?

Kate and Mark discuss their extended kin whom they have not previously considered as in need of information, but who could be at risk of inheriting cystic fibrosis. Kate explains that informing the wider family will be particularly complicated for them because they are not a 'standard' family; there are a number of stepfamilies in the kindred and some family ties are not close. Because of this, the family have not stayed in touch in the way Kate believes families should and instead have gradually drifted apart and lost contact.

> *Mark*: No, there's nobody. I mean, ours have gone their separate ways as time goes on.
> *Kate*: It's not really a standard family though. Is it?
> *Mark*: No.
> *Kate*: I mean, there's three families in a way really, isn't there? [...]
> *Mark*: I mean, they'd be just – They [half brothers] don't, talk do they? [laughs]
> *Kate*: No … But it's interesting though. I mean, I haven't thought about it but they could be carriers, couldn't they?

Mark: It is a slight possibility but only if my stepfather was.

Kate: No, they could be carriers they just couldn't be sufferers. They've got a 25 per cent chance of being a carrier.

The construction of 'family' is an everyday practical accomplishment; families are not naturally bounded entities, but are continuously being refigured and modified. The boundaries of 'family' are drawn and redrawn, with individuals or groups brought within the classification whilst others fade from view. Geographical and practical barriers or internal family rifts mean that individuals are often no longer in contact with some members or branches of their family. Such structural problems mean that many family members who may be at risk of developing or becoming affected by a condition are not informed of their risk or even told that there is 'something in the family'. Instead, they are surveyed at a distance for signs of disease and included in the process of making sense of where the condition has come from, to identify the pattern of who is, and who is not, likely to be affected.

Even if a family member is believed to be at risk, family rifts may prevent them from being informed. This is reinforced by beliefs about who is sanctioned or has the authority within the family to disclose the information. Since her son received a diagnosis of FRAXE, Patty has scrutinized her wider family for potential cases. She identifies a cousin who, as a child, appeared to be 'slow' and considers the risk to his children; she believes there is a chance that they may be affected. She has discussed these concerns with her brother but thinks it unlikely that they will be informed because there has been a rift with that section of the family. Within her kindred, this brother is the final arbiter who can decide who will be informed and, although Patty believes that part of the family may be at risk, she does not consider bypassing her brother and informing them without his consent.

Patty: As I say, there is very few of them that I actually keep in contact with you see. As I say, there might be my one cousin that I, I was going to see him regularly, but … the last time I saw him was when my father died which was nearly three years ago. So during the last three years I haven't really seen anything of him, you know … there is one other cousin as well that had problems growing up, on my mothers side, you know. That was my mother's sister's boy and well he seems to me, they used to call him slow, you know, but they did years ago, you see … When I used to see him, I used to go to my auntie's house and see my cousin, I used to think, 'there's something wrong with him', but I couldn't put my finger on what it was. But he seemed to me, like he was slow, you know, and he grew up, you see, married and had a couple of children. So how do we know that those children haven't got it. He himself, you see, could be affected by the genes, which perhaps he carries. But you see, I mentioned this to my brother and my brother says, well we don't see that cousin now. He sort of went out of favour a bit with the family, you know.

A frequent anxiety was finding an appropriate time and occasion to inform people about potentially devastating information and this was a common rationale for delaying the process. There was also a potent fear of what their reaction would be. Mary has delayed telling the majority of her relatives about her grandson's dignoses because she does not know *how* to tell them and is concerned about how they will react to such news. Disclosure is particularly difficult when it may have implications not only for an individual but also their children; in this case, there is a risk of being affected by, or passing on, a genetic syndrome that causes learning disabilities, which may have a particular stigma attached to it. Mary is worried about how to broach this difficult issue without causing upset and hurt. This is exacerbated because she has little contact with most of her relatives apart from at rare family events such as weddings or funerals. However, she does feel it was appropriate to tell her neighbours.

> *Mary*: I mean, since we've talking about it her daughter is, well ,according to Julia, is the same way and we don't know what if it's going on. It's passing on that way. It's something we have to maybe contact them and say, well, you know, how would you feel being tested and all that? Because you don't know how they'd react. It's like saying 'You're not simple but you've got, there's something wrong with you.' You know it's how, it's a fine balance how you would. She's just happy the way [...] No, I mean, if the subject comes up, you know, I just talk about it. I don't feel bad about it in any way, you, know.
> Julia: I mean, the thing is I didn't know that you'd actually spoken to anybody about it, because you haven't told me.
> *Mary*: Yes like, you know, funnily enough we were talking last night to [neighbours].
> Julia: Yeah, but the thing is they're not family so as far as I'm concerned it's nothing to do with them [...] I don't really want people outside the family, not to not know about it but as far as I'm concerned it's nothing to do with them.

Mary's daughter, Julia, whose son has been diagnosed with FRAXE, suddenly finds that her wish to retain control of the information has been circumvented by her mother. This discussion leads to an exploration of more deeply rooted problems between mother and daughter and wider conflicts within the family. Discussion of the condition and beliefs about who needs to be informed becomes entangled with issues of love, trust and favouritism.

> *Julia*: Yeah, but the thing is see Mum, I mean, people ask me what I do for a living and you don't seem to tell anybody.
> *Mary*: Most probably the subject never come up. I've never been one to brag about my kids, you know.
> *Julia*: No, no the first time you put it out was [sister's] a nurse in America married to John, my son had a pub and I was just married to Chris.
> *Mary*: Oh well, I don't, remember but –

Julia: Well, I do because, I'm not kidding you Mum, that hurt.

Mary: Oh, I'm sorry. I mean, I don't mean to hurt you love.

Julia: Because, I mean, you're quick enough to turn round and talk about [sister] and [brother] but you never seem to talk about me.

Mary: Well, I only talk about you. I've got nobody else here.

Julia: But I never hear you talk about me.

Mary: I know but you're not standing behind me, you're not standing behind me because I always say well 'Julia is a quality controller'. You know, I mean, I think that's an important job, you know. Don't put yourself down love. There's no need to. As I used to say you: you're your father's two eyes. You couldn't do no wrong.

Julia: I know I'm my father's two eyes.

Mary: Because I've never selected a preference you see. I love them all equally. I used to say [daughter] was better because she was my first, [son] as special he's my son and she's special because she's my last. Are you trying to say I don't love you or something?

Julia: Oh, I'm not saying you don't love me, no.

Mary: (*Laughs*)

The discussion raises important issues of ownership, and reveals the calculus of relationships, sharing and knowing within the complex matrix of relatedness. Who has the right to distribute information and to inform the wider family, particularly when other close kindred may also realize who is at risk? Who has the right to withhold information, particularly when disclosure would reveal information about their health status? How are these conflicting rights negotiated? Within a number of families, there was some dispute about who needed to be informed.

Isobel believes her son is at risk of inheriting the condition that led to his father's premature and sudden death. She and her daughter hold conflicting opinions about informing him of this risk. Although in principle Isobel believes he has a right to know, she finds actual disclosure beset by a number of dilemmas that are difficult to reconcile. She is concerned about the effects of revealing the risk of a condition that could have profound consequences for his future life choices. In addition, she finds it difficult to imagine when would be the right time to tell him about this risk. As his mother, she believes that she ought to protect him from the truth and the potential worry and anxiety this could cause. In deciding not to disclose, in her private world she is hoping to create conditions for a normal life, untroubled by the possible risk of premature death. In contrast, her daughter believes Isobel should be 'honest' and tell him about this risk. He is only 2 years old but Isobel is already concerned about what to do and discussions with other family members about this issue have already begun.

Disclosure is additionally difficult because there are a number of competing emotions bound up with the process as family members try to cope with the loss of loved ones in the past and worries about the future of those who are left: the next generation. The visible patterns of onset of a condition within the kindred usually fix the expected pattern of onset of the disease with the next generation. Concern is often linked to key events and for Isobel, it was the sudden death of her partner. She has seen her husband die suddenly at a young age, as did his father before him. Based on this she expects to experience high levels of fear and anxiety when her son reaches his twenties, the age of his father when he died. She sees her future fatalistically mirroring the experiences of her mother-in-law, who saw her husband and son die suddenly. She describes her future of surveillance and worry; she is the next generation of women to worry and watch the next generation of men die.

> *Isobel*: Oh, my daughter, my daughter feels that I should tell Sam [son] the truth no matter what outcomes are, that I should be honest with Sam but like I said to you earlier I've got to protect Sam. I can't have him living with a cloud over his head and thinking, worrying about his future, what's going to happen to me. I've got to take it step by step and just answer questions that he asks in a way to protect him from thinking that anything is going to happen to him ... if it can be found that there was a genetic reason why [husband] and his father died and that Sam hasn't got the same, I don't know what you call it, deformity in the gene, I don't know, that Sam is going to be okay, that there's no chance of him having the same outcome as his dad that would be great. I mean, I could say to him 'Look you've been tested, you're okay.' If there was something found that was found with his father and [son] I would have to say that everything we did was as a precaution, just in case, to make sure that he was okay. I mean, I would lie to him. I wouldn't tell him that there's a big chance that you're going to have a sudden death in your twenties. I mean, you couldn't say that to somebody, you couldn't. Even though I think that's a possibility. I mean, I would do everything to protect him, to make sure he did everything normally and to have a good life and I want him to do everything that youngsters should do without having to worry about his future ... I mean, I'm always going to wait, always, once he gets to 20 that's going to be, I'm going to spend my life, whether people have really given reassurances or not that something is going to happen, I'm going to get that knock on the door ... Because it happened to his mother, because this happened to her it's going to happen to me ... It is but people don't realize how difficult it is, you know. I don't think people realize you need to know.

Isobel is, however, without support in this predicament because her husband's family do not believe there is a genetic condition linking the father and grandfather's sudden deaths and do not want the situation to be discussed.

> *Isobel*: They wouldn't discuss anything. They've closed their minds to anything. They don't really want to know ... his family have closed their minds to any possibility of it being a genetic illness.

Similarly, disclosure is often problematic because it involves broaching 'difficult' subjects that may bring up memories of other painful events in the family. For example, Kate and Mark discuss whether they should inform his mother, Christine, that (contrary to family stories) he is not a carrier of cystic fibrosis and that his children will not be at risk. This appears to be 'good news'. They decide not to tell Christine, however, because they believe the news will cause her to relive her daughter's death from the condition. Because of this, they decide not to mention it, even though this omission is likely to mean that Mark's mother will continue to worry and survey her grandchildren for signs of the condition.

> *KF*: So have you talked to your parents?
> *Kate*: No. Well, it's difficult isn't it. It's a difficult situation with your mum.
> *Mark*: Yeah, I mean, you know, she lost a daughter.
> *Kate*: It's quite raw.
> *Mark*: I mean, I suppose if we told her it wouldn't be you know, and I think it would just rake everything back up, you know. I mean, it would like … I mean, obviously we knew my sister had it but other than that, I mean, nobody really talked about it, the fact that we knew that she was ill. We knew her lifespan wasn't expected to be too long, you know. I mean, she died when she was 23, you know, which was, which we always thought that's a fairly decent age for someone with cystic fibrosis. But other than that, I mean, we didn't know apart from caring for her then nobody really discussed anything.

Influences on Disclosure: Routes of Communication

We found that only a small number of individuals who were considered by the clinic to be at risk of a familial condition appeared to be aware of their risk. However, the family members with this knowledge and charged by the clinic with transmitting information often believed they had fulfilled this obligation. This is because disclosure usually followed the well-established routes of communication within the family.

For example, Julia is close to her sister in Canada and they talk on the telephone and exchange emails regularly. They share their experiences and feelings with each other and have talked about the genetic condition (FRAXE) affecting Julia's son and its implications in some depth. In contrast, they have decided not to inform their brother in England, even though he and his children are at risk of inheriting or transmitting this genetic syndrome because they believe he is not interested. They assume their mother (Mary) will have informed him of his risk, but their mother agrees with their assessment of her son and has not notified him.

> *Mary*: But, you know, I would like to discuss it with him but, I mean, I can't see how it's it would. I don't think it affected him in any way, you know, but, I mean, I should

imagine if I said to him would you have a blood test he'd most probably turn round and say 'When I've got time.'

Similarly, many of the families believed that certain members of their kindred would not be interested in such information or about the wider health problems in the family. Their beliefs were related to making character assessments, weighing up who would act on this information.

The Role of Surveillance

As we have seen in the previous chapter, the process of surveillance is often a means of ruling out the need to inform others. If family members do not appear to be carriers or affected, rather than inform them, those who are aware of the situation continue to watch and wait for any physical signs of the condition to appear. Before embarking on disclosure, the family is surveyed to assess an individual's risk and disease status from a distance and this process can continue for a number of years.

Complex rationalizations were often arrived at to explain why some kin were not at risk and thus did not need to be informed. For example, Julia has assessed her brother and believes he is not at risk of inheriting FRAXE. She believes she does not need to worry about this brother or his children being affected by the condition because they all appear to be unaffected. She has surveyed his children over the years, as they have been growing up, for signs of the condition; she concludes that his teenage daughter and his young son are unaffected. Thus, rather than discussing the condition and the potential risks with her brother, Julia continues to watch and wait for any signs of the condition.

> *Julia*: You know, and I suppose we, I mean, my sister and myself, we're the only ones who can speak to each other and we know how each other feel like. My brother he's, oh, you know, he doesn't give a toss like … Because, I mean, he's got a daughter. She's 19 and, well, she's fine. She's alright she is. We know that and she's got it upstairs. She's got our share of the brains. Oh she's got our share of the brains … And he's married again. He's got another little boy and he seems alright so we know that he's alright anyway.
>
> *Mary*: No. Aye, she had a daughter as well, you see, two daughters and a son. He's out in Australia he is. He had children but we've never heard anything about his children, have we? Mind you, he wouldn't even talk about it if he did. would he?

With the help of her mother (Mary), Julia has also scrutinized the wider kindred for signs of the condition. They consider the branch of the family in Australia and because they believe they do not appear to have any health problems and none has been reported they are reassured that they too do not need to be informed.

Practical Character Assessment

In justifying the sharing or withholding of genetic knowledge, risks or suspicions, family members often undertake a practical analysis of the psychology or character of their relations. We might refer to this as a form of 'lay psychology' for ease of reference. More accurately, we describe it as a process of practical moral or character assessment. In other words, talking about genetic conditions and risks among family members is described as being grounded in assessments as to who can best handle the information. All the family members produced clearly articulated accounts of who could and could not *cope* with the condition or information about their risk status. Such accounts were suffused with theories of moral character and personality type and were used to inform rationalizations of disclosure and non-disclosure of genetic information.

Such accounts were often informed by individuals' everyday beliefs about where the condition had come from and who had passed on the condition to other family members. After surveying their family, Anthony and Rosie believe his father passed the translocation on to his son (Anthony), who has infertility problems, and to one of his daughters, who has a child with severe disabilities, both conditions likely to be caused by the translocation. Anthony and Rosie have decided not to talk to Anthony's father about the effects this condition is having on their lives. It has severe implications for them, Rosie has had multiple miscarriages and they are currently undergoing a long process of invasive interventions and treatment for infertility (pre-implantation genetic diagnosis). They take this approach because they believe he could not cope and would blame himself. They agree that, although Anthony's father does not explicitly avoid the topic, he never mentions the issue and they interpret this as a sign that he does not want to know. This is associated with the 'problem' of men, who are generally characterized by many of the women within these kindred as not being able to discuss such issues. Rosie acknowledges that her husband is an exception.

Anthony: We haven't involved my father in all this at the moment because I mean until we understand it ourselves because obviously we want to put it across to my father in such a way, not for him to think that it is his fault which is obviously not the case because he couldn't do much about it.

Rosie: But he tends to take it on himself, isn't he?

Anthony: Yes, there's not a lot of, I wouldn't say there's a lot of discussion between my father and ourselves, my mother more so but that's still not exactly.

Rosie: Your dad just seems, you know, to carry on: 'I don't want to know in case it upsets me,' type of thing, you know.

Anthony: He hasn't purposely avoided the subject he just, you know, he never, he skirts around it, he never raised it.

Rosie: I don't think men are able to talk about things like that anyway apart from this one (*laughs*), you know.

Rosie believes that a large number of the kindred appear to find it difficult to talk to her about the condition because of the terrible impact this is having on her life. Their approach becomes particularly apparent when family news is related to the condition. For example, when one of her nephews announces his girlfriend is pregnant, she senses that the family find this topic uncomfortable and appear to have delayed breaking the news to her for fear that she would react badly. She senses that they are cautious in their approach to her; however, she wishes this was different.

> *Rosie*: No, me and Anthony talk about it fine. I've got to be honest, I mean, I thought his sisters might have approached us a bit more but they've seem to have kept away as well, haven't they?
>
> *Anthony*: Certainly because my older sister, when my nephew found that his girlfriend was pregnant, found it very difficult. Didn't help to tell me that my nephew was having a child before me.
>
> *Rosie*: And it was like ah.
>
> *Anthony*: Well, congratulations.
>
> *KF*: They were kind of tiptoeing round you.
>
> *Anthony*: Yes, yes, well, I mean, we'd probably do the same, you know, I mean, it's not exactly, you know, but everything is fine now, isn't it?
>
> *Rosie*: Yeah, it's not a problem. It's just, like I say it's treading on eggshells.

There was often a complex process of collusion to protect others. Family members negotiated the boundaries of information flow and fixed limits on the disclosure of information, often on the basis of an assessment of who could and could not 'cope' and concerns about how others would react. The boundaries appear to be constructed carefully to minimize an important dilemma they faced: disclosure inevitably leads to a loss of control of the information.

Patty and her two brothers collude to protect their mother from the knowledge that her grandson has been diagnosed with FRAXE. Patty describes how she has discussed this issue with her brothers and they have decided not to tell their mother about the condition because they do not believe she could cope with this knowledge.

> *Patty*: [Consultant] said that it might be a good idea, you know, to have members of my immediate family tested. But you see my mother is already a big worrier, you know, and she's 73 years old and I talked it over with both my brothers about whether or not my mother should be informed or she'd have to be tested and they said they didn't think she ought to be put through it, you see. Because she does tend to worry a lot, you know ...

Patty and her brothers also imagine what their mother's reaction to the news will be because she is prone to anxiety and worry. They believe that if they disclose information about the condition to her, she will react badly and worry even more. Patty remembers her own experience of finding out about the condition; she experienced strong feelings of guilt at the thought that she may have passed FRAXE on to her son and feels her mother will react in a similar way.

> *Patty*: She might have the same reaction as what I did when I found out that I was carrying this gene and that I had actually passed it on to [son] ... She might feel guilty, you know. She might think – I know what she's like you see. Her mind will start going over and over, you know.

In making the decision, Patty and her brothers also consider the potential practical implications that will be involved if their worst fears about their mother's reaction are realized. They believe that if their mother is informed of the genetic risk the burden of care will fall heavily on Patty's brother Philip, who lives nearest to her. They also agree that if circumstances were different they could tell their mother or would be less worried about her reaction. One brother suggests they could have informed their father, believing he would have dealt with the information appropriately and would have supported their mother, who, since his death, worries more than ever.

> *Patty*: My brother in [South of England] that lives the closest to her said that she'll never stop phoning him up, he'll never have any peace (laughs). Because she'll just sit and think about it. She'll think about perhaps the effects it's had on my children, you know, and if she was proved to be positive, you know, that she is a carrier you see and then she'll think to herself, 'Oh, I've passed that on to [me]' you know.

The decision made by Patty and her brothers also has repercussions for disclosure amongst the wider family and has led to the creation of a complex set of rules among the siblings about when, where and to whom they can discuss the condition and its effects. Because their mother lives near another branch of the family they decide they cannot risk informing them for fear that they will pass on the information to her. Patty believes they should be notified because they are at risk of transmitting the condition on to their children, however, she agrees to withhold the information.

> *Patty*: So nobody else, er, on my side of the family have been told because I spoke to my brother about it and he said, the trouble is, he said, if you go telling people down in [South of England] right, that live near my mum, it's likely that she's going to get to hear about it, you know. So, it's a bit of a problem really, you know. We've keeping it under wraps [...] So you see, my brother is very hesitant, you see, about letting anybody living close to my mother know, because as I say they might connect, you see. You know, they may not keep it to themselves. They may say, yes, we won't tell

her, but then it might slip out in a conversation or something like that, inadvertently, you know. I mean, I've nearly done it myself a couple of times. I've nearly said something to my brother when my mother has been around, you know.

Thus, the three siblings agree that it is more important to protect their mother and they resolve to withhold the knowledge. They dare not lose control of the information.

The Problem with Men

There was often a belief that men 'can't talk about things like that'. This was a common refrain and meant that communication and disclosure was left to (or appropriated by) women. Interestingly, women also used this belief to justify their failure to inform the men in their families about the conditions. Men were often described as feckless and irresponsible family members who, even if informed, would not act on the information appropriately.

> *Julia*: Everybody is aware but until they have to do it I don't think they will, you know … But no I don't think, I think men really they can't, they can't talk about things like that, you know, generally can they? (*laughs*).

Alan has been referred to the clinic for a degenerative eye condition, Best's disease. There is a strong family history and his wife (Dawn) is concerned that any children they have may be at risk. However, she does not expect other men within the family to be interested in identifying their risk of inheriting the condition.

> *Consultant*: And you've got cousins, Helen and Jenny, both diagnosed?
> *Alan*: Helen more than Jenny.
> *Consultant*: They were diagnosed together?
> *Alan*: My mother told them and they were diagnosed. Helen is worse. She needs things specially adapted.
> *Consultant*: And Jenny?
> *Alan*: I think she's got it but it's a lot milder.
> *Consultant*: How about their father?
> *Alan*: He's not affected (*they discuss that he hasn't had the test*).
> *Dawn*: He's the type of person to bury his head in the sand.

There were a range of reported motivations to disclose genetic risk information; rather than being driven by altruism, this process was often a way for individuals to clarify their own risk. Patty has singled out one member of her family as an early candidate for disclosure (of FRAXE) because if she is a carrier this would establish Patty's mother as the likely source of the condition. Additionally, because this woman is a nurse, she may be the most likely to respond appropriately by having the genetic test and passing on the information. However, Patty's brother judges that this cousin does not need to know; she appears unaffected and has no children who could be at risk.

> *Patty*: There is one cousin [...] she's a nurse; she's got something to do with the mentally handicapped. I think she goes around, you know, she travels about and so she's more medically aware and she might accept things a bit more, you know. But I haven't really been able to have a good chat to her. I did mention it once to my brother 'I wonder if [she] ought to be told' and he said 'Well, she hasn't got any children' he said. You know, he said she's not likely to have any now because she's about, probably in her forties, you know, and he said, and I think her husband didn't want children. So they never had children anyway but he said 'You won't really find out much from that because she hasn't had any children' and I said in that way it might be better mightn't it because if she is a carrier of the gene, there's more chance of this on my mother's side. Because you are trying to establish whether it would be from my mother's side or my father's side. But if she is a carrier of the gene then it is more likely to be on my mother's side, isn't it, you know.

There is a complex process of negotiation of who would benefit from knowing. For the brother, disclosure appears to have no benefits; however, for his sister, it may help to establish who is at risk and where the condition came from.

This motivation is sometimes the start of a process involving others in the search for answers, either explicitly by encouraging them to attend the clinic and be tested (if a test is available), or tacitly through surveillance and the wider process of looking at family members for signs of the condition. Individuals and family members often held deep-seated and powerful beliefs that someone within their kin would inevitably be affected by the condition. Although they did not want to disclose the risk, they nevertheless wanted their anxieties about others confirmed or laid to rest. Sometimes individuals tried to employ other tactics to assess their risk, as in this case below.

Nick attempts to persuade his clinicians to collaborate with him in a deception that will allow his children to be tested for Subarachnoid haemorrhages without their consent. In a manner similar to that expressed by Isobel earlier in this chapter, who is concerned about her son's risk (her husband and father-in-law died of cardiomyopathy), Nick is struggling to reconcile the issue of disclosure with the simultaneous desire to protect his children. He discusses this problem with the clinicians and suggests a way in which they could collude to protect his children whilst identifying their risk. He suggests that the clinicians conspire with him to tell his children 'a little white lie' that they are attending the clinic to be tested for a genetic kidney disease rather than a condition that may have led to the sudden death of their mother and two other close relatives. Following an extended consultation in which they discuss this issue at length, the clinician declines and urges Nick to talk to his children about his concerns.

> *Nick*: I think the way I would go down it at the moment is say that there may be a kidney – the thing is I'd have to have back-up from the medical side, you know what I mean, to sort of back me up so if I said 'Your mother might have had a genetic kidney infection and it's best,' that would lighten the load. They wouldn't be so worried about that if I'd said you know 'There could be a possibility of you inheriting or having a stroke like your mother.'
>
> *Consultant*: If you said that you'd come to see a specialist because your wife and her brother had both had strokes.
>
> *Nick*: That would set the clock going over that.
>
> *Consultant*: You're worried about that.
>
> *Nick*: You see, I'd have to say a white lie, you know, because they'd [clicks his fingers] hit on it then.
>
> *Consultant*: But how is talking about kidneys going to …
>
> *Nick*: Well, it would throw them off the track a little bit, if they were thinking oh kidneys, something could be done about that, you know, and if I'd, if I approached them and said 'Look, look your mother died of a brain haemorrhage it's possible that it might carry on down the line genetically,' you know, it would cause them total stress. [long silence] … Doctor I've racked my brains; this is on my mind all the time.

The absence of a female partner thrust this man into the realm of emotional and practical work. Whilst women were seen as performing and gatekeeping the boundaries of disclosure their notable absence did put reluctant men, as some described them, into the main frame.

Nick is sure that his children have failed to connect the sudden deaths of their mother, aunt and uncle. As he talks about this dilemma, he breaks down and cries. He describes the fear and anxiety he faces every day that his children may also die suddenly from the condition. Rather than disclose their possible risk, he watches and observes his children closely, monitoring their health and discouraging behaviour he thinks may exacerbate the onset of the condition such as having a poor diet and smoking.

> *Nick*: I don't think they put two and two together to be honest. I don't think they made any association. I don't think they know about the third one. If they knew about my wife's auntie … [crying] It's a difficult thing to live with thinking your children could go before you … I don't know whether it's just best to say nothing or … So I don't know, you know, which way to turn. I feel it's too serious to ignore and then the thing is it may be nothing. Hopefully it's nothing and then it would cause all this distress to them, and maybe I'd cause more problems by doing that, I don't know. It's such a difficult decision to make; it's Catch 22. I couldn't, I couldn't openly come

out and say about the brain haemorrhages. That would destroy them I think ... I have a terrible gut feeling like that they have, that it is genetic. I've just got that feeling in me.

Nick's failure to disclose the potential risk is linked with wider problems of communication within the family; he believes his children are unable to discuss their feelings about important emotional events that have occurred within the family such as the sudden death of their mother. His concern about his children is linked to his practical moral assessments of their ability to cope with painful events and episodes in their lives or manage such potentially devastating information about their potential risk. Individuals with such knowledge often reported expending considerable energy in hiding their fears from other family members and living in a state of high anxiety.

> *Consultant*: Well, I'm not persuaded that they are at very high risk.
>
> *Nick*: I've got this gut feeling, doctor. I've got to be honest, I've got this feeling within me and when I'm looking at them sometimes I think how much longer are you going to be, you know, especially my oldest ... but at the same time it's difficult to approach them with, isn't it, really, you know ... I could be setting them off and they'd start worrying about something and maybe there's nothing to worry about and then, you know, on the other hand may be there is something serious to worry about where something could be done about it.

The clinician has provided Nick with some reassurance that there may not be a link between these sudden deaths. However, the immediacy of the pattern within his family mean that he does not feel reassured and for him the premature loss of his children has become inevitable. Thus, he continues to watch and wait in silence.

Interestingly, men often played a key role in deciding who should or should not be informed within the kindred. Although disclosure was usually 'women's work', women often deferred to male relatives to decide who should be informed and men's decisions held sway even if the women disagreed. Patty's first thoughts about disclosure were to seek the advice of her brothers. Although she believed her mother and cousins had a right to be informed about the condition affecting her son, her brother's belief that they must not be told prevailed.

> *Patty*: Yes, my brother doesn't think that members of my mother's family down there should be told because it might get back to her you see and then she'll say to us, 'Well why didn't you tell me? Why did I hear it from somewhere else. Why didn't you tell me?' and then, you know, so as I say, she builds up things in her mind. She was speaking to me the other day on the phone and she's a terrible worrier, you know ... because I know the way that my mother worries I thought I'd better speak to both my brothers first and see how they feel about mum being told and they we're both in complete agreement

with each other, you know. In a way, I thought she should be told, because I thought she had a right to know, but on the other hand I could see their point of view. She will worry, she will worry about it and she might go on about it all day.

Thus, we can see the complex rationalizations these individuals and families made to inform disclosure. A range of techniques was employed to inform this process, surveillance to establish who was believed to be at risk and assessment of the character of kin to identify who could best handle the information. In addition, there was often a belief that 'the men can't talk about these things'. However, men often appeared to play a key role in fixing the boundaries of risk information.

Practical Ethics: Protecting Others

The assessment of character is but one aspect of everyday ethical work. The work of relating to family members often elicited practical moral work on the part of our informants. The powerful bonds of love and the desire to protect others lay at the heart of their engagement with the condition and those who were believed to be at risk. These individuals often found it hard to reconcile family members' right to know with their duty to protect them from knowledge of the condition. Based on their own experience and by observing others' reactions, many thought that it was often better not to know about a condition in advance or to have their actual risk assessed. They were aware that knowing the risk of developing the condition often failed to provide any additional benefits (for most of these conditions no treatments or preventative measures are available), and introduced a number of negative impacts on people's lives.

Carla and Claudia both have polycystic kidney disease and have made similar decisions about when to tell their daughters about their risk of inheriting this condition. Their approach is informed by their own and others' reactions. Based on this experience, they do not believe their daughters will benefit from knowing their risk in advance. Carla decides to inform her daughter when the time is right (she is only 4 years old) and Claudia informed her daughters when they were teenagers. They have both decided, however, not to encourage their children to be tested and to inform them in a 'bland' way, taking care not to alarm them.

Carla describes how she has seen the effects of predictive testing on her family and believes testing has caused them to give up hope and to focus their lives around their disease, its onset and their deterioration. She is disparaging, believing that they have become over-concerned about their health and make the condition a central feature of their identity. She does not want this future for her daughter.

> *Carla*: Yeah, because her father didn't want to come because he's panicking at the house. He didn't want to be here because he doesn't want bad, do you know what I

mean. He doesn't want to know either so brilliant. Because a lot of our family have had their children checked, most of them ... But you see them sitting on it and they're dwindling on it ... Well that's what I said to you [mother] isn't it, that I don't want to be sitting in the house and then constantly 'Oh I've given this kidney disease, to her, oh this, oh and that's the way I see the family. Most of them thrive on it. Do you know what I mean?

Claudia has attended the PKD disease support group and, based on her experience and observations of how others have coped with predictive risk information, she believes it is preferable for individuals not to know their risk of developing the condition in the future. She was the first to be affected in her family and received her diagnosis in her forties when she first displayed symptoms. Thus, although she has informed her daughters, she hopes she has done this in a way that will minimize their anxiety and fear.

Claudia: I was beginning to meet people with polycystic kidney disease and the people that hadn't known they were getting it were ... seemed to be a lot happier than the ones that did, if you follow me. I didn't know I was going to get it because there was no history of it so it did come out of the blue and it was a bit of a shock but until then, until I was 40 ... my life was fine, er, and I didn't have that sort of coming, weighing above me, waiting for it to happen ... So it worked for me and it certainly worked for the other people I have met that didn't know. So I haven't encouraged my children but neither have I discouraged them. I've sort of tried to be as bland as possible about it (laughs).

Discussions about who can and cannot cope with risk information often take place within the context of traumatic events within the family such as sudden deaths and bereavements. As we have already seen, two parents, Nick (who is concerned that his children will inherit the subarachnoid haemorrhage that killed his wife and two other family members) and Isobel (who is concerned that her young son will inherit the cardiomyopathy that led to the deaths of her husband and father-in-law), struggle with the dilemma of whether to tell their children that they may be at risk of inheriting a condition that led to the sudden death of one of their parents. Although their clinician encourages them to tell their children, they are held back by the expected enormity of how this will affect their children and how they are likely to react. Both parents acknowledge that it is hard to talk to their children about the condition because they themselves are still struggling to accept the deaths of their partners and the possibility that their children may experience a similar fate. They both fear the worst.

Isobel acknowledges the importance of honesty in her relationship with her son; however, for her the most important part of her duty as his mother is to protect him. Knowledge of the condition and the decision about whether to disclose are a constant burden; she knows the information will have a powerful impact on his life.

> *Isobel*: But I need to know for my own sake as a mother that I'm doing everything I can because it might be, whatever it is, if it's not treatable now it might be treatable in the future if we can find out what it was, you know, and then I can say to [son] – I can be honest with [son]. I can't be honest with [son] as things are now … as he gets older he's going to come up with his own thoughts on what's happened and he's going to put two and two together. He's not a dumb child. He's quite bright and he's going to put two and two together and come up with the same as me. I'm sure he will … he's going to ask questions. He's going to ask questions and, I mean, it would be nice if I could be honest with him but at the end of the day I've got to protect him and I've got to assess the situation as it arises. I've got to do everything I can to protect him and I've got to assess it so, I mean, I don't want him to be driven mad really by it all.

Similarly, Nick worries about the impact of the information he has and tries to devise ways in which he can minimize its effects on his children. He does believe he has a close relationship with his children; however, in this instance he is held back by the potentially life-changing and devastating effects the information may have on their lives. He considers complex ways of avoiding disclosure while also easing his own anxiety by trying to discover his children's actual risk.

Appropriate Behaviour

Issues of blame and responsibility were at the forefront of discussions within families about what action to take in light of information provided by diagnoses and known patterns of transmission. Those who were already parents by the time they had received their diagnosis tended to say that they were not to blame because they had not received a diagnosis or their risk of transmitting the condition until after they had their children. However, although they often stated that they could not be blamed for transmitting the condition onto the next generation, many also spoke of their feelings of guilt and described complex rationalizations that included responsibility, fate, chance and luck.

However, this group often switched their focus to the behaviour of the next generation, urging them to act on the information in an 'appropriate' way. There was often a belief that those who knew about the condition had a responsibility to 'get rid of it' and 'wipe it out' (Rosie and Anthony). Parents often had strong beliefs about how their children should react and modify their behaviour, often advising them not to risk having an affected child.

For example, Patty has advised her daughter Theresa not to have children. Although she experienced feelings of guilt when she found out that she was a carrier and had passed FRAXE on to her children, she does not believe that she is in any way responsible. However, she believes Theresa is in a position to make an informed choice and urges her to make the right decision. Theresa is 20 years old and they have talked about this issue in some depth. Aware of her daughter's desire to have children in the future, Patty is nevertheless adamant that her daughter should not have children and should not risk transmitting the condition, arguing that Theresa would not be able to justify her actions to future children if they were affected. Patty has pointed out the moral and practical problems she feels her daughter will face if she decides to take the risk and have children. Her view is based in part on her own experience of caring for three children with learning disabilities; as she says, 'it's not an easy life'.

Patty also feels strongly that her daughter has an important duty to act on the new information and prevent the condition from affecting future generations of the family. The condition or the 'faulty gene' responsible must be eradicated from the kindred.

Similarly, even though she did plan to have more children, Julia has decided against this because there is a risk that they may be affected by FRAXE. Her decision is made in the context of her guilt that she may have passed the condition on to her son and concerns about how she could justify her actions if another child was similarly affected.

Julia additionally sees her position in a fatalistic light; she believes she was meant to have only one child. Similarly, within the setting of the clinical consultation, others such as Alan spoke fatalistically about their risk of transmitting a condition to any future child. Alan and Dawn decide to throw their 'hat in the ring' and take the risk.

> *Alan*: If we have children will they be affected, about passing it on? Whether I'm affected, its just the way its going to be, but I wouldn't want to pass it on.
>
> *Consultant*: Its dominant, if you have the changed gene you have a 50 per cent chance of passing it on. In your family its interesting. (*looks at pedigree.*) It tends to be more like [cousin] earlier and more severe.
>
> *Alan*: I've been told that the males aren't carriers, only females.
>
> *Consultant*: No, but you could understand it given your family, but for your cousin to have inherited it, your uncle must be affected … any other concerns about children?
>
> *Alan*: Just that they'll pick it up from me.
>
> *Consultant*: How would you feel if there was a 50 per cent chance? How would you react?
>
> (*no immediate reply*)
>
> *Alan*: Probably throw my hat in the ring and have a go.

Parents often made assumptions about what action their children would take in response to risk information, often assuming they would 'do the right thing'. Even though she has not explicitly discussed this with her, Claudia believes her daughter will assess her risk (of polycystic kidney disease) before having children.

> *Claudia*: I suspect [daughter] will want to know, you know, if she has got this illness before she goes ahead with having children.
> *Consultant*: Yes.
> *Claudia*: I have a feeling but we haven't really discussed that.
> *Consultant*: Yes, I mean she's obviously thought about these things in depth and understands them and it's very likely she would raise it isn't it?
> *Claudia*: Yes, I think so. She is a very, you know, thoughtful girl.

Sometimes couples had received clear instructions from their clinicians about what behaviour was considered to be appropriate in the light of their diagnosis. Matt recounts his experience of being diagnosed with muscular dystrophy thirty years ago. When the consultant provided the diagnosis he indicated that an appropriate response would be to choose not to get married or have children. However, Matt got married and had a daughter. He and his wife decided to take the risk of having an affected child based on the natural history of the disease, which is a late onset condition. Their decision was reinforced by their hopes that a treatment or cure would be available by the time their child reached the likely age of onset.

> *Matt*: Right, we went to see a specialist called [consultant] and he was the most rude, abrupt man I've ever met, you know. And what he said to us 'Right don't get married, don't have children,' boom, boom, end of story and we were out, you know. But he had a reputation for being very arrogant, you know, very, you know, very unpleasant man but of course we didn't listen to it. Well, you know, I mean, you know, obviously we realized that there could be problems, you know, but we decided to go ahead anyway and have a child and [daughter] was a result sort of thing. But we knew, even if any of the offspring had muscular dystrophy that it wouldn't affect them any earlier than it affected me, you know. I mean I was sort of in early twenties before I realized that I had MD and it didn't affect me in any way at all and of course any other people born in the family it would affect them at the same time. So you see so it gives, even if they're born with muscular dystrophy it would be twenty odd years before it would affect them in any way, you know, so it's not […] we just talked one day and we just, you know, we talked about having another child sort of thing and then we just decided to go for it really, you know, knowing that as I say anybody, any children we had wouldn't be affected for many years and, you know, and we thought by that time we thought well there's bound to be a cure, you know. And eventually as I say there will be but, you know, that was our, our way of thinking at the time, you know, so it didn't bother us too much.

In contrast, Matt describes his brother's decision-making. Although Matt describes his brother's decision not to have children as a responsible act, he is also rather scathing about his brother's life, which he describes as quite lonely. His brother lives in a bungalow and has had a string of failed relationships with various carers. Matt believes these relationships have failed because of the decision not to have children and that it is now too late for his brother to have a family because his disease has progressed too far. Thus, those family members who make what appear to be the 'right' decisions are not envied by others and are sometimes pitied.

> *Matt*: Well, my brother ... he moved to a bungalow where he lives on his own now, a purpose built bungalow, you know, a lovely place and he has carers now and he's had several relationships with carers, you know, since then but, you know, one of them wanted to have a child, you know, but he said no. He said it's not worth the risk. He didn't want anybody to go through what he'd been through. So and his last relationship has just sort of fizzled out at the moment, but I can't see him getting, having kids anyway, you know, because of the way he looks. I think it's very responsible on his part.

Many focussed their attention and concern on who might be affected in the future within the next generation. However, this anxiety was often modified by the hope that medical advances would have been made before the next generation developed symptoms and a treatment or a cure for the condition would be found.

Rosie and Anthony look at future generations and 'hope' and that the translocation will not affect them. They acknowledge that this process of surveillance will continue for many years; however, they do believe that in ten years medical advances and new technological developments will become available to cure or treat the condition.

> *Rosie*: I hope that it doesn't take off in another, through the other nieces and nephews.
> *Anthony*: Well, this is it but at least, I mean, with this technology with us now may be when they, I mean ten years down the line when they're going to go for it, it might be more advanced again, you know.

A number of individuals also suggested time frames in which medical advances should occur; these were usually associated with the age of onset of the conditions or future events such as members of the next generation starting to have families of their own. Isobel, for instance, is concerned that her young son faces the early death that affected his father and grandfather. Her son is only 2 years old and she considers the time when she will need to tell him about his risk. She hopes that by then a treatment or cure will be available and, in addition, she believes she does not have to start worrying about the onset of the condition until he reaches his early twenties, the apparent familial age of onset.

Similarly, Matt recalls being diagnosed with muscular dystrophy. At the time, the consultant suggested that a cure or an effective treatment would be found and although that has not happened Matt is grateful that a positive future was provided in the context of his diagnosis.

> *Matt*: Yeah, so thirty years I've been diagnosed. Yes, so they [family] came down to see me at the hospital. I said, 'I've got some bad news.' I said 'I've got muscular dystrophy,' and of course we'd heard of it but it didn't mean anything to us, you know. Oh yeah, oh alright then, oh you know. 'Oh I've got to come out of the army.' 'Fair enough,' you know, 'how's it going to affect you in the future?' I said 'Well I might end up in a wheelchair.' But at the time a doctor said to me, he said 'It's not a problem.' He said 'there will be a cure within ten years,' and that was thirty-one years ago. Obviously there wasn't but I'm very glad he told me that because it was a positive, rather than a negative, if you see what I mean, and then it gave me, by the time that ten years came along I knew a lot more about it then and I knew that, you know, ten years on realistic sort of thing it was going to take a lot longer [...] we didn't find it difficult to talk about then because it wasn't a problem as such, you know, it was easy to talk about sort of thing because that was in the future and of course the future is now, you know. You're in the future.

Looking back, Matt believes that the doctor's suggestion of a cure was a useful device that helped him to accept his diagnosis. However, things have changed and he is now severely disabled by this condition.

We can see how these processes of disclosure of genetic risk information are embedded in the everyday realities of practical kinship. All of these individuals expressed extremely high levels of anxiety in recounting the moral, ethical and practical dilemmas they faced in disclosing such information. As part of these processes of decision-making, they all employed a range of techniques of assessment and a practical analysis to assess who was at risk and, in addition, the psychological character of their kin was scrutinized to identify who could best handle the information. These practices allowed both individuals and family groups to define, limit and draw boundaries around the family. This was part of a wider control of the flow of risk information, not only in terms of who is informed, but also in terms of managing the ways in which other family members respond; knowledge provided individuals with additional moral and ethical power to dictate appropriate responses.

In the following chapter we go on to describe in depth how one extended kindred manage their everyday beliefs about inheritance, their processes of surveillance and their practical and ethical approaches to disclosure.

–6–

Family Narratives

Introduction

To explore contemporary ethics and the dynamics of genetic disclosure we describe the biographical narratives of ten members of one kindred affected by an inherited degenerative condition. This kindred was described by the clinical genetics team as an 'open family' who were 'quite happy to come to the clinic together' and was presented to the research team as a kindred from their clinical caseload that could be enrolled as a 'good example' of effective communication and disclosure of genetic information. From the perspective of the clinical team, the effective transmission of genetic information from the proband through to the wider kindred had been accomplished.

However, as we have previously stated, we need to problematize such accounts of kindred as 'open'. Family and kinship work are accomplished through self-presentation and narrative accounts, which are occasioned performances for different audiences. For example, the performance of 'family' and 'family communication' for the clinical team will differ from the performance given to other family members, the researchers and so on. Using this kindred as a case study, we examine their narrative accounts to reinforce and illuminate the communication and disclosure of genetic risk information.

The Condition – a Mitochondrial Disorder

This family is affected by a degenerative disorder that follows mitochondrial inheritance. Mitochondria are minute organelles within each cell in the body which carry out many essential metabolic reactions, especially those involved in the supply of energy to the cell. These organelles carry their own DNA in a tiny circular chromosome, and there will be many mitochondria (and mitochondrial DNA molecules) in each cell – especially in tissues that have high energy requirements such as the brain, heart, muscle and brown fat. The mitochondria are often described as the 'battery pack' within the muscle and they convert oxygen transferred from the red blood cells into energy. When the mitochondria fail to function normally, their host cells become unable to carry out their functions sufficiently well; this results in organ malfunction or damage, sometimes even in the death of cells.

Within this particular kindred, the mitochondrial malfunction is caused by an alteration in the sequence of the mitochondrial genome, a single, small DNA molecule, in a proportion of the mitochondria. Just how severely an individual with the mutation will be affected depends upon the proportion of mitochondria with the mutation, and this proportion can vary both between tissues and over time, the abnormal mitochondria often accumulating in muscle tissue with age. Thus family members can have quite different experiences of the same disease process.

Early symptoms for the women within this family have included fatigue and musclar aches and pains. As a result of these symptoms some of the women have had difficulty working and been labelled 'lazy'. Even though receiving a diagnosis has not led to an effective treatment for these family members, having a biomedical explanation for their illness has been beneficial, providing them with 'a psychological boost' (Consultant) and enabling them to refute accusations (primarily from employers, clinicians and social services) that they are 'idle malingerers'. Because this condition is so rare, it is of interest to both clinical and scientific research teams and this has led to the family's participation in research that may contribute to the development of an effective therapy in the future.

In addition to fatigue and muscle aches, there are a range of different problems that can result from this mitochondrial DNA mutation. The most prominent additional problem within this family has been the growth of brown fat lipomas around the neck, across the shoulders and between the shoulder blades. Brown fat is very different from the more familiar white fat tissue, which can also give rise to fatty lumps called lipomas, and it is a particularly active tissue. One important function it has is to consume energy to maintain the core body temperature. Some brown fat lipomas can become extremely large and unsightly, needing removal for that reason alone, but they can also threaten to compress the trachea and constrict breathing – which is of course a serious potential hazard.

The condition affects both males and females but is transmitted only through females, because sperm contribute virtually no mitochondria to the next generation – all the mitochondria come in the cytoplasm of the oocyte, the egg cell. This results in the maternal, cytoplasmic or matrilineal pattern of inheritance, with all the children of affected women going on to develop the condition (at least carrying the abnormal mitochondria) but none of the children of affected men.

Genetic testing is available for this condition; however, mothers will inevitably pass on to their children at least some of the abnormal mitochondria. What we do not know is just how many (what proportion) of the mitochondria in each egg cell will be affected by the mutation in the mitochondrial DNA – and even if we did know, we could not predict the effects this would have on the child because we could not predict how the different copies of the mitochondria would be distributed in the developing embryo and fetus. Essentially, we know before testing that all offspring of an affected woman will carry the mutation, but it is not possible to predict with any confidence which members of the kindred will be clinically affected or to what degree. Any test carried out on someone with this type of condition will only confirm the diagnosis; it will not reveal the severity of the condition, the way it will affect the individual or the likely age of onset. Thus, a large number of this extended kindred will have inherited the condition from their mothers, although to what extent they will be affected, or the age at which the condition might begin to manifest, could not be predicted. There is no proven effective treatment available for this condition.

The Kindred

This family group all live within a 10-mile radius of each other in a cluster of small villages in north Wales. The proband, Veronica (45 years old), and her three sisters, Lindsey (47 years old), Maggie (52 years old) and Suzanne (57 years old), were all interviewed. They have attended the clinical genetics service and been diagnosed with the condition and are at different stages of disease progression. Their mother and their eldest sister have died of the condition (although they did not receive a clinical diagnosis). They also have two brothers who live in England. They see them only a few times a year at family occasions such as weddings and funerals and because they are 'very private people', these sisters did not want them to participate in the study. Although the brothers too will have inherited the condition, only one has children and his two teenage daughters are not at risk. Only one member of the subsequent generations, Lindsey's daughter, Sally, attended the clinic during the project and received a diagnosis.

Veronica has two daughters, Jenny (24) and Angie (28), Maggie has one daughter, Susan (23), Lindsey has one daughter, Sally (26), and all were interviewed. Suzanne has three daughters whom we were unable to interview. Additionally, the sisters' niece Carrie (23), whose mother died of the condition, was also interviewed. All but one (Angie) of the women within this subsequent generation have young families. There are also four sons within this kindred: Maggie's son, Ian, Lindsey's son, James, Veronica's son, Mark and Carrie's brother, Ben, who are all in their twenties. They too will have inherited the condition from their mothers; however, we were unable to approach them to ask for their participation. Thus Doug, Lindsey's partner, who is not at risk, was the only male member of the kindred we were able to interview.

Veronica (the proband or index case) is divorced and lives in a small terraced house with her son Mark, daughter Jenny and 4-year-old granddaughter. She has had to give up work because of the severity of her condition. Her elder daughter (Angie) and two of her sisters live in the next village. Both her daughters work in the same local supermarket. Within the family, she is closest to her sister Lindsey, who lives in a small town nearby; they see each other almost every day.

Lindsey and Doug live on a very bleak council estate where many of the houses are boarded up. Inside, the house is well decorated in a very traditional style and feels very cosy. Lindsey is obviously very house-proud. She works part-time at the local hospital, although she is unsure how long she will be able to continue working and her partner has taken early retirement. Her son and daughter (Sally) live on a nearby council estate in the same small town with their young families. Sally lives with her partner Richard and their 1-year-old son. Lindsey visits Sally every day.

Maggie appears to be the matriarch of the family. She is the most severely affected by the condition, is unable to work and needs help around the house. She lives in a semi-detached house with her husband and her son has just bought a house in the same village with his fiancée. Maggie's daughter, Susan, works at the local pub and is a single mother with three young children; she lives a short car drive away and visits her mother to help her around the house every day. Maggie is also in regular, if not daily, contact with Veronica and Lindsey.

Suzanne, the eldest surviving sister, is recently widowed and lives approximately ten minutes away from her sister Veronica. She appears to be very close to her three daughters who all live close by; two of which have young children and visit her regularly. She does not see as much of her sisters and the wider family.

Carrie is separated from the father of her two young sons (3 and 5 years old) and lives with her new partner in a terraced house in a small village about 10 miles away from the rest of the family. Her brother, Ben, lives nearby with his young family and she sees them regularly. Carrie does not have much contact with most of her aunts and cousins, but remains close to Maggie, who was present during the birth of her eldest son. Her mother died 5 years before we met her and since then she has had little contact with her mother's family or with her father, who she believes treated her mother badly during her illness.

Beliefs about Inheritance: Substance and Routes

The kindred present a number of lay theories that explain where the condition may have 'come from' and how it has been transmitted through the family. They variously describe both the 'substance' in which the condition is believed to reside and various 'routes' that are attributed to transmission. However, we are not suggesting that they have a literal belief in such routes and substances; rather these are well-established idioms used to express the principles of inheritance, particularly in relation to this condition.

Substance

A number of the kindred describe blood as the substance in which the condition and other traits reside. For example, described in Chapter 3, it was hoped that Veronica would be free of the condition after she had a blood transfusion and received the blood of a police officer. The next generation of women similarly refer to blood as the substance transmitting the condition. Veronica's daughter, Jenny, recalls how the family often referred to 'bad blood' during discussions about the condition and in their descriptions of the mechanism by which it has been passed on through the family 'line'. Lindsey agrees that it is in the blood that the condition resides. However, these women are not fatalistic about the onset of the condition; there is only a risk, not an inevitability, that the condition will be expressed and will develop within individual members of their kin.

> *Jenny*: They'd say 'Oh, bad family blood line.'
> *Lindsey*: Yeah, it was basically sort of a case of 'Well, you've got it in your blood but it's just whether it actually comes out or not.'

This is part of the process of looking for patterns to make sense of where the condition has 'come from' in the family. Suzanne recalls seeing similar symptoms in her parents and grandparents and traces the transmission of the condition with the blood: it is a 'blood-y thing':

> *Suzanne*: Like they wouldn't have remembered the auntie but I remember her. My mother always used to say it's the bad blood on both her parents' side. She always said that. Because my grandfather used to have these lumps on his head and all like these cysts, you know, and they cut them off but they said 'no' they weren't cysts' the ones the girls had, hormones or some blood-y thing.

This account of 'bad blood' is not just the focus of the family lore relating to the specific condition, but is also associated with the transmission of a number of other traits that have been observed in the kin over a number of generations. Many spoke of depression, low self-esteem and lethargy as character traits within the family and associated these with the inheritance of the condition. For example, Carrie links the high rate of depression and Prozac use within the kin with the condition. Similarly, her aunt Veronica believes depression is common within the women in the family and wonders if this is associated with the condition.

> *Carrie*: I don't know if my auntie mentioned but most of us are on Prozac at the moment as well.

> *Veronica*: Like we all seem to suffer with depression and low self-esteem and did this illness affect the nerves because it is the nervous system isn't it? […] Suzanne is

really lethargic and depressed and I mean she's got a beautiful house, plenty of money and don't want to know, she just sits there, comes back, takes the kids to school, comes back and just sits there crying. And I wonder well is it, is it there all the way through the genes like?

Routes of the Condition

For many of these family members, an important part of the process of making sense of the condition is to identify its origins, where the condition started in the family. Beliefs about the original condition are passed between family members and become part of family lore: the story of how and why the condition manifested itself within this kindred – why it happened to them. For example, Suzanne, in reflecting on where the condition has come from evokes a frightening gothic image of her grandmother's sister, '*always in black*' who was physically who was 'all screwed up' and 'twisted'.

> *Suzanne*: When I think back and I remember an aunt I was telling them, it was my grandmother's sister. Oh, and she couldn't speak and she was all screwed up and I really remember her and she was always in black. I used to be frightened to death of her and her speech an' all.

Suzanne goes on to describe how she believes the condition originated from an aunt from her mother's family and has been transmitted through the following generations of women. She suggests that this pattern of inheritance will continue through to successive generations of women in the family.

> *Suzanne*: I remember this auntie vividly and I often think, I wonder if it really stemmed from there because that was my mother's mother's sister, so it was obviously in the line all the way down.

Although the search for the origin of the condition is an important part of the process of understanding why the family has been affected, it also has implications for surveillance and risk assessment. It provides the family with tools to identify who is affected, and to see the future trajectory of the degenerative condition within the kindred. Family stories and memories of the previous generations mean these family members believe that they know the progression of the condition and what happens to those affected in the later stages of the disease. Suzanne, Lindsey and Veronica discuss their sister Maggie. Although they have all been diagnosed with the condition, Maggie appears to be the most severely affected. Suzanne, Lindsey and Veronica observe Maggie's symptoms and see the similarities with their aunt and mother's condition. However, they see not only Maggie's future, but also potentially their own.

Suzanne: In fact some days I look at Maggie and I think 'Oh my God you're like auntie', you know, but you wouldn't dare say it because they wouldn't have known her. I mean, she died when I was quite, well 10 or 11. I vaguely remember her then, you know, because I remember this lady in black and, oh. she was so twisted ...

Lindsey: Veronica said 'Oh, she's so upset.' I said 'Why?' because I thought she'd just had another lump in her neck she'd had out and she said 'No, she's like Mammy now.' She said 'It's right across her back I think and she's really depressed.' I said 'No, I haven't seen that.'

All the kin believe the condition is transmitted through the female 'side' of the family. For example, Maggie believes the pattern of inheritance within the family has originated from her mother's 'side'. This corresponds to the biomedical model of the matrilineal inheritance of the condition.

Maggie: Er, none of them have shown any. My mother's brother's children, they seem to be all right. It seems to be the women in the family, my mother's, my mother's side, seem to be at younger ages getting this.

There is also the suggestion in Maggie's comment above that both the risk of inheritance and the severity of the condition appear to be increasing in the younger generation. Within this kindred, there was a common belief (or hope) that the condition could 'skip' a generation. This mode of inheritance appears to be similar to the biomedical model of 'penetrance'. In general, penetrance refers to the extent to which individuals who must possess the abnormal gene show no manifestations, but may still transmit the condition to their children.

Jenny: Perhaps skipping them. It's like they haven't really said that it's ... they haven't actually said 'It's connected with your mother.' They'd just say 'Oh, it could be connected with your mother.'

Susan: I don't want to end up like this. But I will, won't I? Waiting for it to happen. That's why I don't want to know. So I'll have the blood test but I don't want to know.

Maggie: But perhaps it could skip generations. It could miss a few generations.

Susan: Well, I'll have the test done but ...

Maggie: Right-o then.

Gender differences in the pattern of inheritance were also noted. Only women in the family appeared to be affected and, thus, the women were believed to be more at risk. As Jenny notes, 'It's more in the woman.' So far, the men in the family and their children did not appear to be affected. Maggie similarly reflects that only the women in the family appear to be affected, and concludes that this means the condition does not affect the men.

Jenny: They've told her that it's more in the woman and like she can't pass it, she could pass it onto Mark – that's my mother's son – but he couldn't pass it onto his children.

Because they've got one brother and there's nothing wrong with him.
Maggie: But er, like [the consultant] said it doesn't, doesn't come out in the male.

This perspective can be contrasted with the biomedical model of inheritance that distinguishes the mode of inheritance – in this case 'matrilineal inheritance' – from those who can be affected – both male and female members of the family.

Even though a number of these women were aware that the condition could be 'passed on' to the men in the family, they were often unclear about what this actually meant within their family. For example, as Sally says, although she is aware that her brother cannot transmit the condition to his children, she is not sure whether he will be affected by the condition.

Sally: I did when [the consultant] said first of all, but then when he said that he can't pass it onto his kids I felt a bit better but then I thought: do the men, do the men get those lumpy things [lipomas]?

Surveillance

This kindred perform accounts of family as a site of mutual surveillance in which members are continually inspected, compared and scrutinized for signs that they have inherited, or are developing, symptoms associated with the condition. Their accounts are suffused with explicit descriptions of surveillance, through the close inspection of other family members. Acts of surveillance make up the social reality of the family; their 'lifeworld' of living with the condition is tacit and hidden. Their knowledge of this familial disease and the ever-present threat of its development and its effects represent how the family is defined and constituted.

There appears to be a continual comparison within and across the generations for signs that indicate a family member's risk of developing the condition or the disease stage they have reached. Both the comments individuals make about their health and their own observation of their behaviour and health status (emotional and physical) are used to make these assessments.

Self-surveillance

There appears to be an ongoing comparison of the self with both previous and future generations. Maggie recalls observing her mother's manifestation and development of the condition, and compares them with her own experience. She is acutely aware that she is following her mother's disease trajectory in many ways.

Maggie: But a lot of the things my mother used to say, 'Oh, I can't go out today. If you put me in the wheelchair we'll just go to the shops.' And she'd 'Oh, stop now because everything is spinning', and that's exactly how I feel and I think to myself now I know how she felt ... There we are.

The next generation of women also assess and survey themselves and their health. These daughters look to the previous generation of women, their mothers, and see their future. This leads them to scrutinize themselves continually for signs of the condition. For example, these two sisters, Maggie's nieces, both worry that they too may be displaying early signs of the condition.

> *Jenny*: If I've been bad with my legs and I get tired I do think that I could have the same as them. Like my sister did say 'Oh, if I've got it I don't want to know.'

> *Angie*: Oh. he just laughs at me and says, he says, because we we're on about it the other day and we just try and laugh and joke about it, you know, if we're having a laugh or whatever. And I said 'I'm sure I've got it', because I'd been to the gym and I was really tired and that and my boyfriend he just said 'Oh, for God's sake you haven't. You're just saying that now, you don't know.' But I do think that I, not that I'm paranoid or anything like that but I, I tire quite easy as well, but it's not some, it's not a real problem for me at the moment.

Surveillance of Others

There is also the continual surveillance of other family members; mothers look to the next generation of women, and particularly their daughters, for signs they associate with onset. In the same way, the younger generation look to their mothers and aunts for indications of the various stages of the disease from onset through to the later stages of this degenerative condition. Surveillance also takes place within the generations. Sisters and cousins observe each other, looking for early signs in those thought to be at risk and assessing the progression of the disease in individuals already affected.

All four sisters scrutinize their daughters and nieces and worry that they will develop the condition. For example, Suzanne is apprehensive that the 'bout of nerves' her daughter experienced following her father's death could be an early warning sign of the onset of the condition.

> *Suzanne*: Well, I don't know. As I say, I've been concerned about the youngest one [daughter] and we've had this bout with her nerves, whether it's, I hope it's not going to, you know, carry on. But they seem to think it's because she's just kept fighting all along when her father died and then when everything stopped like, all the different things after and then that stopped and she just boompf, you know. I hope it is only that and not any of this.

Lindsey similarly experiences worry and anxiety that leads her to constantly check her daughter's health.

Lindsey: Thank God. But Sally is the one in my life. I worry about her. Yeah, she's my biggest worry. I usually phone her about six times a day to talk to her, to make sure she sounds alright and that, because if she's not well I can tell by her voice and I go 'Right and I'd better go up and see her', but she's my biggest worry she is.

Thus, a series of pasts and futures within this kindred are continually scrutinized and assessed in the present.

Seeing 'it'

Such family work is also part of the process of identifying signs or symptoms that family members can associate with inheritance in order to project the condition's future trajectory within the kin. Maggie and her daughter, Susan, exemplify this work in their comments below. The following extract demonstrates the way in which subtle physical or behavioural traits are used to indicate the presence of the condition within family members.

Susan: I don't think I've got anything wrong with me.
Maggie: Well, that's nice, that's nice to know you've got that attitude.
Susan: I don't think I have, to be honest with you.
Maggie: Not even with the depression as young as you are?
Susan: Yeah, but that could be ... it could be, yeah. But when I went to my counsellor the first time, she said, didn't she? Because my uncle had died and my auntie?

Throughout her account, Maggie describes her surveillance of her kindred and believes she can 'see' the onset of the condition in the next generation of women in the family, most particularly in her daughter and her brother's daughters. She comments on the depression Susan experiences, associating this with the early onset of the condition. Although Susan denies she is developing the condition, her mother prompts her to reconsider; she believes her depression is an early sign.

Through the retelling and passing-on of family stories, information about the condition is transferred though the family. The kin communicate subtle (and not so subtle) information about the condition to each other through mutual surveillance and their additional commentaries and assessments on the similarities or differences between their various signs and symptoms. They also voice their worries and concerns about who is, or is not, at risk, and who should be encouraged to attend the clinic; they focus their concerns onto those who they believe must be 'worried about'.

In a later interview, Susan describes how she deals with this scrutiny. Although her mother and aunts continually suggest that her lethargy and depression are 'symptoms' of the condition, she believes they are due to events in her past, particularly the deaths of relatives and a close friend. She consciously tries not to think about the condition or look for signs associated with its onset. However, the scrutiny does mean that there are times when she does link her depression with the condition and her account is overshadowed by feelings of anxiety and of having 'bad days'.

> *Susan*: They reckon like the sleeping. I can fall asleep easy. They reckon that's a symptom and because I'm on Prozac antidepressant. But it's nothing to do with all that, you know, it's the past and that, isn't it?
>
> *KF*: Mm and they ...
>
> *Susan*: They're going 'Oh, it's this. It could be to do with this', and 'See we used to have that', and I'm thinking 'Oh'. You know, at the end of the day I don't want to know. I would like to know if I've got it but I don't want to sort of like dwell on everything. You know, you have like a bad day. 'Oh, it's the illness,.' Do you know what I mean? I'd end up making myself worse.

Family members already affected presented information about their signs and symptoms. In turn, the undiagnosed presented their signs to be inspected, assessed and adjudicated on by other family members.

> *Veronica*: Like we all seem to suffer with depression and low self-esteem and did this illness affect the nerves because it is the nervous system, isn't it?
>
> *Maggie*: Oh God, aye, mm. Like I have to psyche myself up to go anywhere. Like last night I was thinking 'Oh right, I know I've got to go up to [the hospital].' And I think my sister's daughter now, Molly and Sally they're very, they are very lethargic but Suzanne is very, er, depressed. Everything is – well, there you are. It's the same bloody thing, isn't it? You just haven't got the oil
>
> *Veronica*: One of them will come and say 'Oh, I feel knackered today', and I think 'Oh well, it's your age.' But then when you take stock and watch them, how they move about and some of the little things they do, I think 'Oh, there's something there like.'

A family member acknowledging that they of experience depression, exhaustion or fatigue reveals to other kin they are likely to develop or are displaying the first signs of the onset of the condition. Both Veronica and Maggie describe the signs of depression and lethargy as the main clues they use both to identify the origins of the condition and to determine who is likely to be affected in the future. Using these indicators, they believe they can 'see' the onset of the condition in the next generation of women in the family: their daughters and nieces.

Seeing Your Future

Members of the family look to previous and current generations for signs of the future trajectory of the disease; they see their future in those who have gone before, who are more severely affected by the condition or have died of the condition. As Veronica notes, she is experiencing similar symptoms to those of her sister and mother who died of the condition, such as tiredness, dizziness and muscle weakness. As time passed, the later stages of the condition meant that they were severely disabled by the time they reached their forties. Veronica sees a similar future for herself.

> *Veronica*: I'm not really sure to be honest. I can't really understand all they say and with my mother and my sister [who died] they were both like us in the younger days and then both in wheelchairs by the time they were 43. And they, it starts off that you feel tired and weak and then your right side tends to give way a bit or you keep falling to the right. If I get tired or I'm walking I feel as if I'm dizzy and I just keep going to one side, hitting the wall or the lamppost and things. And in my mother and sister's case they were like that for years, going round the house, getting on with things but by holding on to walls and different things until eventually they were both in wheelchairs.

Maggie and her daughter, Susan, also predict similar futures. Susan surveys the previous generation of women, observes her mother's manifestation and development of the condition and has a corresponding expectation that she and her cousins will develop the disease will in their forties. Her mother agrees.

> *Susan*: But it's all 40 it hit you lot, isn't it? So by the time you're coming to 40 you'll be thinking 'Oh here we go.'
> *Maggie*: They reckon life begins at 40. What the hell went wrong for us lot? (laughs). There we are, such is life.
> *Susan*: We have to sit there and think 'Oh well we're 40. We're going to get this. We're going to get that by the time we're 40.' I don't want to end up like this. But I will, won't I, waiting for it to happen. That's why I don't want to know. So I'll have the blood test but I don't want to know [...] Yeah, like as soon as Veronica turned 40, I thought 'Oh.'

More widely in the family the generation of women who have been diagnosed with the condition continually survey, assess and compare their symptoms, the severity, and stage of the disease progression. Three sisters (Veronica, Lindsey and Suzanne) all agree that their other sister, Maggie, is the most severely affected. Of the later symptoms, they find the most visual symptom, the large lipomas or 'lumps', the most upsetting to witness and dread a similar future. Here, Suzanne compares herself with her sisters. She notes that her eldest surviving sister, Maggie, is the most severely affected because, as well as having the lipoma she has problems with her speech (a later stage of the condition), Suzanne identifies Lindsey as the next most affected sister as Lindsey has developed the most visible sign of the condition, the 'lumps'. In comparison, Suzanne believes that she is mildly affected because she does not have the lipomas.

> *Suzanne*: Yes, (laughs) I'm not too bad. I mean, Maggie's speech and everything is dreadful, you know. And my other sister, I haven't seen her for a while Lindsey, she's got, she's going back in to see about having the lumps, like my mother had across her back, out now, but touch wood, I haven't got that.

Family members are able to witness the stigmatizing effect of these visible signs of the condition. They see their own future in the public reaction to their kin who are more severely affected.

> *Veronica*: Where my other sister's lumps, Maggie's lumps are more, where Lindsey's are on her neck and she wears a blouse, I mean, Maggie's are on her face, everywhere, her arms, her back, you know. And we've gone out with her for meals or gone, and people can't, they look, they point, they comment until in the end you just feel like quarrelling with them. It is very upsetting. And as Lindsey said, she don't want to hurt Maggie but she said if she looked like Maggie there's no way she'd go on holiday or even go outside the door because it is very upsetting.

Thus, not only does Veronica see people's reactions to her sister's visible signs of the condition, but she also witnesses her own possible future.

Disclosure

As we have previously discussed, assumptions were often made by the professional practitioners about the nature of disclosure within families and what 'family' consists of in the context of genetic information. The notion of disclosure often implied the unproblematic transfer of information about the potential risk of inheriting a genetic condition. In contrast, we found the experience of disclosure within families and this extended family to be much more complex. Veronica reports that she and her family are 'open' and that she is an 'open book' and believes that most of her kindred know about the condition.

> *Veronica*: Well, we're all pretty open anyway, you know. If I, I tend to be an open book, though. If I've got a problem I tell everybody and I say what's what like.

It would, however, be unrealistic to assume that within such an 'open' family there are overt episodes of 'sharing' or 'transmitting' genetic information. The disclosure of genetic information within this kin does not consist of a number of specific instances of communication where information is unproblematically provided to a willing recipient. As Veronica's daughter Jenny explains, it is a process that has no clear boundaries and is always partial in nature. In contrast to her mother's account, Jenny sees disclosure differently.

> *Jenny*: It's funny, isn't it. Like we're a close family but then things like that you don't talk about them.

Jenny believes that most of the information she has about the condition has been overheard during visits to her mother. She has been able to listen in when her mother and her aunts are talking together. In addition, her mother will occasionally mention aspects of the condition to her. She is aware that her knowledge is partial and that they have never discussed the condition in any depth.

> *Jenny*: No, no. I think they probably don't know any more than what I know about her. Like, you know, picking up bits of conversation if I'm in the room or not really being in on the conversation they don't, they do know a little bit […] eah just picking up little bits […] No never, even when my mother [Veronica] first found out like it weren't sort of like 'Sit down, I've got something to tell you.' It was just sort of going up there for a cup of tea and, you know, you're popping in anyway and then just, she just was saying a little bit about it.

More widely within the kin, discussions about the condition were often partial and it is important to note that the actual condition was never named by any of the kin, but referred to as 'it' or 'this thing'. This may be because knowledge of the condition is part of a wide set of shared and tacit everyday knowledge within the kindred (cf. Cox and McKellin, 1999).

> *Sally*: You know, but none of them ever know the name. They always say 'Maybe you've got what I've got.' They don't know what the hell it's called. They don't name it. Well I don't know if they know the name themselves do they, you know, because I haven't got a clue what that name is.

> *Lindsey*: But they don't, no they don't, they don't name it by name any time they mention it, you know. They just say like 'What we've got.'

In the process of disclosure, individuals often incorporated a number of devices such as humour to disguise their concerns that a family member may be showing signs of the condition. Veronica believes her daughter is experiencing the early symptoms of the condition. In addition, as we have seen earlier, Jenny is also worried that she is affected. However, despite this concern, they tell us that they are able to discuss their fear briefly and only through the use of humour.

> *Veronica*: Well, as I say joking again I said, she said 'I hope I haven't got what you've got.' She said 'I'm not going to end up in a wheelchair, all lumps over me', and I said 'Well', I said 'You know I can't help that. It's not my fault.' But she does suffer with a lot of pain in her legs and swelling and all, which my mother's feet and legs always swollen. And yours did yesterday, didn't it? (to Jenny)

Family members also disclose their concern through remarks such as 'I hope you haven't got what I've got', which, while appearing to be casual, are suffused with high levels of fear and anxiety.

Beliefs Informing Disclosure

The kin held a number of beliefs about who is at risk of developing the condition and who needs to be informed. The focus of concern within this kindred was the women in the family; the men were generally not considered to be at risk or receptive to information about the condition.

For example, Maggie is not concerned about the men in her family. She is part of the older generation and because she has seen the condition affect other family members, she believes she can see where the condition is 'kicking off' within members of the kin. She has previously described her concerns about her daughter, Susan, and her two teenage nieces are also a focus of her concern.

> *Maggie*: And I notice with my brother's girls now. I mean, they're only 18 and 14 but there is something there. I mean, perhaps I'm being an old witch or something [...] but it is, it's there, you know, you can see it kicking off. Their mothers don't notice it, but I, whether it's because I'm an older generation and I've seen so much, I'm thinking, you know, it is there.

Within this kin, the focus of concern and anxiety is all younger female members, irrespective of their parentage. However, although Maggie's anxiety is focussed on her two nieces, according to the biomedical model of inheritance they will not inherit the condition from their father. In contrast, their father, Maggie's brother, will have inherited the condition from their mother (who died of the condition). Maggie and her three other sisters show no concern for their brother's future health.

In addition, even though the biomedical model of inheritance indicates that her son and grandson will inherit the condition, Maggie does not believe they are at risk. Because of this she is unconcerned that her son appears to know nothing about the condition. She reports that she did hint to him, before the birth of his son, that 'there are lots of things in the family'; however, because he did not respond, she has not offered further information about the condition. She believes he is the type of person who would not be interested in such things.

KF: And so you've a son. Does he know or …?

Maggie: No, I don't think he knows anything. When his girlfriend was pregnant I did say 'Oh right now you know there's a lot of things in the family.' 'Oh yeah, like what?' and I said 'Well, there's this wrong and there's that wrong.' 'Oh.' He never said any more about it. That is Ian, isn't it?

Similarly, Lindsey is also unconcerned about the men in the family; she does not believe her son and grandson are at risk of inheriting the condition and was only motivated to discuss it with her son before the birth of his first child. She describes experiencing a period of high anxiety prior to the birth of her grandson; she was concerned that if this child was a girl she would inherit the condition. At the time, she was prompted by her fear to hint to her son that her condition may be familial, although she has not discussed it further with him and admits that they find it hard to talk.

Lindsey: He just knows there's something going on like but he's not exactly sure what. He knew my mother was in a wheelchair like and pushed her about and that, but no, not really.

KF: Do you think, do you get the feeling he'd want to know or …?

Lindsey: Yeah, James is come day, go day, nothing bothers James (laughs). It's funny, it's hard to talk to him somehow. You know, I call him and I'll say about 5 minutes to him and that's about it. But he wouldn't pass it onto his child and he had a boy after so I was glad they had a boy.

Lindsey describes the relief she experienced when both her children had sons. She does not believe her son or grandsons are at risk and thus the focus of her concern is her daughter. It is interesting to speculate what she would have done if she had had a granddaughter.

The next generation of women acknowledge that they are the focus of the flow of information and that the men in the family are not expected to know or want to know about the condition. Here, Sally is unconcerned that her brother, James, appears to know little about the condition.

Sally: No, I don't think it has. I think the girls know more than what the boys do. Because I think they think that it's not going to affect the boys as bad as the women, so I think they, the girls know more than, they definitely more than what the boys do definitely, they do (laughs) […] I don't think James knows anything, I really don't. If he does I'd be well shocked. I will be well shocked if James knows anything at all, you know. I think he knows my mother's got lumps. I don't think he's seen them. I'm not too sure, but I think he knows she has got lumps.

However, the men within this kindred do appear to be concerned about the condition and that they too are developing early signs of onset. For example, Carrie has similarly assumed her brother does not want to know about the condition and believes that he is not at risk. However, despite this, she recounts a story that indicates that he is experiencing fear and anxiety that he too may be developing the condition. He had developed a 'lump' and she believes he was extremely anxious that this may be the onset of the disease. He was so concerned that a friend persuaded him to see his general practitioner.

> *Carrie*: I don't know, I don't really know because, I mean, my brother is not very talk-ative about anything at all. He's really in on himself, but I know he's worried about it. And he had a lump on his back, because they've all got these lymphomas and he had a lump come up about 2 years ago and he was really petrified and he would not go to the doctor at all and he was really, I mean his friend dragged him to the doctors in the end and the doctor said, she said 'There's nothing wrong with you,' she said 'It's just fatty tissue, like you know don't be so silly and sort of like go away.' And, you know, I mean, that upset him then because he was really, really panicking. It was the same thing and fatty tissue that's what they said to my mum, fatty tissue and that's what she used to call it to us 'It's just my fatty issue.' So he was really pan-icking about that. I don't know if he's still got the lump or not. I mean, I don't talk to him about it because I know it upsets him.

Carrie recalls this episode with some hilarity and remains unconcerned about his health; in addition, she has no idea whether he still has the 'lump' that may be a potential symptom of the condition. They do not discuss this event or the condition.

Practical Psychology

At the level of the family, the accounts of genetic risk also inform the moral and ethical work these women perform. All these family members produced clearly articulated accounts of who could and could not *cope* with the condition or information about their risk status. These accounts were suffused with theories of moral character and personality type and were used to inform rationalizations of disclosure. For example, Maggie and Lindsey both believe their sons cannot 'cope' with this information about the condition. Maggie believes her son (Ian) would react badly and would not be able to handle this information; however, as we have already seen, she is very insistent that her daughter, Susan, acknowledges her risk and seeks testing. Lindsey also believes her son, James, is not interested in knowing more about her condition, whilst she judges her daughter must be pro-tected from this knowledge because she has other health problems and a young family to look after.

> *Maggie*: Because he [son] hasn't got that er, he hasn't, he hasn't got the attitude for it. He's not that way inclined. He'd be one of these things of if you said 'You've got this

wrong with you', he'd go and sit in a corner and wait for it to happen like. He's not very up and at it at all.

Lindsey: Well, we've told them what my mother was like and that and would they want to know. My son said 'Oh I don't care either way like.' You know, he's not bothered either way and my daughter says 'Oh I don't know if I want to know.' It is hard really, isn't it you know, you can't imagine it like, can you until it starts happening. But, er, like I say Sally's got enough to put up with you know what I mean, with her [chronic condition] and the baby and all the rest of it like.

Practical Kinship

Decisions to disclose are informed by beliefs about who is family. The kin make decisions about who they believe needs to know, based on judgements about who is at risk and, in addition, would respond appropriately to the information. Veronica, the proband, is the main driving force behind disclosure so far and has urged her sisters (successfully) and her daughters and nieces (so far unsuccessfully) to seek testing. She has also assessed her wider family and based on this believes that some members of her family do not need to be informed. The main factors she has weighed up are that so far they appear to be unaffected, they are not from her mother's 'side' of the family and they do not have children who could be at risk.

Veronica: But they, their kids haven't got it, not that we know of anyway [...] I think it was on my mother's side.

Who is informed is also associated with the everyday practical maintenance of kindred links, what could be referred to as practical kinship. There are a large number of relatives, whom the family members described here only see at weddings and funerals, thus making it harder to disclose potentially devastating news.

Lindsey: Oh, we do see our cousins but only when there's a big do; you know, like a wedding or something like that. That's when we see the other side really. We might call in and see one of my cousins or two of them perhaps and that's about it. You lose touch don't you. Weddings and funerals like.

Accounts are suffused with stories about who are the accepted members of the kin and who are not, with clear implications for disclosure. The women provide a number of dark and sometimes contradictory stories surrounding the circumstances of the death of the eldest sister, who died from the condition. This has clear implications for their relationship with this sister's husband and her children. Since her mother's death five years ago, Carrie describes how she has become an outsider in the family and only retains sporadic contact with one aunt (Maggie), even though they live close by.

Carrie: Like, you know, that's the way I see it … I mean I felt like an outcast when I lived up there. My mum was only there a week like and I think she went into hospital, er, but I felt like, other than Maggie, I felt like an outcast with them. Valerie wasn't too bad but Suzanne was a very nasty bitch […] They're total strangers now. You know, it would be 'hello' and that's it. There wouldn't be any other conversation. And I think 'well, you want to be like that then fine, do you know what I mean, because we're family' but it's not my fault whose dad I've got do you know what I mean?

Practical Ethics: Focus on the Molecular Test Result

A common focus within discussions about the condition among the kindred was the molecular test result. This focus is interesting because all of the women interviewed and their children will develop the condition; the test can only confirm this, but will not be able to indicate the severity of the condition or the age of onset.

> *Angie*: You know, so … I don't know if I want to know really to be honest. You know, to go and have the tests and like I say there's nothing that can be done so you'd just worry and, you know, then I mean, 'God if I have got it', you know. But you can have the gene, it doesn't necessarily mean that you're going to be …

> *KF*: Do you think, have you thought about what, what might happen, the possible outcomes of if you have a test or what they might say?
> *Susan*: I did sort of but like I just want to go and just say it's negative. But like if he tells me it's positive I'd want something, you know, to get being done so I can see if the baby, see if there's any way you stop the baby from having it.

Family members were engaged in a complex rationalization of the pattern of inheritance; although many of these women spoke of the inevitability of the condition, they believed there was a 'chance' the condition may not affect them. The 'blood test' appears to be a useful focus for disclosure and discussion among family members because it implies a risk of developing the condition rather than certainty. This focus on the predictive test significantly reduces the bad news and shifts the focus onto the clinic.

Communication Breakdown

The risk of communication breakdown between family members remains another underlying issue of the practical ethics of disclosure. In addition to receiving genetic risk information family members are also provided with responsibilities: they are expected to respond appropriately to the knowledge they have been given. Susan is aware that she may be at risk of developing the condition and reports that she feels pressurized by her aunt Veronica and her mother, Maggie, to seek testing.

The problems of communication between Susan and Maggie threaten to break down the communication channels within the kin unit.

> *Susan*: Veronica wants me to have it done.
> *Maggie*: Our Veronica …
> *Susan*: I think she wants everyone to be ill.
> *Maggie*: No, she wants everybody to know exactly what's going on.
> *Susan*: Yeah, but you don't want to know. It's different for you lot because you've got it, but like us lot don't want to know because we'll be waiting for it to happen by the time we're 40 … There's only Veronica. She shouts at me. Because, you know, you block it out so much and she shouts. That's why I said 'Alright I'll go', you know, to keep the peace.
> *KF*: So you feel you're bullied a bit into …
> *Susan*: No, I want to find out, but I don't. I want to find out, well because of Mum and that but I don't want to know because it's my 40th birthday.

> *Susan*: I'll be tested, but I don't think I've got it.
> *Maggie*: Well, next time we go up to [consultant] then you come and have a blood test.
> *Susan*: I'm not sitting there all day to have lectures.
> *Maggie*: They're not lectures, they're very helpful conversations […]
> *Susan*: Well, I'll have the test done but …
> *Maggie*: Right-o then.

Information about the condition also comes at a price; individuals disclosing risk do so with a clear requirement that family members respond appropriately. Disclosure is often accompanied by pressure to contact the clinical service and seek predictive testing.

Surveillance: The Future

For all these family members, surveying the family means they can see their own future; individuals can look at older kin in order to gauge what their own fate may be. However, Veronica and Lindsey both try not to think about the future trajectory of the disease. Despite watching both their mother and sister develop and die of the condition, they cling to the chance that they may not be as severely affected. Carrie, their niece, has also seen her mother die of the condition and similarly tries to close her eyes to the future. All three hope that they will not 'burden' the next generation; they have all experienced caring for a parent with the condition and do not wish that future for themselves or their children.

> *Veronica*: But the thing is with us it don't matter what we know, because like he [consultant] says, there's nothing, there's no cure, there's nothing they can do. So then

you worry 'will it', it might not get as severe as my mother and my sister [who both died], but will it and will you go down the same road as them? I mean as luck has it I'm 45 now. [Sister] was in a wheelchair long before that, wasn't she?

KF: Do you mind me asking about the future and how you, how you feel about that … because you've seen your mum and your sister?
Lindsey: I don't think about it if I can help it.
Veronica: No.
Lindsey: I think I'll carry on going and, well, see what happens when it comes.
Veronica: If I think about it, I don't want my kids to do for me what I had to do for my mother because like I done it because I wouldn't have seen her go in a home or anything but I used to sometimes resent doing it as well.

Carrie: Yeah, it'll be an air bubble into a vein or something (laughs). But no it's, I couldn't, I don't think I could do that. I mean my mum felt like she was a burden. She wasn't, er, but I know how hard it was to help her and do everything for her and I wouldn't have them [sons] doing it for me.
KF: Yes.
Carrie: You know, so, it's a lot to take in, and you grow up very quickly and it's not fair.

For the younger generation of women (for within this kin, surveillance is the responsibility of women), such acts of surveillance of the previous generation lead to an early awareness of their future care-giving responsibilities.

Jenny: I do worry in case I've got to look after my mother, not worry that way but if she went like her sister in a wheelchair and all how she'd cope because my mother is not a strong person […] I do worry about her because I don't think she'd cope if … anything like that happened. And her mother and her sister, her sister died young.

For some members of the younger generation of women, this future is a reality; they are already caring for a parent. Susan describes the demands of caring for her mother (Maggie) and additionally is aware that her mother's health is likely to get progressively worse; the future fills her with 'dread'.

Susan: It's hard enough now. And it's only sort of like recently now she's well you see she gets all nasty like. Yesterday I just went home. I said 'I'm not staying here.' But she's, takes it out on everyone else and like she's bottling everything up and then she just blows but it's like almost stupid things she's blowing off to, you know what I mean? […] and like if anything is wrong I've got to take care of her, and then it's like 'Can you just do this, can you do that. You should have your kids now. You should be doing this and that.' And I'm thinking they aren't aware of it. You know it's like splitting yourself. It's hard work […] I can't remember my Nan, I can, but all I remember is her in a wheelchair. I don't remember her walking or anything. It was hard work because I remember like these. She used to get really nasty and it was like a burden to her. She's always said, my mum, when she gets to that stage she don't want to, she wants to go into a home, but she won't but I'm dreading it. I am really dreading it.

The experiences of this extended family demonstrate how processes of disclosure are embedded in the everyday realities of practical kinship. All of these individuals employed techniques of surveillance to assess who was at risk and, in addition, carried out a practical analysis of the psychology and character of their kin to identify who could best handle knowledge of the condition. These practices were used to help define, limit and draw boundaries around the family as part of a wider need to control the flow of risk information, not only in terms of who was informed, but also in terms of managing responses to knowledge. Members of the extended kin all expressed extremely high levels of anxiety in recounting the moral, ethical and practical dilemmas they faced not only in disclosing information, but in managing the future.

This one 'family' can help to capture and to crystallize the themes we have been exploring on a wider basis, namely, the way in which surveillance informs beliefs about inheritance and what informs and influences the practical everyday ethics of disclosure. This kindred had developed a number of theories to explain where the condition had 'come from' and the path of transmission. There appeared to be a continual process of surveillance of a series of pasts and futures that were scrutinized and made sense of in the present in order to identify who was at risk. Acts of surveillance constituted the reality of this family; living with the condition or its threat was unspoken and hidden. Additionally, disclosure, even within this 'open' family, did not consist of overt 'sharing'. Instead, disclosure was tacit and partial in nature and informed by a number of beliefs, which meant that those who were believed to be at risk did not necessarily correspond with the biomedical model.

–7–

Risky Relations

The book has been an in-depth excursion into accounts of individuals and families reflecting on their experiences of inherited medical conditions. In engaging with these accounts we have had a number of major preoccupations. In this concluding chapter we summarize these and reaffirm some of the principles that have guided our analysis. Our research has been informed by the sociological and anthropological exploration of family, kinship and genetics. The accounts are by no means devoid of relevance for practitioners. Although not 'applied research' in any narrow sense, our research is not intended to be a purely 'academic' exercise. Consequently, having outlined our main themes and conclusions, we indicate the potential significance of our work for policy and practice on the part of genetic counsellors and other professionals.

Our research has been focused on genetics and the implications of genetic medicine for the families we have worked with. We do not, however, wish to imply that genetic medicine represents a completely new departure in the understanding of illness, or that the reported experiences of our family members are uniquely determined by recent developments in genetic medicine. Social scientists have not been slow to explore the possible implications of recent changes in medical and scientific knowledge. In our view, some of the resulting commentary and analysis have been over-heated. There have been numerous arguments suggesting that new biomedical knowledge is having transformative effects, not only on science and medicine, but also on how ordinary social actors understand themselves, their bodies, their potential risks and their relationships.

We have no wish to dismiss out of hand the significance biomedical innovations and their future potential to affect how we think about ourselves as biological and social beings, or even that new biomedical knowledge has the capacity to challenge the very boundaries between the social and the biological. On the other hand, in reflecting on how ordinary, everyday family members think about and respond to the identification of genetic illness within the kindred, we must be cautious about any strong presuppositions concerning the new conditions of predictive and diagnostic genetic testing.

As we have noted in our opening chapter, ideas about inheritance clearly pre-date modern genetics, let alone contemporary biomedical post-genomic science. We have pointed out the long significance of family trees in European iconography, and the interest in descent and inheritance that permeated European courts and the aristocracy. We can detect the cultural significance of inheritance and descent from various sources. Consider, for instance, nineteenth-century fiction. Emile Zola's realist fiction was explicitly conceived in terms of a scientific spirit of inquiry. He himself referred to his work in terms of the 'experimental novel'. The notion of 'experiment' here does not refer to a genre of experimental writing, as might be applied to varieties of avant-garde writing (although of course Zola's style was innovative in many ways). Rather, it refers to the ways in which Zola's realism was directly influenced by scientific writing – notably that of the physiologist Claude Bernard. Zola conceived of the novel as one way of conducting an experimental and disciplined inquiry – albeit conducted in fictional, literary terms – into the intersection of heredity and circumstance. The narrative of the sequence of novels therefore traces how personal traits are transmitted from generation to generation, and how such traits are refracted through the practical contingencies that confront Zola's characters (cf. Davis, 2003). It is not necessary for the transmission of traits to be predicated on a specific notion of 'genetics' (which post-dates Zola's literary work). It inscribes more generic ideas about inheritance that are more deeply embedded in general cultural idioms.

Gilmartin (1998) has made a similar set of observations concerning inheritance in narratives of nineteenth-century English fiction. She demonstrates the centrality of notions of pedigree and inheritance through which were articulated 'the political, class, regional, national and racial repercussions of the family tree' (Gilmartin, 1988: 17). She also reminds us that much eighteenth-century picaresque fiction is concerned with the recovery of lost lineages and the restoration of rightful inheritance and status. A more recent fictional narrative such as Jean Rhys's *Wide Sargasso Sea* (1966) also captures cultural beliefs concerning inherited character, including inherited insanity.

Our cultural categories have not needed to wait for the Human Genome Project or genetic testing. We have had belief systems concerning 'in-breeding' and the transmission of inherited medical conditions independently of molecular biology and the genetic basis of diseases. The 'Hapsburg jaw' was clearly recognized and portrayed among various European royal houses. So too was the haemophilia that was distributed through the European royal families of the late nineteenth and early twentieth centuries.

It is abundantly clear that 'ordinary' families have had ample opportunity to identify their relationships in terms of categories of inheritance. Family resemblance, after all, is a commonplace. The inheritance of physical characteristics has been a taken-for-granted observation, and the absence of physical resemblance *prima facie* evidence of bastardy. Likewise, the inheritance of aspects of character, such as courage, talent, moral stability and sanity is subject to widespread and firmly entrenched beliefs.

Notions about 'bad blood' in families and its manifestations in successive generations are recurrent in the ordinary discourse of family life, generations and inheritance. Lorna Sage's autobiographical work, called *Bad Blood*, captures perfectly some of these local beliefs, couched in the collective memory-work of families, and enshrined in their private mythologies. Recent fiction has also explored the themes of family and memory within a rural Welsh setting (Fletcher, 2004). Indeed, 'families' are clearly replete with secrets, unspoken pasts and innuendoes. The recent UK television series *Who Do You Think You Are?* illustrates this quite dramatically (BBC 2, 12 October 2004). A number of 'celebrities' 'embark on a voyage of personal discovery' and trace their family trees, in a search for their 'origins'. Several discover things about their own family past and their close relatives that they never knew, and about whom there was a veil of secrecy. Things were not talked about openly in front of the children, and on occasions people were written out of the family's collective narrative altogether. While subject to the same contrivances and performed emotions as any 'reality TV', this television series nonetheless encapsulates what may not be 'typical' family stories, but are at least illustrative, in the public domain, of how families may be morally 'risky' spaces, independently of any explicitly 'genetic' aspects. From a research perspective the same may be said on the basis of Elizabeth Stone's *Black Sheep and Kissing Cousins* (2004). Like our own research, this is based on narrative accounts gathered from family members. Through the narratives it contains, the monograph illustrates how families are not only constituted by the relations that are actively maintained, but also by the silences and suppressed relations.

We should not, therefore, be surprised to find that the families we have worked with have well-established arrays of beliefs and practices concerning kindred and inheritance. We should certainly not expect to find that families with a genetic condition respond only in terms of their shared genetic constitution, as defined by health professionals. We have documented in Chapter 3 that the family members with whom we worked have elaborated ideas about the mechanisms of inheritance, and the consequences of such inter-generational transmission. It would be inadmissible to infer that we can identify a unified 'culture' of beliefs, shared across all our families in Wales, and thus essentialize beliefs about inheritance to form a unified cultural system. It is nonetheless striking that interviews triggered by a shared interest in medical genetics should yield such varied accounts of the 'routes and journeys' of inheritance. Equally, it is striking – though by no means unexpected – that our respondents should have ideas and accounts about the kinds of traits and characteristics that are inherited and manifested in different family members and generations.

These mundane ideas about inheritance are embedded in everyday practices of family and kinship. In some ways we have tried to make the idea of 'family' a more diffuse, more problematic, category than it often is in the professional literature. Families are not bounded entities. The 'English' and 'Welsh' families are quite loosely defined, in contrast to many systems of kinship and affinity in which categories and degrees of membership are more precise (e.g. classificatory kinship), and in which kinship groups may operate as corporate entities. That does not mean, however, that people like our informants do not entertain understandings and ideas about kinship, about lines of descent and about patterns of inheritance. We have, therefore, analysed how family members describe patterns of descent and how these are mapped onto the 'biological' phenomena of inherited conditions. Again, our emphasis has been on how ideas of medical genetics are refracted through more generic patterns of belief about relatedness. This is by no means unique to the field of genetics. We know from other research that everyday, mundane beliefs are, to say the least, under-determined by current scientific understandings. For instance, outside of the restricted context of the science curriculum, students display pre-modern scientific ideas in their everyday reasoning (such as the belief that heavier objects fall more quickly than lighter ones). Likewise, as authors such as Cecil Helman (2000) have shown, one can readily identify pre-modern medical belief systems in people's practical beliefs and practices: humoral physiology is detectable among the English patients Helman worked with, for instance.

We do not altogether disregard recent analyses of well-informed or even 'expert' patients (Prior, 2003). There is no doubt that some individuals can acquire as much systematic knowledge of a very limited field – such as the one specific condition they themselves experience, or that afflicts a close family member – as a specialist. Equally, networks and interest groups can acquire a degree of knowledge about their own particular problem or issue that surpasses that of the general practitioner. The generalist has neither the opportunity nor the motivation to read a great deal of research literature about a particular medical condition, and in the course of a basic medical education and everyday general practice, a professional may encounter very few cases – if any – and may thus not acquire anything beyond a basic 'textbook knowledge'. On the other hand, we do not mean to imply that our informants were in any meaningful sense 'lay experts' in their own condition, or in medical genetics more generally. What we have encountered here, and what we have described in the course of the preceding chapters, is an array of beliefs and practices, some of which are informed by the advice and counselling received from genetic counsellors and some of which derive from broader cultural repertoires.

In pursuing these analyses, we have not departed from current anthropological and sociological research on 'the family' more generally. As we outlined earlier in the book, family and kinship have become increasingly salient in recent research literatures. This partly reflects the fact that 'family' relations have become central to analyses of such diverse phenomena as gender roles, domestic violence, technologically assisted reproduction, surrogate parenthood, divorce and step-parenting. Indeed, the once tidy categories of family relations have been decomposed into a more varied array of social phenomena and analytic topics. New biomedical technologies and their clinical applications are among the drivers for a renewed attention to the intersection of biologically defined and socially defined categories and relationships. Relatedness is recognizable as constructed simultaneously in terms of natural and cultural terms (Strathern, 1992a, 1992b).

Does this mean that genetic medicine and the diagnosed presence of genetic conditions within a family have no consequences? Does new biomedical knowledge have no effect? Clearly not. We are not suggesting that medical genetics have had no consequences or impact at all on the family members we studied. But we are reluctant to ascribe to our findings the interpretation that our families have become enmeshed in a radically new field of knowledge and intervention. Diagnostic and predictive genetic testing have not appeared in a cultural vacuum. As we have been at pains to demonstrate, our family members' constructions of genetic conditions and genetic risks are not determined entirely by the professional constructions of those phenomena, as conveyed to probands in the clinic or in home visits by genetic professionals.

We do not see genetic information being transferred from the professional medical domain into a family that is a *tabula rasa*. If individuals and their families are not 'experts' necessarily, we must acknowledge that their knowledge and practice are underdetermined by medical orthodoxy. This is, perhaps, unsurprising. After all, however carefully genetics services deal with individuals and families, and however much time is devoted to home visits and counselling sessions, such allocations are all but insignificant compared with the amount of time that individuals can spend talking to others, such as other family members, friends and neighbours. There is, therefore, nothing strange in the conclusion that the formal transmission of genetic information does not totally constrain the interpretative frames expressed by our informants.

The knowledge derived from medical genetics, and from the Human Genome Project, figures prominently in many commentaries on the contemporary condition. It is too often asserted that there have been radical transformations in the systems of medical thought, or medical practice, or general cultural understandings, brought in the train of genetic science. It is, we believe, too easy to extrapolate from relatively high-profile or extreme cases (such as Huntington's Disease or familial cancers) to suggest that we are witnessing wholesale transformations in thought and action. We are not, therefore, convinced that we are experiencing major changes that result in new defintions of personhood, or that reflect a radically new sense of 'risk' and 'anxiety'. The bulk of genetic conditions, as diverse as neurofibromatosis, polycystic kidney disease, FRAXE and cardio-myopathy, inhabit uncertain molecular terrains that generate 'uncertain risks' leading to 'messy' prognostic progression from the realm of the genotype to the phenotype. Thus in the bulk of such cases the implications for notions of risk, health and illness, not to mention self-identity, are markedly different from those that emerge when there are diagnostic tests that can predict disease onset as in the case of Huntington's Disease.

It would, in other words, be erroneous to extrapolate from the extension of genetics services and the identification of a growing number of genetic bases for inherited condition to a general state of *geneticization*. The term 'geneticization' has been used in recent years to denote a variety of sociological and anthropolog-ical analyses. While there are moves afoot to variously conceptualize the shift from 'healthy' to 'at risk but as yet not ill' ranging from the notion of 'predicting dis-eases before symptoms appear' (Nelkin and Tancredi, 1994) to 'people as patient before their time' (Jacob, 1998) and 'the potential, perpetual patients' (Finkler, 2001) there is seldom critical focus on those who do not experience being at risk in these terms (Bharadwaj, 2002). It is not our intention at this stage of the argu-ment to open up all the possible meanings that have been applied to geneticization. Here we are engaging with those usages that equate geneticization with an increas-ingly pervasive use of genetic science, with a concomitant reductionist episte-mology that increasingly attributes to genetics a major role in determining health and illness, life chances, and self-identity. To this extent, therefore, we propose and argue for a more nuanced interpretation lacking in certain quarters of social science research eager to argue in favour of a rapid penetration of biomedical knowledge and practice in contemporary everyday life. It is, we suggest, problem-atic to argue that 'we' have all become subject to the power of biomedical know-ledge that is rapidly geneticizing our identities (Dreyfuss and Nelkin, 1992; Lippman, 1992). Consequently, in our analysis we have consciously resisted the somewhat attractive, but too glib, a trend to make epochal claims about the dawn of the genetic age (Conrad and Gabe, 1999) and the century of the gene (Keller, 2000) while attributing agency to new medical and biomedical technologies in shaping everyday experience of selves, bodies, health and illness to formulate genetic-based identities (Armstrong et al., 2000). On the contrary, we agree with Novas and Rose (2000: 491), who rightly reason in favour of locating genetic iden-tity in a more complex field of a bewildering array of identity claims and practices to the extent that even when regulatory practices utilize biological conceptions of personhood, genetic identity is rarely hegemonic.

While within the domain of sociological and anthropological accounts it has become routine to talk in terms of geneticization and/or medicalization of personal and interpersonal social relations, it is far from clear how the realm of molecular genetics and the local moral worlds of practitioners shape and become shaped by the presence of risky diagnosis and resultant kin relations. In this respect, the foregoing chapters bring into focus the potential, possible and indeed very probable implications for everyday clinical practice and diagnostic modalities. The complexities are numerous and effect multiple assumptions ranging from the very categories of family, pedigree, and kin groups to the notion of risk communication and disclosure.

The notion of family that is employed within the clinical domain is by far the most complex one. As we have shown in Chapter 2, the task of constructing and scrutinizing the pedigree or family tree and of writing subsequent medical histories with the view to constructing diagnostic, predictive test trajectories and generating the calculus of risk, produces boundary objects. These boundary objects inhabit multiple social worlds and are therefore particularly amenable to contextual, contingent meanings of 'family'. In other words, family and pedigrees as understood in the domain of kinship networks, and that of the laboratory and the clinic, can give rise to multiple connotations of family and kinship. In this respect there is potential for simultaneous and multilayered meanings of family to co-exist through the process of consultation and counselling as notions of what constitutes family in the everyday experiences of 'the patient', the laboratory scientist and the clinician, while existing in tandem, seldom encounter each other. The picture is even more complex if the local social world of the family is examined. The boundaries that conceal, reveal, include and exclude certain categories of kin, potentially disrupt but most often interrupt the 'risky' communication. In our experience, clinicians can on occasions presuppose free-flowing unobstructed channels of communications, which can exist but only in the altered, truncated and pruned social matrix of social relations that skip certain generations, relations and distant or near kin connections. The family can further shrink in the context of specific genetic disease or risk information. That is, the network of people receptive to information and seen as able to deal with or respond to a risky prognostication is informed by a complex set of ideas detailed in chapters 3 to 5. Journeys and routes or a palpable sense of where the condition is 'coming from', its origins, and beliefs about inheritance pattern often diverge from the medical beliefs about inheritance. Once again, the disjunction is one between the pedigree constructed and ratified in the clinical domain and family trees rooted in the memories of individual 'patients'. The consultant clinician and laboratory expert draw centrally on 'kinship memory'. The implication for clinical practice can be potentially significant depending on how and in what context an individual invokes memory of the kindred. Very often, differing beliefs about where the disease entity is seen to be coming from and the approximate risk calculus obtained within the clinical setting can affect patient and professional engagement. Our research also suggests that there is need for a space within the clinic where the burden of knowledge can be shared and not remain a crippling emotional subtext in the lives of people enmeshed in a network of risky relations.

The work of the clinic generates a variety of genetic risks, and as we have shown, risks are tentatively mapped onto the relations of kinship, as established by the cartography of the pedigree. Medical genetics thus generates a possible calculus of risks, defined in terms of biological relations. But this is not the only calculus that is in play. As we have seen, there is a complex *moral* calculus that encompasses family members' judgments concerning others' rights to knowledge about shared genetic constitution, or to participate in family-based discourse about risk and inheritance. Risk is thus a medical and a moral issue simultaneously.

These are issues that go beyond a sociological or anthropological analysis. The construction of relatedness that we have explored in this study has direct consequences for health professionals and genetic counsellors. The calculus of risk is a real concern for practitioners. For a health professional working in genetics, families can be regarded as 'risky' for a number of reasons. Individuals who seek genetic counselling may be at substantial risk of developing an inherited disorder. The sense of 'risk' can be accentuated, particularly when future reproductive decisions have to be made or when a family member becomes affected by the condition. From the point of view of the professional practitioner, risk may also be construed in terms of potential genetic risk. The individual for instance may be perceived as at risk of transmitting the condition to the next generation. The biological, social and moral components of responsibility may be neatly separable in theory. But their separation does not necessarily work in families, especially if there are pre-existing notions about the origin of the family's condition. As we have seen, individuals' and families' ideas about the biological origin of a genetic disorder are not necessarily congruent with those of a genetic specialist. But as we know, those ideas can carry a set of very powerful social and moral consequences in their wake. Both 'sides' of a family may insist that the condition must have come from the other side. This in turn may be embedded in a more generalized tension or conflict between parents within a kinship network. Family members may have their own theories as to where a disease comes from and who will be affected next, as in the notion of 'pre-selection' in families with Huntington's disease (Kessler, 1988). Older family members such as grandparents may decide that a child will inherit the condition from their father on the grounds that they take after him in so many other ways (the shape of his nose; his sense of humour). The pronouncements of genetics professionals may reinforce or conflict with such pre-existing notions. If they conflict with what, say, a grandmother said, then the official genetic professional standpoint may be discredited if it is generally accepted within the family that she is 'never wrong'. If professional opinion reinforces what the grandmother said, then that may be held to confirm how right she is about inheritance. It may further reinforce a sense of how undesirable that side of the family was all along. Thus, information from genetics professionals will be used by family members in a number of very different ways. The interpretations and constructions placed upon professional advice can go well beyond the legitimate scope of its application as understood (or even imagined) by the professionals themselves.

Even in the absence of any such complicating family agenda, it may be very difficult for even the best-intentioned genetics service 'client' to respond to the biological information in a way that conforms to practitioners' intentions and expectations. A study such as this – situated outside the clinic and problematizing how families respond to and talk about genetic information – is potentially of great value in helping professionals understand the 'constructed' nature of social as well as biological 'reality'. The medical information and advice professionals generate and trade in are not produced and transmitted in a cultural void, nor into a field of social relationships that can be assumed to be 'ideal' from the professional's point of view.

For example a family illness may already be recognized and well understood by those at risk, but where the inherited nature of the condition has not previously been understood or acknowledged, or where this information has been withheld within the family, transmission of genetic information to the relatives of those seen in the clinics can be potentially problematic. Along with professional construtions of the 'biological facts' of inheritance run the social questions of causation, responsibility and blame. The biological is refracted through the moral calculus of family relations. The potential moral obligation on family members to transmit information ironically depends on the same family network that has already (perhaps) transmitted the disease. Consequently, the transmission of clinical understandings of pedigrees and biological relatedness is *inescapably* implicated in the same social relations that generated the biological 'facts' in the first place.

It is, therefore, potentially self-defeating for clinicians and other practitioners to make unduly simple assumptions about the families they deal with. They certainly cannot assume that there will be 'open' communication patterns among members of a kindred, any more than they can assume that what is transmitted between family members corresponds to the professionals' own intended meanings. As we have seen repeatedly in this book, when family members actively share an understanding of shared genetic conditions and risks, they do not do so on the basis of discrete items of medically defined 'information'. Genetic understanding is assimilated to other narratives and idioms of collective understanding that include suspicions, silences, innuendoes and secrets, just as much as they involve the exchange of information that conforms with biomedical knowledge. Families, insofar as they can be said to exist as entities at all, are characterized by complex 'awareness contexts' (cf. Glaser and Strauss, 1965), rather than being characterized by open awareness in all cases or throughout the network. While our analytic focus has been on the families, we can extend our research back into the clinic, at least to the extent of suggesting that genetics practitioners need to pay much closer attention to the idioms of kinship and the networks of relations in which they are implicated.

Much of that work is indirect and at a distance. Genetic counsellors are not able to intervene directly in all aspects of a kindred or family network. The rhetoric of genetic counselling places 'non-directiveness' at the core of its professional ethos, so that, for instance, an individual's decision not to have genetic testing is regarded as a healthy outcome as long as they have an understanding of the issues involved. Indeed, it is even possible for genetics professionals to see the informed decision not to undergo such testing as a professional success.

From a professional perspective, a problem arises when a genetic counselling 'client' does not pass on to a relative some item of genetic information that is of potential importance for their health, or that could be relevant to their decisions about reproduction, or does so in a way that departs from the professional's intentions. There may be some concern on behalf of the family members who may be affected adversely by the individual's decision not to share information. This is especially relevant if family members are at risk of a disease for which early medical management may bring major health benefits, or if they are planning to have children but are unaware that each child would be at risk of a serious, inherited disorder. For example, an individual's relatives may stand to benefit directly from regular surveillance for the early detection of tumours in a familial cancer syndrome, or for signs of dilation of the aortic root in Marfan's syndrome (the most serious manifestation of this condition is ruptures in the walls of major arteries); or their family planning decisions may be influenced by the knowledge of risk to their future children, whether or not prenatal diagnosis is available for the particular condition, and whether or not they would consider terminating a pregnancy if the baby was likely to be affected.

The usual response of professionals to this situation – where their 'client' has disclosed their intention not to pass on relevant information to their relatives – is to seek to persuade them to change their mind and pass on the information as they have suggested (Clarke et al., 2005). However, professionals face the quintessential ethical quandary when individuals persist in not making the disclosure. Questions such as 'What should the professional do if the "client" persists in not making the disclosure?' and 'under what circumstances would they be obliged to force disclosure, against the wishes of their "client"?' (Leung et al., 2000; Mariman, 2000) continue to be debated.

While our research does not provide ready prescriptions for professionals to solve such problems, it is clear that they should not interpret these perceived problems and dilemmas in terms simply of an individual's incapacity to understand genetic information or an irrational refusal to co-operate with medical practitioners.

It is clearly vital for professionals to understand the idioms of relatedness that inform family members' interests and practices. As we have emphasized, a moral calculus of ethical conduct is not the preserve of professionals. Equally, practitioners need to treat seriously the belief systems concerning inheritance and inter-generational traits if they are to engage with the social worlds of family members. Our research shows most clearly that health practitioners cannot interpret their work in terms of simple 'information'. They need to be sensitive to the interpretative frameworks that inform the *reception* of genetic knowledge, and its *circulation* among kin and affines.

Arthur Kleinman (1988) has been one of the most prominent advocates of a 'narrative' approach to medical practice as well as anthropological research on patients' illness experiences. He has suggested that clinicians need to engage in a form of 'ethnographic' understanding of the lifeworlds of their patients. We could make a similar observation concerning the needs and opportunities of genetic medicine. In order to understand the awareness contexts and dynamics of family networks, professionals too may need to think 'ethnographically', tracing the journeys and routes enshrined in local beliefs, and also tracing the contours of communication across generations, between siblings and among affines. The crucial difference between a 'narrative' formulation, like Kleinman's, and the professional interests of geneticists lies in the fact that the latter cannot base their professional work and understanding primarily on individual narratives of past experience. They need to engage with the shared and collective narratives of kinship, idioms of relatedness and interpretative frameworks that constitute the *social world* of the family. In that sense, therefore, the work of genetic professionals can and should be more thoroughly ethnographic than the individualistic approach advocated by Kleinman. Genetics is not unique in this context: conditions like cancer (Gordon and Paci, 1997) and HIV (Ezzy, 2000) also give rise to narratives of disclosure, evasion, silence or sharing.

We conclude therefore by reiterating one of the guiding themes of this book. It is vital for researchers and practitioners alike to ground their work in an understanding of everyday family practices that is sensitive to their complexities. It is not adequate for either professionals or social scientists to operate simply with idealized and overgeneralized views of their subject matter. As we have seen, genetic counsellors and other healthcare professionals cannot assume that families are open communication systems, or make too many assumptions about the distribution of knowledge and awareness within family networks. Simple anthropological truisms, such as the contingent and conventional relations between biologically defined and socially defined relations, need to be kept in mind constantly. The nature and consequences of practical kinship need to be recognized, in other words. We intend that professionals can learn from our intensive research something of these contingencies and complexities.

Equally, we need the corrective of empirical research to balance social scientists who claim that new biological and medical knowledge necessarily transforms the social categories of family, kinship, relatedness and personhood. Clearly there is the potential for innovation and transformation, but it cannot be read off from a small number of extreme cases. Our own research suggests that the people with whom we worked have made sense of their genetic risks and constitutions in accordance with a wide variety of frames of reference, and have assimilated their genetic information into a very stable repertoire of idioms of kinship. We certainly cannot derive from this research, or from the families involved, wholesale changes in self-identity as a consequence of genetic medicine, nor extrapolate from their experiences to a dystopian view of biomedical surveillance, an obsessive risk society or a postmodern condition in which the social is suffused by the biological.

Appendix: Summary of Conditions

This summary partially recapitulates details from Chapter 2 in order to preserve clarity.

Fragile X Syndrome Type E (FRAXE)

There are a number of chromosomal sites where the appearance of the chromosome as viewed under the microscope occasionally suggests that a break may (almost) have occurred; these sites are termed 'fragile sites'. To view chromosomes, cells are grown in culture and cell division is then arrested at a stage when the chromosomes have gathered themselves into discrete, condensed bodies and are easier to visualize; in contrast, in their usual state between cell divisions, chromosomes are dispersed as thin threads invisible to ordinary microscopy. The portions of the chromosome on either side of the fragile site condense down in the normal fashion for cell division and are connected by a thin thread where condensation has failed to occur. While a number of fragile sites have no association with any genetic disorder, at least two fragile sites exist on the long arm of the X chromosome which are both associated with intellectual disability. Expression of the gene associated with the fragile site in each case is disrupted when a simple repeat sequence element in each gene expands; the expansion both interferes with gene function and impairs the ability of that section of chromosome to condense appropriately for cell division. One type of fragile X syndrome, FRAXA, is much the commoner and is often associated with a set of typical physical features in addition to very variable learning and behavioural difficulties. Fragile X syndrome type E (FRAXE) is much less common and is not associated with any particular facial appearance and only with a mild to moderate degree of learning difficulty. Both conditions manifest in males more than females, and are transmitted through families in a sex-linked fashion – being transmitted from a man to his daughters and from a woman to half of her children of either sex. In both conditions, but especially in FRAXA, the mutation causing the phenotype is unstable – the repeat expansion that causes the problem itself changes as it is passed from a woman to her children, often expanding and causing more severe developmental problems.

Cardiomyopathy

There are a number of inherited disorders of cardiac muscle that impair the function of the heart. They fall into two main groups, dilated cardiomyopathy (DCM) and hypertrophic cardiomyopathy (HCM). In DCM, the pumping chambers of the heart enlarge because the muscle in the wall of the ventricles contracts inefficiently. In HCM, the muscle in the wall of the ventricles thickens in addition to contracting less effectively, and this thickening can itself cause obstruction to the blood being ejected in systole from the left ventricle into the aorta. These conditions can be inherited in any of the modes of inheritance but most typically as autosomal dominant traits passed from an affected parent to half their children of either sex.

XYY Syndrome

Of the twenty-three pairs of chromosome usually present in the fertilized egg and in each cell of the body, twenty-two pairs are the same in boys and girls – the autosomes, numbered from one to twenty-two. The other pair is the pair of sex chromosomes, X and Y. The X chromosome carries many genes controlling a wide range of bodily functions, while the principal function of the Y chromosome is to impose the pathway for male development. One of the two X chromosomes in females is inactivated early in development so as to ensure that the effective dosage of X chromosome genes is the same in both sexes; the choice as to which X is inactivated is (usually) random. Sex-linked diseases affecting any system of the body (e.g. blood clotting, colour vision, immunity, muscle development) arise in males when one of the X chromosome genes has mutated; they may show in females if a functioning copy of the gene is required for normal function in all cells (if normal function in just 50 per cent of cells – those cells using the X chromosome on which the copy of the relevant gene is intact – is insufficient). Because of this mechanism of dosage compensation for sex-linked genes, there 'should' be few clinical consequences of anomalies of sex chromosome number. There are some genes on the X and Y chromosomes that are exceptions to this scheme, however, so that alterations in the number of X and Y chromosomes can be significant. Some X chromosome genes escape inactivation in females and have an active homologue on the Y chromosome, so that two functioning genes exist in normal males and females. Having an additional Y chromosome, like having an additional X chromosome, is therefore associated with somewhat increased growth (tall stature) and a higher incidence of mild learning and behaviour difficulties – but not with severe intellectual disability or with malformation. There has been controversy about the effect of a second Y chromosome on criminality but the additional effect of a second Y chromosome, if it exists at all, must be trivial compared with the major effect of a single Y chromosome that gives males a much higher incidence of criminal behaviour than females.

Cystic Fibrosis (CF)

This disorder affects the transport of chloride ions across epithelial membranes in the body. This results in thickened mucus that can make it difficult to clear infection from the lungs or to release digestive enzymes into the bowel. CF therefore results in chronic lung damage from infection and poor growth ('failure to thrive') from malabsorption. It also leads to male infertility from its effects on the vas deferens. The outlook for affected individuals has improved greatly over the past 20–30 years but additional benefits may result from early detection through newborn screening or from gene therapy.

Neurofibromatosis Type 1

This is one of the commonest autosomal dominant disorders, largely because the large gene which can give rise to the disorder has a high mutation rate. NF1 leads to the development of café au lait skin marks in early childhood and, from late childhood, the development of numerous benign tumours on the skin, the neurofibromas. Associated with these features is a wide range of other problems that arise in a proportion of affected individuals. About one third of cases have some degree of learning difficulty, and about a third have some significant medical complication including malignancies, brain tumours, hypertension, epilepsy, scoliosis and other bone or joint problems. Most affected individuals therefore suffer from the stigmatizing effects of the physical features and some have to confront serious medical hazards as well.

Subarachnoid Haemorrhage (SAH)

This consists of bleeding into the space around the brain, beneath the arachnoid membrane that wraps around the brain and spinal cord. The bleeding is usually from the arteries that supply oxygenated blood to the central nervous system. Anueurysms are points where the wall of an artery is dilated, and where it may rupture. There are several different types of arterial aneurysm, with different causes and a range of possible consequences. A number of inherited disorders are associated with these weaknesses in the arterial wall, but they can occur for other reasons too – for instance, they can be associated with high blood pressure and high blood cholesterol. One important inherited cause of cerebral aneurysms (and SAH) is polycystic kidney disease (q.v.).

Aortic Aneurysm

Aneurysms are points where the wall of an artery is weakened and has dilated. When this occurs in the aorta, the largest artery in the body that carries the cardiac output to the whole of the body, there is a danger of aortic rupture with cata-strophic consequences. There are a number of inherited (and non-inherited) con-ditions in which the strength of the arterial wall may be reduced and aortic dissection can occur as a cause of sudden death.

Polycystic Kidney Disease (PKD)

This is an autosomal dominant disorder affecting 1 in 1,000 of the population. It leads to the formation and enlargement of cysts in the cortex of the kidneys and sometimes elsewhere in other abdominal organs, especially the liver. It is a common cause of chronic renal failure, often requiring dialysis or transplantation. Overt problems (symptoms) do not usually arise until well into adult life, but cysts may be detected much earlier – often from the teenage years and occasionally even from infancy – if imaging (usually with ultrasound) is employed. Young adults may present with symptoms from the enlargement of the kidneys (simply from their bulk), from bleeding into a cyst or from urinary infection. Later morbidity results from renal failure, cardiovascular disease and cerebrovascular disease, including subarachnoid haemorrhage from intracranial aneurysms. Complications can be delayed and reduced but not abolished if hypertension is detected and treated promptly and if urinary infections are managed effectively. Hypertension and other treatable complications are unusual before the late teenage years; occasionally, an affected individual will develop cysts without ever running into problems from them. There are two genetic loci at which mutations are associated with PKD; the phenotype associated with mutations at PKD1 is often somewhat more severe than that associated with the less common mutations at PKD2.

Chromosomal Translocation – Robertsonian Type

Several of the twenty-two pairs of autosomes (see XYY syndrome for an explana-tion of this term) have small and non-coding short arms, with all their functioning genes being located on the long arms of the chromosome. Two such chromosomes will occasionally fuse together at the centromeres, the junction of the chromosome's short and long arms and the regions at which the chromosomes attach to the cell's chromosomal locomotor apparatus at cell division. This results in the loss of the chromosome short arms and a reduction in chromosome number from 46 to 45 but there is no loss of gene sequences. Chromosomes 13, 14, 15, 21 and 22 may be involved in this process. While the carrier of a balanced Robertsonian translocation will be unaffected – i.e., will be perfectly healthy – they will have an increased chance of having problems with chromosome segregation at meiosis, the cell division leading to the production of eggs or sperm. In particular, there can be increased risks of a trisomy for chromosomes 13 or 21 or the possibility of problems from uniparental disomy (UPD) for chromosomes 14 or 15. UPD occurs when both copies of one chromosome in a child are derived from the same parent.

Charcot Marie Tooth Disease (CMT)

This is a progressive condition affecting the peripheral nerves as they carry impulses from the spinal cord to the muscles and from the sensory organs in the skin and other tissues to the spinal cord and the brain. There will often be no problems apparent at birth, although this can happen, but at some point in childhood or adolescence an affected person is likely to show signs of muscle weakness or wasting – typically in the hands and the lower legs. The condition usually progresses very slowly but in some affected individuals it may eventually lead to a substantial degree of physical disability.

Hemihypertrophy

Hemihypertrophy is one type of asymmetry of physical growth involving a relative enlargement of one side of the body. This may affect the whole of one side of the body or just a part or parts of it, such as the face and tongue, or one or both limbs. It suggests that the larger side of the body is the abnormal side, while in other conditions asymmetry may result from the impaired growth of the smaller side. Asymmetric overgrowth of one side of the body is associated with a risk of Wilm's tumour, especially when the hemihypertrophy is associated with other features of the Beckwith-Wiedemann syndrome. Children with hemihypertrophy may therefore be offered regular ultrasound scans as surveillance for the early detection of a Wilm's tumour.

Becker Muscular Dystrophy (BMD)

This is a sex-linked disorder affecting skeletal muscle and cardiac muscle. The first muscles to become weak due to BMD are often the limb girdle muscles, those that move the limbs on the pelvis and the shoulder girdle and which are essential for standing up from the sitting position and for walking up stairs or up a slope. Some muscles – typically the calf muscles – demonstrate hypertrophy, excessive growth, in an attempt to compensate for the weakness. There may be a dilated cardiomyopathy (DCM) as one feature of this condition. There is a great variation in the age of onset and rate of progression of the condition. Some affected boys show weakness and become unable to walk in the teenage years, while a few affected men may have no symptoms until they are middle aged and they may continue walking until beyond 60 years; the course of the condition in most affected men is intermediate between these extremes. Men are affected more severely than women and often at an earlier age. Women who carry the altered gene on one of their two copies of the X chromosome will sometimes develop a degree of weakness or cardiac problems from the BMD, but usually later in life than affected men. The relevant gene is the same one involved in Duchenne muscular dystrophy (DMD) but the gene alteration in DMD is more severe, effectively abolishing production of the dystrophin protein, while in BMD the protein is very often altered in size or other properties and is usually present although in reduced quantity.

Autistic Spectrum Disorder

Autism is the term used to describe a pattern of behaviour in which young, developing children withdraw from social relationships and become focussed on themselves and on the things around them. There is a wide range of severity of autism, and it is clearly not a single, distinct condition. Some children with other learning or behaviour problems show some mild autistic features and will often overcome them, at least to some extent, while others have profound problems from which they never fully recover. Different again is Asperger syndrome, in which children will often have very patchy abilities – poor social skills co-existing alongside great strengths or even some striking, and very specific, abilities. This range of problems is often grouped together as the Autistic Spectrum. The underlying causes of this range of disorders are unclear, but autism certainly can cluster in families and genetic factors appear to make an important contribution amongst other possible causal factors. Some children have autism in association with another distinct cause of intellectual disability, while many others appear to have no other distinct condition and suffer autism as an isolated problem.

Dysmorphic Conditions Thought Most Likely to be the Result of an Unrecognized Chromosome Anomaly

Many children with unusual physical features and developmental delay remain undiagnosed despite a careful physical examination and a full set of the relevant investigations. This group of children has, however, become somewhat smaller over the years, as both clinical expertise and the scope of genetic tests have developed. Some of the unrecognized disorders – affecting children to whom no firm diagnostic label can yet be applied – will be the result of developmental accidents or the intrauterine exposure of the fetus to drugs, chemicals or infection. Others will represent the effects of mutations at specific single loci. Yet others will be the result of subtle, so far unrecognized, chromosomal anomalies; these will often be small deletions or duplications that are difficult to detect by conventional microscopy. Clinical geneticists think that this group of subtle chromosomal disorders can sometimes be distinguished from the other groups because the pattern of anomalies recognized in a patient would be unlikely to arise from changes in a single gene but might result from the altered dosage of a number of neighbouring, but otherwise unconnected, genes. With the advent of genomic microarray technologies, it is likely that a significant proportion of this group of conditions will become recognizable through testing in the diagnostic laboratory – but for now it remains a question of 'clinical judgement'.

Best's Macular Dystrophy

The Best type of degeneration of the eye affects the macula – the small portion of the retina that gives us central vision, which we use to see what we are looking directly at, and also our awareness of colour. This condition is a progressive disorder inherited as an autosomal dominant trait. There is a variable age of onset, from early childhood to middle age, with a progressive impairment of vision. When looked at with an ophthalmoscope, the appearance of the macula takes on a specific appearance that evolves over time as the condition progresses; this results from the accumulation of fatty material that comes to look like a scrambled egg.

References

Armstrong, D., Mitchie, S. and Marteau, T. (2000) Revealed Identity: A Study of the Process of Genetic Counselling, *Social Science and Medicine*, 47(11).

Atkinson, P.A. (1995) *Medical Talk and Medical Work*, London: Sage.

Atkinson, P.A., Bharadwaj, A. and Featherstone, K. (2003) Inheritance and Society, *Encyclopaedia of the Human Genome*, London: Nature Publishing Group.

Atkinson, P.A. and Coffey, A. (2002) Revisiting the Relationship between Participant Observation and Interviewing, in Gubrium, J.F. and. Holstein J.A. (eds) *Handbook of Interview Research*, London: Sage.

Atkinson, P. and Housley, W. (2003) *Interactionism*, London: Sage.

Atkinson, P.A., Parsons, E. and Featherstone, K. (2001) Professional Constructions of Family and Kinship in Medical Genetics, *New Genetics and Society*, 20(1): 5–24.

Bauman, R. (1986) *Story, Performance and Event: Contextual Studies of Oral Narrative*, Cambridge: Cambridge University Press.

Beck, U. (1992) *Risk Society, Towards a New Modernity*, London: Sage.

Bellé-Hann, I. (1999) Women, Work and Procreation Beliefs in Two Muslim Communities, in Loizos, P. and Heady, P. (eds) *Conceiving Persons. Ethnographies of Procreation, Fertility and Growth.* London: The Athlone Press.

Bestard-Camps, J. (1991) *What's in a Relative: Household and Family in Formentera*, Oxford: Berg.

Bharadwaj, A. (2002) Uncertain Risk: Genetic Screening for Susceptibility to Haemochromatosis, *Health Risk and Society*, 4(3): 227–40.

Blood of the Vikings, <www.bbc.co.uk/history/programmes/bloodofthevikings/>

Bouquet, M. (1995) Exhibiting Knowledge: The Trees of Dubois, Haeckel, Jesse and Rivers at the Pithecanthropus Exhibition, in Strathern, M. (ed.) *Shifting Contexts*, London: Routledge.

—— (1996) Family Trees and Their Affinities: The Visual Imperative of the

Geneaological Diagram, *Journal of the Royal Anthropological Institute*, 2: 43–66.

Bourdieu, P. (1977) *Outline of a Theory of Practice*, Cambridge: Cambridge University Press.

Bowker, G.C. and Starr, S.L. (2000) *Sorting Things Out. Classification and its Consequences*, Cambridge, MA: MIT Press.

Bowler, P.J. (1989) *The Mendelian Revolution: The Emergence of Hereditarian Concepts in Modern Science and Society*, Baltimore, MD: Johns Hopkins University Press.

Cassidy, R. (2002) *The Sport of Kings: Kinship, Class and Thoroughbred Breeding in Newmarket*, Cambridge: Cambridge University Press.

Castel, R. (1991) From Dangerousness to Risk, in Burchell, G., Gordon, C. and Miller, P. (eds) *The Foucault Effect: Studies in Governmentality*, London: Harvester Wheatsheaf.

Carsten, J. (2000) Introduction; Cultures of Relatedness, in Carsten, J. (ed.) *Cultures of Relatedness: New Approaches to the Study of Kinship*, Cambridge: Cambridge University Press.

—— (2004) *After Kinship*, Cambridge: Cambridge University Press.

Clarke, A., Richards, M., Kerzin-Storrar, L., Halliday, J., Young, M.A., Simpson, S.A., Featherstone, K., Forrest, K., Lucassen, A., Morrison, P.J., Quarrell, O.W.J., Stewart, H. (2005) Genetic Professionals' Report of Non-disclosure of Genetic Risk Information within Families, *European Journal of Medical Genetics*, 13: 556–62.

Clay, B. (1977) *Pinikindu: Maternal Nurture, Paternal Substance*, Chicago: University of Chicago Press.

Clifford, J. and Marcus, G.E. (eds) (1986) *Writing Culture: The Poetics and Politics of Ethnography*, Berkeley, CA: University of California Press.

Conrad, P. (1992) Medicalization and Social Control, *Annual Review of Sociology*, 9l(18): 209–32.

Conrad, P. and Gabe, J. (1999) Introduction: Sociological Perspectives on the New Genetics: An Overview, in Conrad, P. and Gabe, J. (eds) *Sociological Perspectives on the New Genetics*, Oxford: Blackwell.

Coster, W. (1993) *Kinship and Inheritance in Early Modern England: Three Yorkshire Parishes*, York: Borthwick Institute Publications.

Cox, S. and McKellin, W. (1999) 'There's This Thing in Our Family': Predictive Testing and the Social Construction of Risk for Huntington Disease, *Sociology of Health and Illness*, 21(5): 622–46.

Cussins, C. (1998) Producing Reproduction: Techniques of Normalization and Naturalization in Infertility Clinics, in Franklin, S. and Ragone, H. (eds) *Reproducing Reproduction: Kinship, Power and Technological Innovation*, Philadelphia: University of Pennsylvania Press.

d'Agincourt-Canning, L. (2001) Experiences of Genetic Risk: Disclosure and the Gendering of Responsibility, *Bioethics*, 15(3): 231–47.

Davis, L.J. (2003) Heredity and the Novel, *Encyclopedia of the Human Genome*, London: Nature Publishing Group.

Davis-Floyd, R. (1992) *Birth as an American Rite of Passage*, Berkeley, CA: University of California Press.

—— (1994) The Technocratic Body: American Childbirth as Cultural Expression, *Social Science and Medicine*, 38(8): 1125–40.

Davison, C. (1996) Predictive Genetics: the Cultural Implications of Supplying Probable Futures, in Marteau, T. and Richards, M. (eds) *The Troubled Helix: Social and Psychological Implications of the New Human Genetics*, Cambridge: Cambridge University Press.

Dean, M. (1999) Risk, Calculable and Incalculable, in Lupton, D. (ed.) *Risk and Socio-Cultural Theory*, Cambridge: Cambridge University Press.

Delaney, C. (1986) The Meaning of Paternity and the Virgin Birth Debate, *Man*, 21: 494–513.

—— (1991) *The Seed and the Soil: Gender and Cosmology in Turkish Village Society*, Berkeley, CA: University of California Press.

Deftos, L.J. (1998) The Evolving Duty to Disclose the Presence of Genetic Disease to Relatives, *Academic Medicine*, Vol. 73(9): 962–8.

Department of Health (2003) *Our Inheritance, our Future. Realising the Potential of Genetics in the NHS*. Presented to Parliament by the Secretary of State for Health.

Dijck, J. van (1998) *Imagenation. Popular Images of Genetics*, New York: New York University Press.

Dreyfuss, R.C., Nelkin, D. (1992) The Jurisprudence of Genetics, *Vanderbilt Law Review*, 45(2) March: 313–48.

Dube, L. (1986) Seed and Earth: The Symbolism of Biological Reproduction and Sexual Relations of Production, in Leacock, E., and Ardner, S. (eds) *Visibility and Power. Essays on Women in Society and Development*, Oxford: Oxford University Press.

Edwards, J. (2000) *Born and Bred: Idioms of Kinship and New Reproductive Technologies in England*, Oxford: Oxford University Press.

Edwards, J., Franklin, S., Hirsch, E., Price, F. and Strathern, M. (eds), (1999) *Technologies of Procreation: Kinship in the Age of Assisted Conception*, 2nd edn, London: Routledge.

Ewald, F. (1991) Insurance and Risk, in Burchell, G. Gordon, C. and Miller, P. (eds) *The Foucault Effect: Studies in Governmentality*, London: Harvester Wheatsheaf .

Ezzy, D. (2000) Illness Narratives: Time, Hope and HIV, *Social Science and Medicine*, 50: 605–17.

Featherstone, K., Latimer, J., Atkinson, P.A., Pilz, D. and Clarke, A.J. (2005) Dysmorphology and the Spectacle of the Clinic, *Sociology of Health and Illness*, 27: 5.

Finch, J. and Mason, J. (2000) *Passing On: Kinship and Inheritance in England*, London: Routledge.

Finkler, K. (2000) *Experiencing the New Genetics: Family and Kinship on the Medical Frontier*, Philadelphia: University of Pennsylvania Press.

—— (2001) The Kin in the Gene: The Medicalization of Family and Kinship, *Current Anthropology*, 42(2) April: 235–63.

Firth, R. (2004) *Studies of Kinship in London*, London: Berg.

Fletcher, S. (2004) *Eve Green*, London: W.W. Norton & Company.

Forrest, K., Simpson, S.A., Wilson, B.J., van Teijlingen, E.R., McKee, L., Haites, N. and Matthews E. (2003) To Tell or Not to Tell: Barriers and Facilitators in Family Communication about Genetic Risk, *Clinical Genetics*, 64: 317–26

Fox, N. (1993) *Postmodernism, Sociology and Health*, Buckingham: Open University Press.

Foucault, M. (1979) *Discipline and Punish*, London: Vintage.

Fox, R. (1996) *Kinship and Marriage*, Cambridge: Cambridge University Press.

Franklin, S. (1997) *Embodied Progress: A Cultural Account of Assisted Conception*, London: Routledge.

—— (in press) *Born and Made: An Ethnography of Pre-implantation Genetic Diagnosis*.

Franklin, S. and Ragoné, H. (eds) (1998) *Reproducing Reprodution: Kinship: Power and Technological Innovation*, Philadelphia: University of Pennsylvania Press.

Fujimura, J. (1992) Crafting Science: Standardized Packages, Boundary Objects and 'Translations', in Pickering, A. (ed.) *Science as Practice and Culture*, Chicago: University of Chicago Press.

Gabe, J. (ed.) (1995) *Medicine, Health and Risk: Sociological Approaches*, Oxford: Blackwell.

Gillison, G. (1980) Images of Nature in Gimi Thought, in MacCormak, C. and Strathern, M. (eds), *Nature Culture and Gender*, Cambridge: Cambridge University Press.

Gilmartin, S. (1998) *Ancestry and Narrative in Nineteenth-century British Literature: Blood Relations from Edgeworth to Hardy*, Cambridge University Press, Cambridge.

Glaser, B. and Strauss, A.L. (1965) *Awareness of Dying*, Chicago: Aldine.

Goody, J. (1983) *The Development of the Family and Marriage in Europe*, Cambridge: Cambridge University Press.

—— (2004) *Comparative Studies in Kinship*, London: Taylor & Francis.

Gordon, D. and Paci, E. (1997) Disclosure Practices and Cultural Narratives:

Understanding Concealment and Silence Around Cancer in Tuscany, Italy, *Social Science and Medicine*, 44: 1433–52.

Gould, S.J. (1989) *Wonderful Life: The Burgess Shale and the Nature of History*, London: W.W. Norton & Company.

Green, J.M., Richards, M.P.M., Murton, F.E., Statham, H.E. and Hallowell, N. (1997) Family Communication and Genetic Counselling: the Case of Hereditary Breast and Ovarian Cancer, *Journal Genetic Counselling*, 6: 45–60.

Hallowell, N. (1999) Doing the Right Thing: Genetic Risk and Responsibility, *Sociology of Health and Illness*, 21: 597–621.

Haraway, D. (1990) *Simians, Cyborgs, and Women: The Reinvention of Nature*, London: Routledge.

—— (2003) For the Love of a Good Dog: Webs of Action in the World of Dog Genetics', in Goodman, A.H, Heath, D. and Lindee, M.S. (eds) *Genetic Nature/Culture: Anthropology and Science Beyond the Two-Culture Divide*, Berkeley, CA: University of California Press.

Helman, C.G. (200) *Culture, Health and Illness*, Oxford: Hodder Arnold Publication.

Holy, L. (1997) *Anthropological Perspectives on Kinship*, Ann Arbor: University of Michigan Press.

Hope, J. (2003) The 3-Parent Family, *Daily Mail*, London, 14 October.

Howson, A. (1998) Surveillance, Knowledge and Risk: The Embodied Experience of Cervical Screening, *Health*, 2: 195–216.

Hubbard, R. and Wald, E. (1999) *Exploding the Gene Myth: How Genetic Information is Produced and Manipulated by Scientists, Physicians, Employers, Insurance Companies, Educators, and Law Enforcers*, Boston: Beacon Press.

Inhorn, M.C. (1994) *Quest for Conception: Gender, Infertility, and Egyptian Medical Traditions*, Philadelphia: University of Pennsylvania Press.

Jacob, F. (1998) *Of Flies, Mice, and Men*, Cambridge, MA: Harvard University Press.

Keating, P. and Cambrosio, A. (2001) The New Genetics and Cancer: the Contributions of Clinical Medicine in the Era of Biomedicine, *Journal of the History of Medicine*, 56: 321–52.

—— (2003) *Biomedical Platforms: Realigning the Normal and the Pathological in Late-Twentieth-Century Medicine*, Cambridge, MA: MIT Press.

Keller, E.F. (2000) *The Century of the Gene*, Cambridge, MA: Harvard University Press

Kessler, S. (1988) Invited Essay on the Psychological Aspects of Genetic Counselling. V. Preselection: A Family Coping Strategy in Huntington Disease. *American Journal of Medical Genetics*, 31: 617–21.

Kessler, S. and Bloch, M. (1989) Social System Responses to Huntington Disease, *Family Processes*, 28: 59–68.

Klapisch-Zuber, C. (1996) Family Trees and the Construction of Kinship in Renaissance Italy, in Maines, M.J., Waltner, A., Soland, B. and Strasser, U. (eds) *Gender, Kinship and Power: A Comparative and Interdisciplinary History*, London: Routledge.

Kleinman, A. (1988) *The Illness Narratives*, New York: Basic Books.

Konrad, M. (2003a) From Secrets of Life to the Life of Secrets: Tracing Genetic Knowledge as Genealogical Ethics in Biomedical Britain, *Journal of the Royal Anthropological Institute*, 9(2): 339–58.

—— (2003b) *Narrating the New Predictive genetics: Ethics, Ethnography and Science*, Cambridge: Cambridge University Press.

Latour, B. (1987) *Science in Action*, Cambridge, MA: Harvard University Press.

Leach, E.R. (1966) *Virgin Birth: Genesis as Myth and Other Essays*, London: Cape.

Leonardo, M. (1992) The Female World of Cards and Holidays: Women, Families, and the Work of Kinship, in Thorne, B, and Yalom, M. (eds) *Rethinking the Family: Some Feminist Questions*, Boston: Northeastern University Press.

Leung, W.C., Mariman, E.C., van der Wouden, J.C., van Amergongen, H. and Weijer, C. (2000) Results of Genetic Testing: When Confidentiality Conflicts with a Duty to Warn Relatives, *BMJ*, 321(7274):1464–6.

Lippman, A. (1992) Led (Astray) by Genetic Maps: The Cartography of the Human Genome Project and Health Care, *Social Science and Medicine*, 35(12): 1469–76.

Lupton, D. (1994) *Medicine as Culture: Illness, Disease and the Body in Western Societies*, London: Sage.

—— (1995) *The Imperative of Health: Public Health and the Regulated Body*, London: Sage.

—— (1999) *Risk*, London: Routledge.

MacEowen, F.H. (2004) *Spiral of Memory and Belonging: A Celtic Path of Soul and Kinship*, Berkeley, CA: Publishers Group West.

Macfarlane, A. (1986) *Marriage and Love in England: Modes of Reproduction 1300–1840*, Oxford: Blackwell.

Malinowski, B. (1987 [1929]) *The Sexual Life of Savages in North-Western Melanesia. An Ethnographic Account of Courtship, Marriage and Family Life among the Natives of the Trobriand Islands, British New Guinea*, Boston: Beacon Press.

Mariman, E.C.M. (2000) Act to Resolve Conflict, *BMJ*, 321: 1464–6.

Mishler, E. (2000) *Storylines*, Cambridge, MA: Harvard University Press.

Nelkin, D. and Lindee, M.S. (1995) *The DNA Mystique*, New York: W.H. Freeman & Co.

Nelkin, D. and Tancredi, L. (1994) *Dangerous Diagnostics: The Social Power of Biological Information*, Chicago: University of Chicago Press.

Novas, C. and Rose, N. (2000) Genetic Risk and the Birth of the Somatic Individual, *Economy and Society*, 29(4): 485–513.

Nukaga, Y. and Cambrioso, A. (1997) Medical Pedigrees and the Visual Production of Family Disease in Canadian and Japanese Genetic Counselling Practices, in Elston, M.A. (ed.) *The Sociology of Medical Science and Technology*, Oxford: Blackwell.

Oakley, A. (1974) *The Sociology of Housework*, London: Martin Robertson.

Ogden, J. (1995) Psychosocial Theory and the Creation of the Risky Self, *Social Science and Medicine*, 40(3) February: 409–15.

Ostor, A., Fruzzetti, L. and Barnett, S. (eds) (1982) *Concepts of Person: Kinship, Caste and Marriage in India*, Cambridge, MA: Harvard University of Press.

Parsons, E. and Atkinson, P. (1992) Lay Constructions of Genetic Risk, *Sociology of Health and Illness*, 14: 437–55

Parsons, E. and Clarke, A. (1993) Genetic Risk: Women's Understanding of Carrier Risks in Duchenne Muscular Dystrophy, *Journal of medical Genetics*, 30: 562–6

Pilcher, J. (1995) *Age and Generation in Modern Britain*, Oxford: Oxford University Press.

Plummer, K. (2001) The Call of Life Stories in Ethnographic Research, in Atkinson, P. Coffey, A., Delamont, S., Lofland, J. and Lofland, L. (eds) *Handbook of Ethnography*, London: Sage.

Prior, L. (2003) Belief, Knowledge and Expertise: The Emergence of the Lay Expert in Medical Sociology, *Sociology of Health and Illness*, 25: 41–57.

Ragoné, H. (1994) *Surrogate Motherhood: Conception in the Heart*, Boulder: Westview Press.

Rapp, R. (2000) *Testing Women, Testing the Fetus: The Social Impact of Amniocentesis in America*, London: Routledge

Rhodes, L.A. (1992) The Subject of Power in Medical/Psychiatric Anthropology, in Gaines, A.D. (ed.), *Ethnopsychiatry: The Cultural Construction of Professional and Folk Psychiatries*, New York: SUNY Press.

—— (1995) *Emptying Beds: Work of an Emergency Psychiatric Unit*, University of California Press.

Rhys, J. (1966) *Wide Sargasso Sea*, London: Penguin Books Ltd.

Richards, M. (1996a) Families, Kinship and Genetics, in Marteau, T. and Richards, M. (eds) *The Troubled Helix: Social and Psychological Implications of the New Human Genetics*, Cambridge: Cambridge University Press.

—— (1996b) Lay and Professional Knowledge of Genetics and Inheritance, *Public Understanding of Science*, 5: 217–30.

—— (1996c) Lay Knowledge of Inheritance and Genetic Risk: A Review and a Hypothesis, *Health Care Analysis*, 4: 1861–64.

—— (1999) Genetic Counselling for those with a Family History of Breast or

Ovarian Cancer: Current Practice and Ethical Issues, *Acta Oncologica*, 38: 559–65.

—— (2000) Children's Understanding of Inheritance and Family. Jack Tizard Memorial Lecture, *Child Psychology and Psychiatry Review*, 5: 2–8.

Riessman, C.K. (1993) *Narrative Analysis*, London: Sage.

Ritvo, H. (1987) *The Animal Estate: The English and Other Creatures in the Victorian Age*, Cambridge, MA: Harvard University Press.

—— (1995) Possessing Mother Nature: Genetic Capital in Eighteenth-Century Britian, in Brewer, J. and Staves, S. (eds) *Early Modern Conceptions of Property*, London: Routledge.

Rosaldo, R. (1989) *Culture and Truth*, Boston: Beacon Press.

Sachs, L. (2004) The New Age of the Molecular Family: An Anthropological View on the Medicalisation of Kinship, *Scandinavian Journal of Public Health*, 32(1): 24–9.

Sage, L. (2000) *Bad Blood*, London: Harper Collins.

Sarangi, S. and Clarke, A. (2002a) Zones of Expertise and the Management of Uncertainty in Genetics Risk Communication, *Research on Language and Social Interaction*, 35: 139–71.

—— (2002b). Constructing an Account by Contrast in Counseling for Childhood Genetic Testing, *Social Science and Medicine*, 54: 295–308.

Sarangi, S., Clarke, A., Bennert, K. and Howell, L. (2003a) Categorisation Practices across Professional Boundaries: Some Analytic Insights from Genetic Counseling. In Sarangi, S. and van Leeuwen, T. (eds) *Applied Linguistics and Communities of Practice*, London: Continuum.

Schneider, D. (1980) *American Kinship: A Cultural Account*, 2nd edition, Chicago: University of Chicago Press.

—— (1984) *A Critique of the Study of Kinship*, Ann Arbor: University of Michigan Press.

Sexton, S. (2002) *Deceptive Promises of Cures for Disease*, <www. TheCornerhouse.org.uk.>

Shaw, A. (2000a) Conflicting Models of Risk: Clinical Genetics and British Pakistanis, in Caplan, P. (ed.) *Risk Revisited*, London: Pluto Press

—— (2000b) *Kinship and Continuity: Pakistani Families in Britain*, London: Taylor and Francis.

Skolbekken, J.A. (1995) The Risk Epidemic in Medical Journals, *Social Science and Medicine*, 40(9): 533–44.

Star, S.L. and Griesemer, J. (1989) Institutional Ecology, 'Translations' and Boundary Objects: Amateurs and Professionals in Berkeley's Museum of Verterbrate Zoology, 1907–1939, *Social Studies of Science*, 19: 387–420.

Stone, E. (2004) *Black Sheep and Kissing Cousins: How Our Family Stories Shape Us*, New Brunswick: Transaction Publishers.

Strathern, M. (1992a) *Reproducing the Future: Essays on Anthropology, Kinship and the New Reproductive Technologies*, Manchester: Manchester University Press.

—— (1992b) *After Nature: English Kinship in the Late Twentieth Century*, Cambridge: Cambridge University Press.

—— (1996) Cutting the Network, *Journal of the Royal Anthropological Institute*, 2(3): 517–35.

Sykes, B. (2003) Women: Do We Need Men? The Y-Chromosome – the Ultimate Symbol of Machismo – is in a Bad Way, *Guardian*, London, 28 August.

VanEvery, J. (1995) *Heterosexual Women Changing the Family: Refusing to be a 'Wife'*, London: Taylor & Francis.

Val, P. and Bruno, F. (2003) Types of Self-Surveillance: From Abnormality to Individuals 'at Risk', *Surveillance and Society*, 1(3): 272–91

Voysey, M. (1975) *A Constant Burden: The Reconstitution of Family Life*, London: Routledge & Kegan Paul.

Walby, S. (1990) *Theorizing Patriarchy*, Oxford: Blackwell.

Weijer, C. (2000) The Ethical Analysis of Risk, *Journal of Law, Medicine and Ethics*, 28: 344–61.

Weir, L. (1996) Recent Developments in the Government of Pregnancy, *Economy and Society*, 25(3): 372–92.

Who Do You Think You Are?, 12 October 2004, BBC 2, 9.00 pm. <http://www.bbc.co.uk/cumbria/content/articles/2004/10/11/family_history_feature.shtml>

Willians, C. Kitzinger, J. and Henderson, L. (2003) Envisaging the Embryo in Stem Cell Research: Rhetorical Strategies and Media Reporting of the Ethical Debates, *Sociology of Health and Illness*, 25(7): 793–814.

Zola, I.K. (1972) Medicine as an Instrument of Social Control, *Sociological Review*, 20: 487–504.

Index